Labyrinths
and
Clues

Labyrinths and Clues

Essays

by
Alan Wall

Odd Volumes

of the
Fortnightly Review
LES BROUZILS
2014

Odd Volumes of

The Fortnightly Review

Le Ligny

2 rue Georges Clemenceau

85260 Les Brouzils

France

ODD VOLUME 4

2014

ISBN-13: 978-0615935782

ISBN-10: 0615935788

These essays were first published in The Fornightly Review's New Series online at fortnightlyreview.co.uk.

TABLE OF CONTENTS

INTRODUCTION

ESSAYISM AND MODERNITY

IT WAS ROBERT Musil in *The Man Without Qualities* who propounded 'Essayism' as the necessary modern mode of thought. Essayism is characterised by an aversion to the axiomatic, a deliberated provisionality, an acceptance of uncertainty, an openness to the possibilities of intellectual adventure and discovery which Musil liked to call 'possibilitarian'. In the face of the ruin or ossification of so many axiomatic schemata, so many ideologies, Musil asks, what is there left to us but provisionality, that testing of theory and practice which is conveyed by the word 'essay'?

An essay means an attempt or a trial; having a go at something with the available intellectual equipment and the current knowledge. Built into its etymology is the notion of uncertainty, the endless seesawing possibilities of proof and disproof. An essay is a testing; its lexical doublet 'assay' highlights this feature. To assay a metal is to test it; to seek to establish its quality, its molecular structure; its mettle. To find out if it's got the right stuff. Now Montaigne used the word *essais* to describe his own provisional and exploratory forays into whatever subject happened to have caught his attention most recently, and Francis Bacon followed this up in 1597 by using *Essays* as the title of his book. Ben Jonson gave us *essayist* in 1609.

But as for *essayism*, this word is used largely negatively in the nineteenth century, where it originates. It seems to signify something to do with the cant of current opinion, particularly the urbane prattle of the periodical press. It is to be deprecated. Musil's retrieval of this abusive word is intended as a redemptive manoeuvre, though *essayism* was not always regarded with favour by his contemporaries. Vladimir Nabokov accused Thomas Mann's *Doktor Faustus* of 'super-essayism', by which he meant that the fictional narrative of that novel was constantly diverted into extended meditations on various topics like polyphony, diabolism, or whatever. The implication of Nabokov's use of this term is that such indulgence in the essayistic mode is really not the business of fiction, which should stay with the narrative, if it knows what's good for it. An equivalent term these days in regard to literature would be 'info-dump', where the writer appears determined to insert a large amount of material which has no necessary relevance to the narrative, even though it might well be a matter of obsessive interest to him.

The argument for the defence might be this. The essay is frequently the monadic unit of original and exploratory thought. Most full-length books, examined closely, will show that they are built out of essay-length units, even biographies, where the continuity between the units can be provided by the external agency of chronology. Most novels are episodic to some degree or another. They are called novels, not books of short stories, simply because the units are joined together with convincing narrative cohesion, and the characterised protagonists remain constant. Even a great deal of poetry will show itself to be essayistic, which is to say that it makes an intellectual journey in regard to a certain subject or congeries of subjects, and brings as much intellectual energy to bear on the matter as language and form allow. We see this admitted occasionally, say in the title of Pope's 'Essay on Man'. But we can look at Blake's *Marriage of Heaven and Hell* as an essay, an exploratory examination of the inter-dependence of the powers of good and evil in the year 1790, seen through the anode and cathode of an electrical circuit called morality.

Moby-Dick is super-essayistic in Nabokov's usage, but then so is much of Shakespeare. What is pressed forward, in terms of dramatic action, when Ulysses delivers his grand speech on order in *Troilus and Cressida*? What is happening here is not the forwarding of the action, the progression of the plot, but a weighing-up of options; philosophical, even metaphysical options. The English and French form of essay takes us back to the Latin *exagium,* which involved a trial of weight; a weighing-up, a testing-out. What we call, when the matter is not too grave or urgent, giving it a whirl. So as to see if we can try to find out what's what.

Now Musil was Viennese, and in one sense his commitment to essayism can be read as an intelligent response to the questions which Viennese culture was putting, not just to him but to the world, in the decades before the Great War. What were these questions? In architecture Adolf Loos regarded ornament as a crime; it had no function but deception, representing the historicist facade which pretends that one age is really another; that one age's technology is really that of another. Everything in a building should be functional, he argued. Le Corbusier would follow him up on this, when he described a building as a machine for living in. Wittgenstein was in the process of formulating something similar in philosophy. So much of what passed for philosophical discourse he thought of as mere prattle, about as much use as that succession of decorative frontages around the Viennese Ringstrasse that so enraged Loos. What is it possible to say, and what are the viable means of saying it? He answered that question in his *Tractatus Logico-Philosophicus*, published shortly after the war. Meanwhile Arnold Schoenberg was stripping down music to its essentials, which did not necessarily include any commitment to tonality. The twelve-tone system is effectively a mathematisation of musical composition; all sentiment can be excluded as a form of unwanted melodic nostalgia.

And there was little enough sentiment in the painting of Egon Schiele, who wished to paint the driven body in the throes of its torments and neurotic compulsions. Meanwhile Otto Wagner had been simplifying architectural motifs in his own way, not as ruthlessly as Adolf Loos, but with a clear sense that we should not treat columns and pilasters as though they had a structural significance, when they clearly did not. In this, Wagner was continuing the architectural themes and perceptions of Sir John Soane in England a century before. The classical orders are to be treated as vestiges, ghosts of an originary principle, to be incised on the surface of the building. They allude to an ideal type of symmetric proportion; they do not support a roof.

And then we have Sigmund Freud. Whatever one's judgement of Freud today, he was attempting to get to the heart of the psyche and its essential mechanisms. In the best essayistic manner, he made all seeming axioms provisional while he explored the matter at hand; nothing was taboo to his investigation. As Loos wanted to get to the heart of architecture, and Schiele wanted to paint the human creature as it really was, without protective clothing or disguises, and Wittgenstein wanted to ask only true philosophical questions which permitted meaningful answers, so Freud wanted to ask the most searching questions of the functioning psyche: what did it want, how did it try to get it, what strategies did it resort to when obstructed? Between drive and repression the historic psyche constructs itself. Freud's wife Marthe fretted that he had become in all but name a pornographer, since the Unconscious does not acknowledge morality, only desire.

Another way of saying this is that Musil was born into the world of Modernism. He must try as best he can to make sense of it, which is what he does through his alter ego, Ulrich. It is in this Viennese milieu that Musil formulates and elaborates his belief in essayism. He is most explicit on the subject in Chapter Sixty-Two of *The Man Without Qualities*. There Ulrich informs us of the welcome return into the intellectual world of uncertainty, contingency, the unknown and the potentially unknowable.

Signifier and signified become problematical when Rimbaud writes 'Le Bateau Ivre'; nothing Baudelaire ever wrote so severs the sign from its expected referent. Even in Baudelaire's masterpiece, 'Le Voyage', the desperate journeyers still stay fixed inside a nautical lexis of secure meaning, however synaesthetic its symbolic implications. It is the journey itself that becomes metaphoric, a figuring of how we flee ennui in pursuit of the experientally new. What Rimbaud's poem announces is a severance between sign and context which presages the dislocated world of Surrealism. The correspondences may still be there, but they have become deranged. This is an entirely new mood. The bedroom turns itself inside out and moves into the street. Dreams are now directing the traffic.

*

Musil's hero and alter-ego Ulrich calls essayism 'the return of uncertainty', and he welcomes it. The essayistic is an inherently uncertain mode; it is a trying and a testing, rather than an assertion of any axiomatic truths. Pope's *Essay on Man*, despite its frequent pomposity and grandiloquence, is tolerable precisely because it is an essay, not a catechism. Ulrich takes this further, into the existential realm, by the procedure he calls 'living hypothetically'. Completion, in life or thought, appears to him illusory; a closure where closer observation and more honest appraisal would demand opening. Every day, every moment, and every thought – all are cast in the provisional mood. To act as though any item of life or thought is charged with plenary significance, as if it could complete itself and then sign its own QED, is a betrayal. We are effectively building a metaphysical cathedral on sand, and the tide is bringing the waves towards us, even as we give the last elegiac wipe to our trowel.

Why an essay, though? The succeeding paragraphs of an essay, Ulrich thinks, explore an issue from different sides. They represent a perspectival adventure. As a mode of enquiry, it is tentative, even aspectival. It is (most importantly) happy to contradict itself when necessary; its own starting-point might well end up being gainsaid during its unpredictable progress. We are exploring possibilities; not asserting dogma. And our progress is the itinerary of a butterfly, not the straight line between two coordinates of a crow. Ulrich relates this to a way of thinking involving fields and constellations, not singular entities with isolable identities. The notion of 'field of force' takes him back to Michael Faraday, and the use of the word constellation links him up with Musil's German contemporary, Walter Benjamin. Georges Braque insisted, to himself as much as to anyone else: 'There are no things; only relations between things.' And A. N. Whitehead said frequently during the 1920s that the biggest illusion modern thought had created for itself was the notion that there had ever been any single meaningful 'thing'. Things are only meaningful in relation to one another, in the field or network of meaning in which they find themselves. The note of C Natural can be the tonic for the key of C Major; it can also be the third of the key of A Minor. Its meaning depends entirely upon its placement. The meaning of everything depends entirely upon its placement, its siting within a constellation. David Bohm believed that using nouns to describe so-called elementary particles was a mistake; it gave the wrong impression; it was the wrong form of linguistic representation. Verbs would be truer descriptively. It would be more accurate to say 'to electron' than to say 'an electron'. Our nominal obsessiveness represents a kind of intellectual possessiveness, which misrepresents nature. We wish to circumscribe the reality and hold it in place. This could be why Yahweh, when asked who he is in *Exodus*, replies 'I am that I am', which in its Hebrew form is the most verbal construction possible. Don't attempt to circumscribe my immense activity, since I am all verb, and cannot be reduced to the status of one of your tame nouns, crouching in its lexical cage. My meaning cannot be thus contained. The circumscriptions of your nouns are too small to contain the immensity of my verbal, ceaselessly dynamic being.

So essayism accepts the provisionality of all thought; and so, we might add, does science, wherever it is effective. Musil's narrative is continually interrupted by essays on any number of subjects. In this it resembles Thomas Mann's *Doktor Faustus*, the book which drew from Vladimir Nabokov the criticism of engaging in super-essayism. Between Ulrich's belief that the only meaningful mode of thought is essayism, and Nabokov's belief that essays should know where they belong, and not go cuckoo-nesting inside fictional narratives, we seemingly confront not a dilemma, but a choice.

In the wider sense which we are using here, Picasso and Braque were two of the greatest exponents of essayism of the twentieth century: they rendered vision itself provisional. They parenthesized the notion of reality, in order to investigate its visual construction. They were looking at how we look. They demolished perspectival constructionism, in order to permit us to examine the way in which we construct our visions out of the raw visual data. The great paintings of Cubism amounted to a form of apperception: we are seeing ourselves seeing. We watch ourselves constructing a visual world, and become vividly aware of the conventions we employ to do so. We are seeing not merely an accomplished image, but the itinerary of perception and representation.

The figure of Wittgenstein hovers about here, like a presiding spirit. And Wittgenstein can be seen to stand in for what has come to be called 'the linguistic turn'. Initially Wittgenstein sought an entirely logical use of language, employing the picture theory. Each statement embodied in its form a truth about what was the case. This was his accomplishment in the *Tractatus*. His subsequent work permitted language its own logic, the logic of usage exhibited by specific 'forms of life'. Language was not a translation of logic through lexis; it was the expression of the way in which we live with, and refer to, each other and the world we inhabit. You must approach the meaning through the specificities of language; you must not assume a separable meaning, which then merely translates itself into language. There is not a meaning separable from, or prior to, linguistic usage. The meaning of a word, said Wittgenstein, is its use in the language. Samuel Johnson had come to a similar conclusion when he published his great *Dictionary* in 1755. We do not express our meanings in language; we discover our meanings through language. We are linguistic creatures and are as dependent on language 'to mean' as we are on the world's atmosphere to breathe.

Borges was entirely an essayist, in Musil's sense, even when he was writing fiction. He never wrote fiction that wasn't essay-length. He frequently wrote fictional accounts of larger fictions, books in fact, that had never existed in the first place, except inside his own texts. All his writing takes the form of critique. In one of his masterpieces, 'Tlön, Uqbar, Orbius Tertius', he critiques the building of a new world, the re-creation of reality. You have to re-write the books, re-organize the metaphysics, establish ground-breaking epistemologies. Borges was writing this story during the years of Nazism, whose ambition was precisely to so restructure reality that any alternative versions were rendered not merely defunct, but illegal.

In essayism we find a concentrated discourse, a mode of heightened and compressed perception, in which language is required to be as luminously economic as it is in poetry. If essayism finds itself within a larger philosophic system, it automatically queries its architectonic credentials. We can see here what brings together work as radically different in other ways as Kierkegaard, W. G. Sebald, Guy Davenport and Robert Bringhurst. The segment of the world being examined has been rendered provisional, defamiliarized by the withdrawal of certainties.

What had happened with Rimbaud was a severing of the secure link between the sign and its world of referentiality. This is a specifically modern form of essayism, a species of comprehensive intellectual and moral alienation, more ultimate (in terms of meaning, anyway) than death. Surrealism picks up this world of severance where Rimbaud left off. And it is possible that the most authentic inheritor of the vision of Blake in *The Marriage of Heaven and Hell*, Rimbaud at the time of 'Le Bateau Ivre', and Surrealism in its heyday, was Bob Dylan. Between 1963 and 1966 Dylan might well have been the greatest protagonist of essayism on the planet. In songs like 'Ballad of a Thin Man' and 'Desolation Row' he severs sign from expectation with a forensic exactitude and force which would surely have impressed André Breton. The Mr Jones of 'Ballad of a Thin Man' is informed verse by verse not only that his answers are the wrong answers, but that all his questions are the wrong ones too. He is domiciled in an antique world of meaning. He wishes to excise the question-marks from life, and thereby escape modernity. Language elucidates nothing for him; it merely further obfuscates the dingy mental fog he already inhabits. The songwriter is engaged here in a form of venturesome essayism; Mr Jones, however, looks upon this region of uncertainty as a guarantee of nothing but spiritual vertigo. All he wants is to be permitted an exit from all this dire confusion, and a return to the world of fixed certainties from which he set out before his fatal encounters. He wishes to escape the world of essayism, and the challenge of its endless uncertainties.

I

RUIN, THE COLLECTOR, AND 'SAD MORTALITY'

EVERY STAMP COLLECTION IS a protest against the Second Law of Thermodynamics. Every act of archaeology laments the dispersion of what remains of us through time and space. Each book collector asserts the justice of ultimate cohesion in a world whose teleology and terminus is organizational and structural degradation. Every burial site refuses to relinquish entirely into time's maw those treasures we have encountered in time. Shakespeare's sonnets negotiate the paradox over and over: we revere those things whose loss we perceive approaching:

> *This thou perceiv'st, which makes thy love more strong,*
> *To love that well, which thou must leave ere long.*

And to protect itself from the charge of whimsicality and greed, collecting itemises and describes; it inventories and delineates; it compares and contrasts. This is not merely a stab against darkness and death, its catalogues assure us: it is science. Here might be a few of my favourite things, but they are windows into what Prospero called 'the dark backward and abysm of time'. Insofar as they shine in the dark, it is so as to illuminate that darkness with bright constellations of knowledge.

And so first we hunt the narwhal or elephant, then we carve on the hacked-off dentition of its ivory the shape of the creature we have slaughtered. Now we will surely be able to see for ever the mammoth in the mammoth's tusk; the ibex in the reindeer's antler. In the caves of Altamira and Lascaux, neither the creature limned nor the ancient limner survive, but the images still do. These are traces time has not yet obliterated, like Shakespeare's sonnets.

THE ENTROPIC PRINCIPLE INFORMS us that heat goes out of the system, any system. Unless Maxwell's Demon has finally come to life, like Mr Punch jumping up after playing dead with the policeman, then we end up with a maximum state of disorder, a grey sea of randomized matter graded down to its lowest common denominator. There might be the odd molecular twitch, a dead memory stirring, an echo of livelier times, but otherwise this is the end, an end that threatens to go on and on; as eschatologies go, this looks like being a lengthy one.

In my end is my beginning: so Mary Queen of Scots said, heading for the scaffold and her own beheading. So was this featureless entropic soup the primeval gruel from whence we all first started out? Milton thought the universe was made out of chaos, not nothing. He agreed with Thomas Harriot on this: *ex nihilo, nihil fit*. Even God can't make something out of nothing. Modern science might, however, be deciding otherwise. If the whole cosmos flipped into being out of a single quantum fluctuation (one potent theory) then everything effectively came out of nothing, though we might need to ponder the significance of the O at the heart of the word nothing: it would appear that there is nothing there except perhaps a world of infinite possibility, which might (on reflection) start to look like quite a lot. Not a vacancy then, more of an arithmetic womb.

In the Greek cosmology, chaos came first, a great commingling of all elements, a sea of indeterminacy that might bear some comparison with a singularity. All that was to come later was implicit here in chaos, though it had not yet found its form. And the first agency of order to emerge from such seething formlessness was Eros. Love finds form in chaos; already the theme of the collector struggling against time's arrow and the tide of dissolution can be discerned in these early myths, for the man with the postcard collection is imposing form upon what would otherwise appear to be no more than a scattering of entropic communications (even though the butterfly collection adds its tiny quotient to the entropic process, with every act of minute assassination). In his tiny Wunderkammer, the collector is Maxwell's Demon; he sorts the faster molecules from the slower ones; he reverses entropy in the delimited space of his collection. Chaos in any case can either be disorder or an order we have not yet perceived. We use the word gas because Van Helmont used the Dutch word for chaos to describe a phenomenon that seemed to him without any observable patterning. Brownian motion and the discoveries of thermodynamics between them established patterns unknown to Van Helmont, and we can now predict the behaviour of gases with considerable precision.

IN 1943, THE PHYSICIST Erwin Schrödinger delivered a series of lectures at Trinity College, Dublin. In these he argued that the metabolism of any organism feeds upon its environment in order to free itself as far as possible from consistent entropic decline. The entropic decline is expressed in the equation: $S^1 - S \geq 0$. This might be the most depressing thing the human species has ever said to itself. Entropy always maximises its life-destroying possibilities. Things go from bad to worse. We're all doomed. Maximum entropy once achieved is the state of thermodynamical equilibrium. Entropy ends where life ends, at the point of absolute zero, minus 273 degrees centigrade. Short of that, things are still going on to some extent. Schrödinger argued that in battling away to minimise the entropy that condemns it to death, the organism always ingests negative entropy: it effectively creates order in an anti-entropic manoeuvre. A plant is continually borrowing order from the sunlight so as to stay alive and grow. The capture and retention of energy is the first principle of life.

So we have here a cosmic dialectic between order and disorder. These two mighty forces are in constant battle and negotiation. At the microcosmic level, the collector ventures continuously into the disordered city so as to rescue some fragments of order, like Aeneas bearing his father Anchises away from the burning ruins of Troy. In his essay 'Unpacking My Library' Walter Benjamin speaks of the life of the collector consisting of 'a dialectical tension between the poles of disorder and order'. We could equally well describe this polarity as that between contingency and causality: every bookshop, every auction, is a field of contingency from which might emerge another proof of causality.

'Collectors are the physiognomists of the world of objects,' says Benjamin. What the collector sets against chaos and dissolution is passion and knowledge: the craving to possess here, according to Benjamin, amounts to a redemption of the lost object into the coherence and focus of the new possessor's loving and knowledgeable gaze. Such passion leads often enough to dissension and conflict. Theft is a frequent accusation; and not infrequently a fact. Thomas Frognall Dibdin published *Bibliomania* in 1809. Inspired by a poem, The Bibliomania, by John Ferriar, a medical man who worked with the insane, Dibdin's book was primarily a study of Richard Heber. Dibdin himself, despite the title Reverend that prefixed his name, was a cheerfully unscrupulous acquirer of bibliographic treasures. He offered to help the clergy of Lincoln Cathedral bring their antiquated library up to date. He turned up with £300 worth of modern volumes. They then discovered that Dibdin had just sold one of the old volumes he had taken away for £1800. He ceased to be a welcome visitor; he became *ex cathedratic*. (Modernization can be a terrible thing: the Bodleian Library Catalogues show that it possessed a Shakespeare First Folio of 1623 until 1635, but the Catalogue of 1674 lists only the Third Folio of 1664. The early one had evidently been superseded, and had gone for ever.)

BUT DIBDIN WAS ANODYNE normality incarnate compared to his subject Richard Heber, who was busily compiling book catalogues by the age of eight. The catalogue, Benjamin points out, is the emblematic focus of order amidst the chaotic realm of the collector's world. By the end of his life, Heber was a bibliomanic eremite, locked behind the doors of his house in Pimlico. On hearing news of his death Dibdin turned up to discover this scene: 'I looked around me in amazement. I had never seen rooms, cupboards, passages, and corridors, so choked, so suffocated with books. Treble rows were here, double rows were there. Hundreds of slim quartos – several upon each other – were longitudinally placed over thin and stunted duodecimos, reaching from one extremity of a shelf to another. Up to the very ceiling the piles of volumes extended; while the floor was strewn with them, in loose and numerous heaps.' In other words, the collection had replaced the world. The collector had built a microcosm, and now lived inside it, regarding the macrocosm as no more than background, or as the catchment area for reality proper: the collection. Baudelaire describes this eclipse of world by collection in the first stanza of 'Le Voyage', where the stamps seen in lamplight are so much more luminous than the daily realities encountered on the street.

The biggest purchaser of manuscripts from Heber's collection was Sir Thomas Phillipps, whose life was dedicated to the acquisition and cataloguing of books and papers. He amassed an army of creditors, frequently bankrupting booksellers in the process, and had to flee abroad for some years. His wife and daughters, and even the governess, were employed as catalogue compilers and forced to live in grave discomfort: books always took precedence. His wife died young, addicted to drugs; anything to dull the pain of the life her husband inflicted on her, which was in effect a species of bibliomanic imprisonment. Then along came the Shakespeare biographer James Orchard Halliwell. He courted Phillipps, but he also courted his daughter Henrietta. Phillipps wanted money for his daughters, to enable him to buy more books, and Halliwell didn't have any. Consent for the match was not forthcoming, so the young couple eloped, eliciting a venomous reaction from Henrietta's father that lasted a lifetime. Halliwell, despite his undoubted Shakespeare scholarship, appears to have been a zealous book thief, and was very nearly prosecuted for stealing manuscripts from Trinity College, Cambridge. He also took a 1603 *Hamlet* quarto from Phillipps's own library. This he mutilated in order to disguise it. A bibliomane he might have been, but hardly a bibliophile, since that word means lover of books. He often destroyed copies in order to enhance the value of the one remaining volume in his own possession.

John Tradescant in the seventeenth century had built up a substantial collection, consisting of all sorts of objects, which together came to be named the Tradescant Ark. This remarkable man, who was responsible for introducing a great variety of trees into Britain, including the acacia, the horse chestnut, the larch, the plane and the mulberry, had an eye for anything of interest in the world at large, in which he travelled a great deal; he was, in Benjamin's phrase, a physiognomist of objects. His collection, which his son, also John Tradescant, dubbed the *Musaeum Tradescantianum,* caught the attention of Elias Ashmole, a voracious antiquarian with an alchemical obsession. Ashmole seems to have convinced Tradescant and his wife Hester that he alone had the means to do their collection justice. He had a document made up which allowed him to acquire the Musaeum Tradescantianum for the peppercorn sum of one shilling. The Tradescants soon came to think better of this deed, and let it be understood that Ashmole had gained their agreement through several varieties of genteel chicanery. After John's death, Ashmole pursued the matter with legal force, and had the case heard at Chancery. The Lord Chancellor happened to be Lord Clarendon, whom Ashmole knew, since he was now himself a Windsor Herald. He won. And so were assigned to him 'the said books, coins, medals, stones, pictures, mechanics and antiquities'. Hester Tradescant subsequently drowned herself. And thus began the Ashmolean Museum, the first genuine museum in Europe. The Musaeum Tradescantianum formed the core of its first collection. Like so many museums its exquisite adornments and venerated items appear to have originated as loot, expropriated from the inattentive and the guileless.

THE COLLECTION EXISTS IN order to hold ruin at bay, so there is an acute poignancy to the ruin of any collection. Particle meets anti-particle; annihilation ensues. Alfred Russel Wallace spent years putting together his collection of animals and plants from the Amazon. The brig on to which they were loaded for return to England caught fire, and almost everything was destroyed. Wallace always was unfortunate; his best stroke of good fortune was to gain the affection and loyalty of Charles Darwin. But what went up in smoke that day in South America is nothing in comparison with the destruction that occurred in a matter of hours when the Library at Alexandria caught fire. Located in the cross winds of a political conflict, it was collateral damage as far as Caesar was concerned. As a result we have seven extant plays by Sophocles; but there were at least a hundred in the library. The others went up in flames, along with so much else. And Caesar continues on his breezy way. In 2003 the National Museum and Library in Baghdad were badly burned and looted. American soldiers stood around nearby, but their brief was not the protection of antiquities. Collateral damage once more, then. Manuscripts don't burn, said the great Russian writer Mikhail Bulgakov, but he was wrong, sadly.

One of the most astonishing meeting-points of antiquarian collector and temporal ruin is the relationship between John Soane and Joseph Gandy. Soane was a brilliant architect and

Joseph Gandy was a troubled artist with a genius for painting buildings. Soane had an uncanny premonition that little of his own work would survive, and he was right. Most of his master-pieces have subsequently been demolished. Soane rebuilt the Stock Exchange, which at the time consisted of a rotunda within the Bank of England. He then commissioned Gandy to paint it for him. Gandy did so, and immediately afterwards painted the same structure, this time in ruins. A little over a century later the building itself was in ruins, demolished to make way for a more convenient space in which money might reproduce itself. In the museum which bears his name at 13 Lincoln's Inn Fields in London, Soane's extraordinary collection of antiquities re-mains like an acknowledgment of universal vastation. 'These fragments I have shored against my ruins,' says the central voice of T. S. Eliot's *The Waste Land*. The words could well be in-scribed over the doorway of the Soane Museum. Fitted into the wall on the outside of the architect's house are some corbels, retrieved from the burnt-out Palace of Westminster.

At the end of his life W. B. Yeats stared back across the col-lection of images and emblems he had incorporated as symbols in his writing. He had frequently recommended rage against the levelling wind (a good image for entropy) but at last he ac-knowledged its inescapability:

> *I must lie down where all the ladders start,*
> *In the foul rag-and-bone shop of the heart.*

SHAKESPEARE HAD BEEN THERE before him, as Yeats well knew. Time in *Macbeth* becomes entropic, that 'tomorrow and tomorrow and tomorrow' which continues for ever in mean-ingless succession, shaping the syllables of a tale told by an id-iot, the randomized prattle of a nature that has come to nothing. All falls into 'the sere, the yellow leaf'. And the sonnets address the war between order and chaos, between form and dissolution, over and over:

Since brass, nor stone, nor earth, nor boundless sea,
But sad mortality o'ersways their power,
How with this rage shall beauty hold a plea,
Whose action is no stronger than a flower?

Sad mortality is the overwhelming force; it is the Second Law of Thermodynamics personified, the man in the black silk hood, 'this fell sergeant, Death'. The legal metaphors in the last two lines, involving the consideration of a case, and the action brought by a plaintiff, show what all our desperate legalities are finally doomed to endure. The magical circle of the collector's vivid attention is temporary at best. Ruin can never be legislated away.

Perhaps one of the most affecting images of the collector staring into the face of dissolution is that of Walter Benjamin in the last days of his life at Portbou. It has long been reported that he had with him a suitcase, which contained a document 'more valuable than his life'. It has been speculated that this document may have been the most complete draft of his immense *Arcades Project*, which was never published in his lifetime, but which may have contained a whole section on the collector and his battle against entropy. Walter Benjamin committed suicide in that small town, rather than risk falling into the hands of the Nazis. The suitcase has never been found. It could turn up, though; there is still time. We have not yet reached absolute zero. Benjamin's battered case could resurface on history's scummy tide one day. A manuscript concerning Ben Jonson's hike to Scotland has recently been discovered, having disappeared for the better part of four centuries. There are still paintings by Rembrandt or Leonardo waiting for the door to open, the light to come through the window at last. Soane's Bank Stock Office was reconstructed within one of the Bank of England's halls in 1989. Joseph Gandy's pen and watercolour drawing of 1798 was invaluable as a guide; the visionary of Soane's ruins had become the means of his restoration. These fragments I have shored against my ruins. To love that well, which thou must leave ere long.

II

CLUES AND LABYRINTHS[1]

IF THE WORD 'labyrinth' does not lead us eventually back to the very earliest human communities, it has a good try. The Greek *labyrinthos* appears to be a linguistic echo from Egypt and Asia Minor. It is possible that it relates to *labrys*, a double-edged axe, emblem of the Cretan royal family. No one is certain, since tracing the origin of the word 'labyrinth' is itself an etymological labyrinth.

It creeps into something like modern English as *laboryntus* in Chaucer's *House of Fame* and has become by the early fifteenth century *laberynthe*, a maze. Except for specialised usages the terms 'maze' and 'labyrinth' then become almost indistinguishable in English. Fanshawe's seventeenth-century Horatian translations talk about clews and mazes, so we are back with the Cretan labyrinth and Ariadne's bobbined thread, which permitted Theseus to find his way out of the maze after he had executed his monster. Such a thread was a clew, or ball of yarn, providing us with our modern word 'clue'.

THE SENSE INITIALLY was of a structure designed to baffle and disorientate; to prevent curiosity; to hide that which must not be found, either because it was sacred or because it was shameful. It may not always be a minotaur in there (and see below), but there will be something whose immediate disclosure is either undesirable or forbidden. It could be a monster, a priest or a crocodile. The secondary sense is of any structure or series of structures which, whatever their primary purpose, have the effect of baffling us as we try to find our bearings. Instead of finding our route, we stand amazed. 'Amazed' caught on quickly and stayed; 'labyrinthed' was introduced, but never won through – it sounds too clumsy. 'Amazement' worked well, though in modern usage we are more likely to say 'labyrinthine' than 'mazy'; three centuries back, it would have been the other way around. And then there are the mazes and labyrinths whose function is purely ludic and recreational, whether in Versailles or Hampton Court. These are structures designed for those with time on their hands, time to get lost during luxurious and lengthy afternoons.

What are the earliest known sightings? The first structure known to be entitled labyrinth was a vast building in Northern Egypt, constructed some time around 2000 BCE. Herodotus was astounded by it. It had been built at a vast expense of human labour, just above Lake Moeris, opposite Crocodipolis. There were fifteen hundred rooms on the top floor, according to Herodotus, and fifteen hundred below. The lower ones he was not permitted to visit, since they contained the tombs of kings and sacred crocodiles. A later traveller, Strabo, appears to confirm much of what the frequently unreliable Herodotus says, and describes the Egyptian labyrinth as a work equal in scope to the pyramids. There was a sacred crocodile in the lake, which was tame and came whenever called. It was fed flesh, honey and wine. Pliny too confirms that Egyptian labyrinths were the 'most stupendous' works ever constructed.

The Romans built a village over the site, using the labyrinth itself as a quarry for the purpose. Others, including Louis XIV's Antiquary, came much later and noted the sad state of the ruins that remained. Flinders Petrie identified the actual site with accuracy in 1888. It appeared that it might well have been intended, like so many other grand buildings in Egypt, as a sepulchral monument, probably for King Amenemhat III, whose mummified remains, together with those of his daughter Sebekneferu, were entombed in a nearby pyramid.

BUT THE LABYRINTH which has come to us in legend and myth, and from which we take the name, is of course the Cretan one. King Minos had a son named Androgeos who went travelling in Attica, and was treacherously slain by the inhabitants of that region. Minos imposed a dire penalty. The Athenians had to send seven youths and seven maidens every nine years to Knossos. These would then be inserted, one by one, into the labyrinth, the bafflingly complex structure erected by that technological genius, Daedalus. He had built this fearsome edifice, not for pleasure or even wonder, but for incarceration. The wife of Minos, Queen Pasiphae, had copulated with a beautiful white bull and brought forth the miscegenated hybrid, the minotaur, which had a man's body but a bull's head, and which was characterised by fearful strength and even more fearful appetites.

Theseus was the son of the King of Athens, Aegeus, and offered to become one of the fourteen votive offerings to the minotaur on the next marine consignment. He would then devise a means of killing the troublesome and ravenous therianthrope. Reluctantly, the King complied, insisting that Theseus should show that he was victorious on his return journey by changing the black sail on his boat to white.

On his arrival in Crete, Theseus was helped by Ariadne to kill her half-brother. She had fallen in love with this foreign prince at first glance; a goddess was imposing her curse here, as so often. The thread she supplied let him find his way out of the labyrinth after the killing. She had asked only that he take her away with him after his heroic deeds were completed. She had, after all, just arranged the assassination of her half-brother. He did take her away, but abandoned her on Naxos, the first island the sailors came to after Crete. At Delos the sailors performed a notable dance called the Crane Dance, in which they re-threaded their way through the labyrinth in ritual form. This dance was performed by the islanders for thousands of years after Theseus's departure. There seems to have been a fair amount of revelry on board – and presumably a few jokes about the lovelorn Ariadne whom the skipper had so casually dumped – and on their approach to the mainland Theseus forgot to change the black sail to white. His father Aegeus, watching from the cliff, assumed he had lost his beloved son to the monster, and threw himself into the sea, thereby giving it the name it still holds: the Aegean.

This is the legend. From the beginning there were alternative accounts. Philochorus insisted the labyrinth was no more than a run-of-the-mill dungeon. The youths were kept there until they could be awarded to victors in the sports held in honour of Minos's murdered son. The minotaur was neither more nor less than a fanatical and brutal military officer, who happened to bear the name Tauros. So he was, then, Minos's Tauros; thus do we elide our way towards a minotaur. Plutarch quotes a work of Aristotle which has not survived: in that the youths were not slaughtered but instead employed as slaves, a routine transaction for those days. Plutarch points out that Minos was a noble ruler, famed for his justice, who in no way deserved the calumnies Greek tradition had inflicted upon him. But rationality was condemned to the margin and the footnote: there was after all a better story to be told. In the Darwinian scheme of narratives, it is the strongest tales that survive their telling.

And this particular tale has continued to be told. The labyrinth, like Bluebeard's chamber, is of just as much interest whether it arose from some vestiges of historical occurrence, or expresses instead a psychological necessity to tell and re-tell such narratives. What the imagination chooses and retains is not necessarily that which is vouchsafed by history, and yet we continue to hunt down whatever history might offer us as col-lateral in the form of archaeology, as if still determined to prove the legend true. At the beginning of the eighteenth century the French botanist Joseph Pitton de Tournefort explored the cavern at Gortyna, long thought to be the original labyrinth. Some said it was merely a quarry used to build the local settlements, but Tournefort thought it too inaccessible for such a purpose. It was certainly an easy place to get lost in, and the locals finally sealed off most of the passages, for fear of losing their children in there. Tournefort's book about his travels and his excavations, *A Voyage into the Levant*, was translated by John Ozell and published in London in 1718. It contains this vivid account of the labyrin-thine experience to be had there: 'If a man strikes into any other Path, after he has gone a good way, he is so bewildered among a thousand Twistings, Twinings, Sinuosities, Crinkle-Crankles and Turn-again Lanes, that he could scarce ever get out again without the utmost danger of being lost.'

STILL, KNOSSOS ITSELF remained to be explored; ruined walls made of enormous blocks of gypsum, which still bore elaborate engraved marks. Arthur Evans (not yet Sir) finally got there in 1900, and started to excavate. He found what he believed was a large palace, and the objects discovered within it were of such significance that Evans decided they were the products of an ancient civilization of sufficient import that it deserved a name of its own. That name, Evans ruled, was 'Mi-noan'. Here he found pictographic inscriptions, which he con-cluded had existed prior to the Phoenician, and therefore offered an alternative system of foundations for our written language. He also found a large area for dancing, an *orchestra* in the orig-inal sense, which is to say a place for the chorus of dancers. Im-ages showing bull-leaping were numerous. This seems to have been a highly dangerous sport which consisted of a young man catching the horn of a charging bull and leaping over him. Evans speculates that this lethal activity might well have involved training up young captives (rather like gladiators) to provide a sport that might have had a ritual significance too.

And so we could have arrived, by a sequence of crinkle-crankles, at the origin of the story of the Cretan labyrinth, and the sacrificial death of the young, particularly since some centuries elapsed between the destruction of these buildings and the first written accounts of the legend. Evans himself concluded that a mighty earthquake had ruined Knossos around 1600 BCE; modern archaeology tends to disagree.

He did find one other thing that gave him pause. Thirty feet down from the palace floor there was an artificial cave, with three big steps leading into it. It gave the impression of being the rough dwelling of some formidable beast.

LABYRINTHS APPEAR ON Egyptian seals and amulets. And around 500 BCE there are Knossian silver coins, some of which bear an image of the minotaur on one side and on the other a symmetrical meander pattern, a labyrinth. One shows the minotaur dancing on the obverse; on the reverse is a swastika labyrinth. The minotaur, the labyrinth and Theseus and his weapon, then become recurrent motifs in western art. They appear as a graffito at Pompeii, and mosaics in Caerleon, Salzburg and Cormerod in Switzerland. Each image registers a complicated structure which at its heart houses the minotaur. Theseus is duly making his way there, or has already arrived, and is clubbing the monster to death. The motif begins to appear in pottery: Greek kylices show Theseus and his many exploits, including the killing of the minotaur. Smaller versions appear on ancient gems. There is a series of drawings called the Florentine Picture Chronicle, ascribed to Baccio Baldini. In one of them, all aspects of the minotaur story are seen simultaneously. The collection was once owned by John Ruskin, and is now in the collection of the British Museum.

The labyrinth wends its way into Christian churches. The basilica of Reparatus in Algeria appears to date from the fourth century CE. It has a north-western pavement eight feet in diameter which is a square labyrinth. At its heart is not a minotaur, but a composite of letters made out of the words SANCTA ECCLESIA, which can be spelt out in almost any direction. Many more such pavements were built during the twelfth century. There is a labyrinth one hundred and fifty yards long (if you walk it through) at Chartres. The French words for the labyrinth were sometimes *daedale* or *meandre*, but sometimes *Chemin de Jérusalem*, which shows how the ancient iconography could be translated into Christian teleology.

The centre was often known as *ciel*. In Rheims, Chartres and Amiens the figure inhabiting the centre is neither the minotaur nor Theseus, but apparently the architect. Thus does Daedalus reclaim his centrality in this particular story. The name *Chemin de Jérusalem* may give credence to the notion that such labyrinths in churches may have been miniature pilgrimage routes, ritualistic enactments in microcosm of the macrocosmic pilgrimages that went on outside. In which case they would be the equivalent of the Crane Dance performed at Delos by Theseus and his merry crew. It is possible the labyrinth on the church pavement had to be traversed on your knees. Since it has been calculated that the average church labyrinth would take two hours to traverse in this manner, it is possible that it is meant to represent an enfolded *via dolorosa* – Chateaubriand calculated in his *Itineraraire de Paris à Jérusalem* that it took him two hours to walk from Pilate's house to Calvary. On the other hand, the figure of the architect at the centre of some of these labyrinths might signify that it was an elaborate mason's mark, acknowledging Daedalus as the greatest of all masonic masters in the secrets of the craft.

AND SO THE labyrinth continues to flourish, as a turf maze or that topiary variety known as a hedge maze. The Christian vision is wary: in the Middle Ages labyrinths are often seen through Christian eyes as emblematic of hell. Virgil, a great source for medieval Christian writers, has a labyrinth inscribed over one of the entrances to the Underworld in the *Aeneid*. For the alchemists, the labyrinth represents the dangerous journey that the adept must make through the *opus alchymicum*. Such a labyrinth is not negotiable without a clue or clew.

The maze-like etymology meanders. In Ruskin's time the origin of the word was thought to be *laura*, a passage, a mine or often a cell set aside for monks and hermits. In *Fors Clavigera* Ruskin provides this intriguing definition: 'coil-of-rope-walk.' That ties in neatly with contiguous corridors and Ariadne's thread, and Ruskin must have mused upon it as he gazed upon the Florentine Picture Chronicle which he then owned. Max Mayer suggested *labrys*, the double-headed axe, as the origin. And there, it would appear, we rest for the present.

CHAUCER GIVES US the story itself in his 'Legend of Ariadne':

> *This wepen shal the gayler, on that tyde,*
> *Ful privily within the prison hyde;*
> *And, for the hous is krinkeled to and fro,*
> *And hath so queinte weyes for to go –*
> *For hit is shapen as the mase is wroghte –*
> *Thereto have I a remedie in my thought,*
> *That, by a clewe of twine, as he hath goon,*
> *The same way he may returne anoon,*
> *Folwing always the thread, as he hath come.*

Here we have the association of labyrinth and maze, we have the clew of twine or thread that will yield us in time the word 'clue', and we have the marvellous word we encountered before:

'crinkle'. The crinkle or crinkle-crankle or crinkum-crankum all denote a structure of sinuosities, twists and baffling turns.

More frequently we have labyrinth used as metaphor for a place of great danger and confusion. So Suffolk in *Henry VI Part One*, after entreating Margaret of Anjou to consider taking the King's hand, tells himself off for desiring the royal dainty for himself:

> *Thou mayst not wander in that labyrinth:*
> *There Minotaurs and ugly treasons lurk.*

The word 'maze' is more frequently threatening in Shakespeare than it will become later. A Latin comedy called *Labyrinthus* was performed at Cambridge before King James I. Pepys in 1684 saw a theatrical production entitled *The Labyrinth*, and declared it 'the poorest play' he'd ever seen. That one appears to have disappeared into the black hole fate had prepared for it.

IN MORE RECENT times we have Joyce's Dedalus, seeking to escape the labyrinth of nationhood and religion, so that he can soar instead in the region of art. And there is the best of Michael Ayrton's work, sculptures featuring his minotaurs. They are usually positioned inside a rudimentary labyrinth. The minotaur (that embodiment of our rage and power and lack of understanding) stares out at the geometrized labyrinth, but knows that he himself can never be geometrized. He is, quite literally, incalculable. Picasso's minotaurs span fifty years of his prodigious output, and are surely meant to be read as self-portraits. Desire, rage and tragedy interlink here like cross-hatchings on a metal plate. Kafka's castle in his eponymous novel is the labyrinth rendered into modernity; as his trial is the labyrinth rendered virtual as a system of baffling and punitive legality.

It is impossible to read any of these texts now without acknowledging the figure of Freud, the suspicious hermeneut, whose antiseptic eye lurks behind them all. He showed how an ancient text could be read as an allegory of the psyche when he re-read *Oedipus* with such radical revisionism in 1899. He could surely have concentrated instead on the labyrinth, had he so chosen. Let us say that the labyrinth is created with extraordinary ingenuity by Daedalus so that the past might be buried; the past where the shameful events once occurred. And yet the past still needs feeding with present life; hence the tribute every nine years – seven youths and seven maidens. The minotaur's appetites like those of the unconscious tend towards bisexuality and androgyny. The labyrinth is the site of a crime instituted by desire. It was Pasiphae who loved the bull. Minos in his grief had the labyrinth built by Daedalus to hide from the light of day the fearsome creature who had come out of the king's wife's loins. So the labyrinth is a monument to love, built at one remove; the superego is erasing the traces the libido has left. We push the things of light into the darkness. In Freud's terms it is the region of the unconscious where the repressed is forced down. It comes out into the light of day in the form of a return of the repressed, not all the time, but intermittently. Maybe once every nine years.

There is an intriguing doubling of this narrative in the various folk tale accounts of Bluebeard. Bluebeard's chamber is also the place where the past is hidden, where the crimes are put away, but which must still be fed by bodies from the present. Bluebeard needs a new bride from time to time, to join the old ones he has already slaughtered in his chamber. And yet desire, which would always like to start anew without memory or guilt – to do it right this time, and cleanly – implicates the present in the past and vice-versa. The new bride must be given the keys to the chamber, and there she will find the image of herself, the murder of that desire she presently represents. She too is a living totem of sexuality and death, just as the previous brides were before their execution. Thus does the repressed crime irrupt into the present; thus does desire discover once more its inescapable criminality.

AND SO FINALLY we come to Borges, whose name is linked for ever with the word 'labyrinths', but who never actually assembled a book with that name on its cover. Books did appear with that title, in a number of languages, but they were edited by others. Even more curiously, when *Labyrinths* was put together – not by him – the two pieces he'd written that actually contained the word 'labyrinth' in their titles were left out. Now that could perhaps be thought of, from the editorial point of view, as labyrinthine. Borges was however greatly preoccupied with the theme; or perhaps we should say themes. Let us start from the assumption – a fair one – that the labyrinth is manifold. Blake insisted that he must either make his own system or be imprisoned in another man's. Yeats reckoned that 'a man is lost amidst the labyrinth he has made/In art or politics', though it is hard to see why he needed to restrict the self-made labyrinth to those two realms.

For Borges reality was a labyrinth, and knowledge certainly was; the Tower of Babel had been refashioned as a library. All of Borges' ruminations on the library emphasize its infinite possibilities. Knowledge pursued through books is emblematic not of the finite but of the infinite. Human beings create labyrinths every time they build a city.

Science came to regard nature as a labyrinth, which is to say, as a structure whose meaning is not self-disclosing. At the time of the doctrine of signatures, it was still possible to believe that nature's identity was inscribed in a series of correspondences, designed to communicate identity and use to the intelligent reader of signs. But we live in the age of the standard model, and it took a great deal of questioning of observable nature to arrive at such modern physics. It is little more than a century since we first discovered that the atom was not indivisible; it is precisely a century since we found it had a nucleus. Learning the structure of the inside of matter, how it was made and when, has been one of the most titanic struggles of the human mind. It was such a mighty struggle because nature did not present itself to the human eye as transparent meaning: it is labyrinthine.

In *The Great Instauration* Francis Bacon is explicit:

> *But the universe to the eye of the human understanding is framed like a labyrinth, presenting as it does on every side so many ambiguities of way, such deceitful resemblances of objects and signs, natures so irregular in their lines and so knotted and entangled...*

And a little later Bacon makes the allusion as explicit as it can be: 'Our steps must be guided by a clue.' To put the matter bluntly, if God wanted us to understand this book of nature, then he also wanted us to undergo a great deal of hard study first, and to spend a great deal of time about it. Whenever revealed religion has argued with the findings of science, it has always had to apologize for its anathemas at a later date. Religion has tended to rubberise its own dogma to accommodate science, never the other way about.

THE FIRST IMAGES we traced in the caves of the Upper Palaeolithic were created below ground in labyrinthine stone corridors. What precisely we were doing down there, and whether or not we were in a shamanic trance at the time, continue to be questions that greatly preoccupy modern anthropologists and ethnologists. What is beyond dispute is that some of these images feature therianthropes, creatures which are part human and part animal. The head is most frequently the animal part of these figures, and it tends to feature horns: like the minotaur.

If a single image could form the filament between the complex neurological mappings inside our brains and the vast complexities of the cosmos and the quantum states, it would be the labyrinth.

Of course, if it really is a labyrinth we are exploring here, then there is still a question which might turn out to be of some relevance. When we get to the heart of this vast baffling structure, will we actually be meeting a minotaur, preparing its maw for yet another welcome feast, or will it be the figure of Daedalus, architect of this mighty maze, with his masonic code book open on his lap? Or could it turn out to be that most formidable motor of our astronomic constellations, a black hole? In which case, we will be about to pass through a darkness as intense as that of any shaman.

CHAPTER NOTES

1. This essay has made considerable use of *Mazes and Labyrinths: Their History and Development* by W. H. Matthews.

III

THE JANUS FACE OF METAPHOR

We as yet do not know enough about our thinking through, by, and with metaphor.
– Harold Bloom, The Anatomy of Influence.

WHEN THOMAS SPRAT, in his *History of the Royal Society*, said he wished to rid all scientific writing of 'this vicious abundance of phrase' – meaning all figurative language, but metaphor primarily – he was misunderstanding the nature of language. Rid language of metaphor and it falls apart. In fact, it is impossible to speak without metaphor. Even if we trained ourselves to avoid figures of speech altogether, catachresis inhabits the lexicon: our etymologies constitute a riot of metaphoric transfer. We cannot escape metaphor, and so we have no alternative but to try to find the most appropriate metaphors in which to situate ourselves. Consciousness of metaphor means that we understand the structuring of meaning to which language is conditioning us.

Metaphor in the strict sense, in Aristotle's sense, is the creation of a figurative image which combines two different entities or concepts into one word or phrase. Ideally, the two differ-

41

ent entities should each inhabit a different genus, as in 'Achilles is a lion'. If I say, as Glenn Gould once did, 'Bill Evans is the Scriabin of jazz', that is not a metaphor, since both halves of the statement belong to the same species, making it a comparison, and the etymology of that word contains the notion of equality; of comparing like with like. It is the unlikeness between the two terms in the figure that shapes a metaphor.

Such figured images frequently pass quickly into common usage and become clichés. A cliché is all too frequently a metaphor that has lost all force, friction and tension. The generative power of a metaphor comes from the dissonance between the two hemispheres that go to make up the whole figure, combined with the consonance achieved. Metaphor is created out of pattern recognition, the perception of shared identity in apparent dissimilitude.

We can distinguish here between two types of pattern recognition: routine and radical. Routine pattern recognition lets us function in daily life. We know that the traffic lights change through red to amber to green; responding to such stimuli does not require thought, merely reflex. Radical pattern recognition on the other hand is audacious. It permits discovery, whether in the writing of poetry or the exploration of science. Radical pattern recognition is an overcoming of generic dissonance, so as to acknowledge identities where none were perceived before. As William Carlos Williams put it:

> *A dissonance*
> *in the valence of Uranium*
> *led to the discovery*
>
> *Dissonance*
> *(if you're interested)*
> *leads to discovery*

But the dissonance here must be framed by a larger consonance; otherwise what is encountered would not be discovery, but a mere scattering of data. However apparently miscellaneous the details, we perceive an overarching set of resemblances in the family structure.

*

A DISTINCTION BETWEEN TWO TYPES OF METAPHOR.

IN FICTION AND poetry, metaphor is used to defamiliarize the familiar; in science it is used to familiarize us with the unfamiliar. In both cases a dissonance is encountered, but this fundamental and crucial difference means that literary metaphor is the reverse manoeuvre of scientific metaphor: it is trying to estrange our perception of the familiar so that it becomes momentarily alien and surprising. In Ezra Pound's formulation, the original figure makes it new; in William Blake's words, we see (if only momentarily) through the eyes instead of with them. We escape our entrapment in perceptual conventions. Scientific metaphor, on the other hand, invariably seeks to find comprehensible parallels in the known world for what appear to be exotic concepts and events. It is seeking, not to enhance the frisson of dissonance while finding similarity, but rather to neutralize it through homology.

When Marianne Moore says that the swan 'turns and reconnoitres like a battleship' (technically, it's a simile) the image is meant to halt us, make us re-think the swan. We had never thought of the swan in the light of a battleship's stately movement through the water before. It is meant to slow down our perception of a sight well known to us in order to enhance and render vivid our daily perceptions. This is defamiliarization or estrangement in Victor Shklovsky's sense of *ostranenie*.

In science we take the unfamiliar – for example the behaviour of atoms in Brownian motion – and translate it into a realm we find more familiar and predictable, more domestic even, like the behaviour of billiard balls on a billiard table. We are making an attempt to visualize what often defeats visualization in its own terms; so we carry over the one situation into the far more familiar one, where we can make images (the etymology of metaphor is after all a carrying-over). We think largely through images. There are exceptions to this – the musician and the mathematician, for example – but mostly we need to create an image so as to facilitate understanding. And the image we create is often generated by a metaphor.

Metaphor in science is so closely related to modelling and analogy as to be frequently inseparable from them. When Richard Feynman gave his testimony at the enquiry into the Challenger disaster, his most effective moment was an exemplary instance of modelling and miniaturisation. Into a glass of chilled water he dropped a small O-ring. After a moment it snapped. And that, in larger form, was exactly what had happened on that very cold morning when the Challenger had been launched. Larger O-rings had been chilled beyond their tolerance, and had ceased to insulate the craft from the meteorological conditions outside. The glass and the rubber band here functioned the way all metaphor is meant to do in science. They clarified a set of structural relations through a moment of condensed exposition. The modelled moment mimics the panorama of data to be expounded, but compresses it, and lets it emblematize the larger situation to which it alludes. It operates as a figurative form in which to concertina a large amount of information and so make it instantly lucid and intelligible. This is what an effective scientific metaphor does too.

LITERARY METAPHOR.

SINCE THE TERM 'metaphor' was first used in regard to poetry, let us consider for a moment why it is so crucial to writing; why, according to Aristotle, it is the defining quality of poetry – its creation the mark of true genius. Only by understanding how metaphor works in literature will we be able to see how its use in science tends to be so radically different. Scientific metaphor is in effect the obverse of the literary trope.

Metaphor tends to find two different situations and discovers a parallel or parallels between them which can usually be expressed in images. It finds, as Aristotle puts it, similitude in dissimilitude. We are thus observing pattern recognition in action as a transcendent power of discovery. Since he created some of the most potent metaphors in the language, let us consider Shakespeare. In *Macbeth* the King is informed of the death of his wife. By this stage he cannot sleep at all. We are told, in a vivid metaphor, that 'Macbeth does murder sleep'. His wife can sleep but is haunted by the murder of Duncan so relentlessly that in her sleepwalking she re-enacts her desperate attempt to wash the blood off her hands after the crime. And now, with a mighty battle looming, she dies. What Macbeth says in response to this is one of the most famous passages in literature:

> *Tomorrow and tomorrow and tomorrow*
> *Creeps in this petty pace from day to day,*
> *To the last syllable of recorded time:*
> *And all our yesterdays have lighted fools*
> *The way to dusty death. Out, out, brief candle,*
> *Life's but a walking shadow, a poor player*
> *That struts and frets his hour upon the Stage,*
> *And then is heard no more. It is a tale*
> *Told by an idiot, full of sound and fury*
> *Signifying nothing.*

What are the different hemispheres, the seeming dissimilarities, brought together here in metaphoric images? First we have time as some sort of exhausted beast crawling along the highway of existence until the chronicle should at last be ended. All wisdom, all tradition (all our yesterdays) amount to no more than a road of folly leading to extinction. The candle of existence might as well gutter, since life itself is nothing but a shadow, and then the poor player who is actually strutting and fretting his hour upon the stage, here at the Globe, tells us that life itself is no more than such a player as himself. And what does he have to say? That life is meaningless, a tale told by an idiot, that signifies nothing whatsoever. Here the theatre, the Globe – 'this wooden O', as it is called in *Henry V* – is the microcosm, and the world outside it the macrocosm. Each image reverberates back and forth, from the larger world of London and Europe to the smaller world of the theatre which is modelling the macrocosm. The model enacts the structure of the larger world in which it is contained, as Feynman's glass of chilled water represented the weather on that fateful morning when the Challenger blasted off. Macbeth is a man speaking lucidly about derangement, and finding reverberating metaphors in which to do so.

Another of Shakespeare's audacious acts of metaphor-making can be found in Sonnet 73:

> *That time of year thou mayst in me behold,*
> *When yellow leaves or none, or few do hang*
> *Upon those boughs which shake against the cold,*
> *Bare ruined choirs where late the sweet birds sang.*

The poem goes on to compare the ageing man to the evening of the day, and a dying fire, whose embers, which once provided vigour, now smother the remaining flames. So we have a series of metaphoric manoeuvres: from man's life to the rhythm of the seasons, the diurnal transit from light to darkness, and the flaming and quenching of a fire. In 1930, in his book *Seven Types of Ambiguity*, William Empson introduced a previously unknown register in the reading of this poem. He ponders on the bare ruined choirs and the sweet birds. Shakespeare was born a mere twenty years after the dissolution of the monasteries, and the weathering remains of such mighty religious buildings in Warwickshire must have struck him forcibly. The evidence seems to point to the Catholic sympathies of his father, John, and it is at least possible that the religious atmosphere of his youth was, let us say, *elegiac*. So Empson claims that Shakespeare's lines, while bearing the superficial meaning of trees in a forest losing their leaves in the autumn, while the birds leave to migrate to somewhere warmer, also carry a deeper and more socially ruinous burden. The choirs of the old despoiled monasteries and priories: here is where choristers once sang. All we see now are the ruins of those buildings, the Gothic tracery of whose windows mimicked the branching of trees. The birds that have fled are the choristers who once sang inside these ruins during religious services, and no longer do so. They sat on lengths of wood too, as do the birds, and their song has now flown, along with the avian migrants.

So if 'bare ruined choirs' describes a forest in autumn and finds a metaphor through a resemblance between birds sitting in a row along their branches and the rows of choristers dressed in their chaste finery, we have a subtle lament for what has recently been lost in England. Only the bare stonework of the tracery now remains. Empson reverses the journey of the metaphor to find its origin in the destruction of ecclesiastical property that took place under the stewardship of Thomas Cromwell, with Henry VIII's compliance. Empson claims that the ambiguity in the word choir prompts Shakespeare to the elaboration of its metaphoric outgrowth.

Ambiguity was for Empson a register of the variousness to be found in the world, rather than a confusion of meanings which needed to be riddled out, and ideally reduced to one. Unusually among literary critics, he had started from a scientific background. He was keenly interested in the discoveries going on in modern physics, and he had read Eddington's mighty book *The Nature of the Physical World*. Jonathan Bate in *The Genius of Shakespeare* points out that what Empson took from all this was a simple premise that then operated in his work throughout his life: ambiguity is not an indeterminacy in finding 'the one correct reading'. Ambiguity has now been found in nature in the form of wave/particle duality or complementarity, and it is there in language too. Ambiguity is a deepening richness of meaning.

In trying to find a single 'correct' meaning and consigning all others to quibbling footnotes, we are merely robbing the text of its metaphoric multifariousness. As in light's dual wave and particle properties, we are obliged to see not either/or but both/and.

So let us remind ourselves what Shakespeare is doing here in Sonnet 73. The time of a man's allotted life is figured as a year. The metaphoric transfer is then explored for further parallels: the leaves in the autumn lighten in colour then fall from the boughs of trees, just as hairs whiten and then fall from the head of an ageing man. The boughs shake against the cold, as an old person's limbs shake with the onset of physical frailty. Then the metaphor generates an image which properly belongs to neither actual dimension of the original metaphoric pair – the bare ruined choirs, where late the sweet birds sang. This elegiac image might well conjure the ruined choirs of medieval monasteries. The metaphor has generated a third term, unimplied by anything in the nature of the original perceived similarity. This meaning might be gratuitous, but it is appropriate. It has grown upon the site of the original metaphor itself. We might call this a metaphoric outgrowth.

This highlights a quality of metaphor to which Aristotle in *Poetics* and *Rhetoric* was oblivious: the original metaphoric pair does not remain untouched by the metaphoric process. By entering into the linguistic metamorphosis, the terms of comparison are placed in a novel constellation, in which all the significant nodes subtly alter, gaining new connotations, making unexpected connections, forming new networks of connotation. The metaphor, in other words, is not merely a passive tracing of an existent perceived parallel, as Aristotle argued, but is actively generative of meaning. It is seminal.

This last point was part of the burden of Max Black's essay 'Metaphor', published in 1954. Metaphor is not simply a detection of patterns of meaning, nor is it a mere figurative distortion of meaning: it is productive of meaning in its own right. When we employ metaphoric language, we are engaging in metaphoric thought, whether consciously or not. And this is highly significant in terms of metaphor in scientific discourse. So what work is metaphor then doing in scientific discourse?

METAPHORIC PARALLELS.

WE MIGHT NOTE here that if what Macbeth says were to be true, then science would be impossible. If it really *were* a tale told by an idiot, signifying nothing, then there would be no point in pursuing any form of intellectual enquiry.

When we describe the vastness of what is around us by using the words cosmos and cosmology then we are already speaking in the metaphoric register, and we are flatly contradicting Macbeth. 'Cosmos' comes from the Greek word for order; cosmetics, interestingly enough, is the art or science of restoring order to a face or body. Cosmos is a useful word because it draws our attention to the grand act of faith on which science is based: the conviction that order prevails, and that our enquiries will therefore not be fruitless when we start out on our quests for pattern recognition. The same recurrent structures that provide us with metaphors also provide us with physical laws.

However deranged the world he is describing, Macbeth at least retains faith in one notion of the science of his time: the correspondence between the macrocosm and the microcosm. His own life has been an extinction of meaning; the larger world he propounds in his images must therefore reflect the same extinction. In the seventeenth century the correspondence between macrocosm and microcosm was a tenet of the age's science. As above, so below. As in the large, so in the little. Galileo had pursued the matter of falling bodies. They all fall, he reckoned, unless a contrary force should be exerted upon them. Newton formulates this falling in his laws of motion, having first observed a metaphoric correspondence: the apple that fell in a garden in Lincolnshire, and the moon. The celestial body was falling too, but the universal force of gravitation stopped it leaving us and disappearing into the darkness out there, just as it had stopped the apple floating upwards. As above, so below.

The doctrine of signatures is a vast and complex metaphor in which everything in the world exhibits and articulates the universal interrelations of character and meaning. It survives in various poetic doctrines, such as Baudelaire's notion of correspondences, where it announces a synaesthesia which will be further echoed in Rimbaud's deregulation of the senses.

AN ASIDE ON THE TWO FUNCTIONS
OF METAPHOR IN SCIENCE.

They are hermeneutic and heuristic.

Function 1. To explain the matter in hand to non-specialists.

Difficult scientific concepts are explained by reference to something better known. To show how light finds the most economic route through the space-time continuum we use domestic objects: a rubber blanket is envisaged, with a metal ball rolling across it. It will make its way down the fold in the rubber, taking the most economical route. This is a transposition from an exotic thought, and one that is hard to visualise, to a more available set of images, images that we find predictable and explicable. Let us call this metaphoric manoeuvre imagistic domestication; it's a kind of homely modelling. The same thing happens if the teacher picks up a series of tennis balls and contrives a makeshift orrery on the table to demonstrate the movement of the planets or the force of gravitation. This thing here, which you know, represents that other more remote thing there, which you don't know anything like as well (the essential manoeuvre of scientific metaphor in explanatory writing). Now there is a crossover area here between modelling and metaphor, which we might try to elucidate.

When Einstein conducts one of his thought experiments, he is modelling in his mind the universe as he conceives it. He imagines that he is travelling on a beam of light. He is holding up a mirror twelve inches from his face. What happens? he asks himself. There is nothing to be seen in the mirror. At 186,000 miles per second, nothing can overtake me; nothing travels faster. So, if my image cannot travel faster than the speed of light, then it can never arrive at the surface of the mirror. That's the thought experiment, based upon the Einsteinian model. And if I now create a phrase to encapsulate it and say 'travelling at the speed of light is an endless stare into an empty mirror' I have created my metaphor. One thing – the speed of light – is another – a stare into an empty mirror; each belongs to a different intellectual genus.

Function 2. To test hypotheses, examine models and their functioning, and to reveal means of describing new phenomena.

The scientific process of exploration often says about a newly observed phenomenon: '*This* looks remarkably like *that*, so let's assume for a moment that the same laws apply, and see what happens.' The old model becomes the metaphoric framework for the testing of the new concept. If this is really like this, says the scientist, then we should expect the following to happen; we should observe a parallel form of behaviour. In literature and the arts a metaphor holds good until it loses its surprise, which is a function of its dissonance – the frisson generated by the remaining dissimilarity in which the similarities are embedded – but in scientific thought a metaphor is tested to destruction. Then another metaphor or model will have to be found, more adequate to the recent data.

A famous example of this is the development of the Bohr-Rutherford model of the atom. Since the nucleus had now been discovered and since electrons appeared to orbit this massive but tiny atomic centre, the model that put itself forward was the planetary one of the solar system. So let's view the nucleus as the sun, and electrons as orbiting planets. This was, in Mary Hesse's formulation, a positive analogy. But in fact what was being metaphorized were two dissimilar phenomena, since the planetary system's motions work in terms of gravity, whereas inside the atom it is electrical forces that obtain. And so the metaphor started growing ragged and incoherent very quickly; it went from positive analogy to negative analogy. If the model was a planetary one, then how come the electrons were not continually losing energy in their orbits, as one would expect? If the inside of an atom were really functioning according to its metaphoric other half then the electron would soon lose its necessary energy and spin counter-clockwise into the nucleus. And in any case, since the force of the nucleus is positive and that of the electron negative, why don't the two simply get together as soon as possible? Either way, there would be no atom. The metaphor only works if (however remotely) *this* can still be said to be *that*. Here this and that have started to become radically at odds with one another; they are now pushing apart, further and further into the field of negative analogy. The solution to this dilemma was the development of what we now call quantum mechanics – a different model of understanding. But the route to that understanding went through an exploded metaphor. In science a metaphor can be of maximum use while it is being demolished. And sometimes it is not the positive analogy which yields the richest results, but its negative sister. Dissonance, as Williams reminded us, leads to discovery.

WHY IS LANGUAGE INHERENTLY METAPHORIC?

WE HAVE ASSERTED that language is inherently metaphoric. Let us try to substantiate the statement. We have just been speaking of the nucleus. The term was first used in our modern sense by Ernest Rutherford in 1912. It is usually said to be the word for kernel, and in fact goes back to the Latin *nucula*, the diminutive of *nux*, a nut. At the beginning of the eighteenth century a nucleus was normally used to mean one part of the head of a comet. And if we trace the word kernel back to Old English we will find it originated in the word corn. So, these inorganic items making up the universe have been introduced to us through organic transfers inside metaphors. There is no way out of this. You can switch to German, but there you will find that the term is *der Kern*, so we are back where we started, and where we started is a constant metaphoric burden: we translate inorganic matter into dynamic organic entities by means of metaphors which are frequently unconscious. We speak of the life and death of a star, when such an inorganic entity has no life and no death either; it might have a beginning and an end, but the narrative impulse presses us to enliven the proceedings by metaphoric injection. We do this so much that we seldom notice we are doing it at all.

The essence of metaphor is interactive and projective imagery. Single words themselves frequently contain their own metaphors and just as frequently hide them. The dandelion comes to us courtesy of the French phrase *dents-de-lyon* – teeth of the lion. The yellow spears that surround the corolla resembled (or were thought to resemble) the teeth of the great cat. We borrowed it and Englished it; meanwhile, French itself has moved on. The French refer to the same plant now as *pissenlit*, which is not so much a metaphor as a dire prediction of diuretic effects to come. Similarly with daisy: we can trace it back to the year 1000 and the day's eye is there inside it. The little yellow disc only opens when the big one in the sky is shining. The plant opens its eye on the day. And a window is the wind's eye, a loophole for the eye to peer out and the wind to blow in. And if we talk about the cosmos, then as we said, we are speaking of order, whether we explicate it thus or not. The iridescence in Newton's *Optics* is only there because of the Roman goddess Iris, whose physical attribute was the rainbow.

MODERN LINGUISTICS.

MODERN LINGUISTICS STARTING with Ferdinand de Saussure tells us that we do not need these histories buried inside words, these strict etymologies, in order to use language efficiently. The history of language is found in its diachronic dimension; the way it actually works at any moment represents its synchronic identity. Language works as an engine of differences; it generates meaning by distinction, not by reference to origin. As long as I know that this is a dandelion, and not a lupin or a thistle, then I am using language correctly when I use the designation. And it is usage that dictates meaning, not etymology. Even Samuel Johnson had to acknowledge this in his great dictionary of 1755.

However, metaphoric potency is a ghost hovering behind the schema of Saussurean linguistics, and we see it particularly in regard to science and its metaphoric usages. The history of science lurks inside any word that science uses or has used. We still speak of the 'atom'. The word takes us back to Lucretius, Democritus and Leucippus and that early Greek notion that the universe was made up of tiny bits of matter. It was a tradition that continued, setting itself against the idea that the ultimate Elementals were earth, water, fire and air. By the time John Dalton was busily identifying elements in the early nineteenth century this was the chosen word to describe our ultimate particularities. When you reached this barrier you couldn't get any further. Hence the adaptation of the Latin *elementum*, meaning rudiment. The notion of substance without further structure seems to have been spelt out fully for the first time in Sir Humphry Davy's *Elements of Agricultural Chemistry* in 1813.

But the history contained in this word 'atom' is now a metaphor transcended: 'a-tomos' in the (transliterated) Greek meant unsplittable, something that could not be cut. But in the 1890s Thompson discovered the electron; in other words, he discovered that in fact there was a structure inside the atom, that it was not indivisible and homogeneous matter. Then in 1911 Rutherford discovered the nucleus. Since then the construction of the Standard Model in physics has found particle after particle. We still say 'atom' as we still say sunrise and sunset, though hiding in all those words are antiquated conceptions of the world about us. We still say planet – though the word indicates, if we are to trust its etymology, a celestial body that wanders among the fixed stars.

Perhaps the most notable metaphors we use are the names of constellations. Perseus, we say, that notable hero, and Cygnus the swan, Orion the hunter, and Monoceros the unicorn. Creatures that never actually existed continue their lives in the night skies of our observation. And how did we name them? Through pattern recognition and imaginative union. Metaphor works through a pendulum motion of the mind; it functions, as we said, through projective and interactive imagery. We join this to that and thereby form a single image. We perceive a pattern in the night skies and we find a similarity between that and a creature, real or imagined, here on earth, and so we create the metaphor of a constellation. It is only there in our perception of it; it only has its name because we have brought together two radically different realms. Once we have navigated our way through the Neolithic, we can even put a plough up there, but we couldn't have done so before. The identification and naming of the constellations indicates that there is an instinct for unified perception in us that goes very deep. It is what led to Spinoza's speculations about a substance underlying the whole universe. It is what led finally to the construction of the Standard Model. Coleridge tried to describe this imaginative force that we radiate: he called it the 'esemplastic' power – that intellectual drive which shapes disparities into unities. This is the ability of our minds in their most vivid moments to perceive nature as ultimately unified, and to help it towards that unity by our own metaphoric skills. Metaphor is a way of asserting the existence of the infinite correspondences that constitute our universe. Every time we invent a new metaphor we assert that we still use the word 'cosmos' precisely, because it means order, and we are finding order in our latest metaphoric discoveries.

METAPHOR: LIMITATION AND OPPORTUNITY.

TO USE METAPHOR creatively we must be constantly aware of the dangers of using it blindly.

An unexamined metaphor controlling our thought is a limit placed upon our imagination, because it directs and shapes perceptions and analyses, without our being aware of the structuring that is occurring. Wittgenstein in the *Brown Book* points out how Saint Augustine in *The Confessions* broods about the meaning of time and time passing. All his problems in this regard, Wittgenstein says, come from the operative metaphor he is employing: the river. Thus does time bring all things to us and take them all away again. Thus does it flow both behind us and before. Because Augustine never foregrounds the metaphor of the river in his own thoughts, they remain in thrall to the entailed imagery of the river flowing. Identify the metaphor you are inside (to use another spatial metaphor) and you can at least start getting your bearings. But delude yourself that it is not a metaphor, merely a transparent filament between yourself and reality, and you are trapped, like a metaphoric fly in metaphoric amber.

When Heisenberg first began to formulate what came to be known as the Principle of Uncertainty he was prompted by his profound unhappiness with the phrase 'the path of the electron'. Others thought this was a straightforward description of the truth; he reckoned it was a pernicious and misleading metaphor. The problem here was like the problem Wittgenstein identified in Augustine's thinking about time. A metaphor is so pervasive that it is not seen as a metaphor at all; it is assumed to be merely a transparent filament connecting us with the observable world. But 'path' here, as Heisenberg realised, is a Newtonian notion, with an attendant repertoire of expectations: a specified object makes its way across a designated region which can be mapped. Given sufficient information, then at any moment we should be able to give the coordinates for its sequence of positions, and so ascertain its velocity. But this is not the situation regarding observations in the subatomic world. Here there is an inherent limitation placed upon the amount and nature of the information we might acquire, and this affects our understanding of the phenomenon. And the phenomenon, as Niels Bohr made plain, must include the apparatus of observation: the manner of our observation cannot be separated from the character and behaviour of what it is we actually observe. Neither can our thoughts be separated from the figures of speech in which they find their shape and meaning. This is why Bohr always insisted 'We are suspended in language.'

We end up, on the far side of all these considerations, with a different way of thinking about the electron and all other particles too. An astute awareness of the functioning of metaphors was the beginning of this process. Here the break-out from a limiting metaphor, which like most limiting metaphors went largely unobserved by its users, finally permits discovery. The old metaphor is carrying the baggage of an antiquated world of conceptualisation. Old metaphors will inevitably constrict new intellectual energies. They turn our thoughts into clichés – that's why Wallace Stevens in *Adagia* recommended the creation of new metaphors as the only escape from cliché.

METAPHORS IN MOVEMENT.

WE MIGHT REMIND ourselves for a moment about some words in science – specifically, words which carry a portion of the history of science inside themselves. They have often become metaphoric; they can't help that. But what is interesting is how the specific metaphoric resonance changes from one point in history, one moment in science, to another. The nature of the metaphor, its current usage, models the larger world of scientific conceptions in which it is situated. And here I would like to quote two different people. The first is the French painter Georges Braque:

There are no things; only relations between things.

That was what a lifetime in painting had taught him; that is effectively what Cubism means. And the second quotation is from A. N. Whitehead:

The misconception which has haunted philosophic literature throughout the centuries is the notion of independent existence. There is no such mode of existence. Every entity is only to be understood in terms of the way in which it is interwoven with the rest of the universe.

He is saying the same thing as Braque, though under a different rubric.

Meaning is not isolable; it always functions as one aspect of a world of meaning. Metaphor is the most vivid way in which we demonstrate this to ourselves, since metaphor only works relationally. All meaning is relational, and so is endlessly in dialogue with its manifold determinants, as the following brief examples show.

Electricity. Take the word 'electricity'. The word could well take us back all the way to the Sanskrit *ulka*, a meteor: shining things. Anyway, it certainly takes us back to the Greek *electron*, related to *elector*, the bright sun. More shining things. Through the Latin *electrum* meaning amber we get to *electricus*, and its sense of a power which amber generates. This takes us to *electricam*, which William Gilbert employed when in 1600 he wrote his thesis on the magnet. Then throughout the eighteenth century (much preoccupied as it was with matters electrical) we have electrify and electrification. 'Electricity' itself was a word devised by that notable neologist, Thomas Browne. So when a negatively charged particle is discovered in England in the 1890s, it receives the word electron. If we go back to Johnson's Dictionary in 1755, we find under Electricity: 'The name of an unknown natural power, which produces a great variety of peculiar and surprising phenomena. See AMBER.' One hundred years later there will be no more talk of unknown powers. The word 'electricity' shows us how the meanings of our words alter with the state of our knowledge. Our metaphors and their usage are indicators of changes in the epistemological rules.

Particle and Wave. Whatever uncertainties were starting to beset the mind at the start of the twentieth century, most intelligent people at least knew one thing: energy and matter can either arrive as a wave or a particle, but neither can be both at once. That was not possible. What the double-slit experiment shows is that light behaves both as wave and as particle. And it was science that brought us to this epistemological impossibility. Science here rewrote the possibilities of being and manifestation. It demonstrated that two contradictory states could be simultaneously inhabited by the same fragment of matter. It all depended on what questions you asked; the apparatus is part of the phenomenon, as Niels Bohr had insisted. Wave/particle duality or complementarity is a vindication of the essential metaphoric perception: nature is not singular but aspectual. It responds to the intellectual criteria in which our questions situate it.

We seldom mean only one thing when we speak or write. Ambiguity is inherent in our patterns of meaning; it is not the result of a failure of interpretation on the part of the auditor or reader. We only learned this in relation to Shakespeare after physics had learnt it in relation to nature. Ambiguity is a sister to metaphor. Both assume that meaning is manifold rather than singular.

CONCLUSION.

Bishop Sprat wanted to get down to the singleness of meaning he believed underlay the disfigurements of figurative language. Like Adolf Loos, he believed that decoration was crime, and he thought metaphor was merely decorative. We could achieve a language of ultimate plainness, with no ambiguity whatsoever. Language, however, isn't like that; it seeds itself and sprouts unpredictably. There is no single meaning; no isolable facts, as Whitehead pointed out. Ambiguity, manifold polysemous possibility, is inherent in language, but we have now discovered that it is inherent in nature too. Complementarity shows us that doubleness is neither disguise nor subterfuge, but the actual face (or faces) that nature shows us under observation. Light must be either a wave or a particle, cried Bishop Sprat's descendants, but they were wrong – light turned out to be both. Metaphor tends to work by acknowledging the fact that language seldom inheres in a single, discrete meaning. It achieves meaning by polyvalency and accrual.

Meaning in metaphor presents itself as if it were the obverse and reverse of a coin. Whichever side you flip, you'll still end up with the other side too, even if it is momentarily hidden from observation. Living as we do in the age of complementarity, we should regard the creation of metaphor not as a decorative diversion, but an exploration of the way in which meaning is most creatively constructed. Heads only means heads in opposition to tails. It is a particle, most certainly, until you start asking it wave questions – at which point it will become a wave. But even as a wave, heads can mean nothing without tails, and vice versa. We are to double-business bound.

I V

NEWTON'S PRISMS

FIVE INTRODUCTORY REFLECTIONS.

1

NEWTON IN HIS room in Cambridge arranges the prism so that white light is rainbowed into the discrete colours it comprises. Then he fixes up an inverted prism, to test that the separated beams suffer no further alteration. Thus does the symmetry of nature demonstrate itself in a single room in Trinity College, Cambridge, in the seventeenth century.

Light arrives as corpuscles, or particles, he reckons; though he allows for the possibility that it has some of the character of a wave. Others insist that light propagates itself entirely as a wave. So in Newton's representational world light is particulate. We only see light as it arrives in infinitesimal speeding units from the sun. He has a clinching question for those, like Huyghens, who insist that light is a wave: how come it can't go round corners then, the way sound can?

2

THE 'TRUTH' OF any fact is its demonstrability within a system of representations. No fact is ever singular, or discrete; it is relational. 'There are no things,' said the painter Georges Braque, 'only relations between things.' Nothing is inherently true or false. It appears in a field of relations out of which truth or falsehood is generated. To stand outside any representational world and describe it is to designate it either as myth, ideology or bad science. And to describe any representational world as any of these is to imply that one is situated, even if partially, in a different representational world, since only this would permit the distance required for such external characterisation.

Newton knows that waves have certain characteristics: they can go round corners, for example. Light does not appear to do this; even when refracting, it always travels in a straight line. So the colours coming out of Newton's prism in his room in Trinity confirm a world of representation in which light is particulate, made up of individual corpuscles.

3

IN THE EARLY years of the nineteenth century, Thomas Young conducted (or arranged to be conducted) an experiment which is the prototype of the double-slit experiment. This crude demonstration appeared to show that light forms patterns of diffraction and interference. If it does this then it is exhibiting the behaviour of a wave. There was considerable hostility to Young's deductions, partly because of the great authority which accrued around Newton's name and reputation, and partly because of hostilities between the Royal Society and the Royal Institution. The criticisms effectively shut Young up on the subject, but the nineteenth century found more and more evidence to support his notion that light comprised a form of electro-magnetic radiation, and expressed itself in waves. As the century wore on, Young's wave theory of light seemed to be vindicated.

4

IN 1900, PLANCK discovered that light arrives in quanta – tiny discrete units of energy. If light is discontinuous, then it cannot be propagating itself as a wave, since one of the defining characteristics of a wave is its seamless continuity. In 1905, Einstein demonstrated that the photo-electric effect is only possible because photons (a term not used in this sense at that time) are granular, and can knock electrons out of a metal sheet, provided they arrive at the right wavelength.

What we now appear to have placed before us are two representational models, in contradiction with each other, both insisting that their terms include the 'nature of light'. This crisis took nearly a quarter of a century to resolve itself. It did this by abandoning 'either/or' and choosing instead 'both/and'. It is known today as the principle of complementarity. Light is both wave and particle. Ask wave questions and you will receive wave answers; ask particle questions and you will receive particle answers.

5

'LIGHT IS PROBABLY the undulation of an elastic medium.' Thus Thomas Young. This medium was thought to be the ether. Both Newton's corpuscular theory and Young's wave theory could be traced back to antiquity. There were proponents on both sides for thousands of years. However, all appeared to be agreed that light could either be a wave or a stream of particles, but it could not be both at the same time. Energy could transmit itself either as wave or as particle, not as both simultaneously.

So the crisis that needed to be resolved within this system of representations was an epistemological one: how could one type of energy or matter be both wave and particle at the same time? The 'resolution' of this dilemma expressed itself as quantum mechanics, and Niels Bohr coined the word complementarity to permit an approach to the apparent contradiction.

But how much complementarity can any representational world sustain without fissuring? And which types of representations are to be permitted as complementary; which will be simply deemed contradictory? In the space between 'complementary' and 'contradictory', our intellectual worlds either cohere or disintegrate.

Newton's corpuscular theory of light can be accepted as valid modern science; his alchemy and his Biblical numerology cannot. They are seen as material from entirely other worlds of representation, worlds which are simply incompatible with the 'modern scientific world view'. Similarly, Newton's prism is still with us, but John Dee's shewglass is not. In that he paid skryers to observe creatures from elsewhere; angels came in the night and spoke the language of Enochian. Such data we cannot include in our modern intellectual world view. We consign it instead to the region of the antiquarian and the occult. When John Dee stared into his crystal he was convinced that he was seeking truths there as valid as any Newton might have observed emitting from his prism. We beg to differ. At this point we say, complementarity must now end, and contradiction begin. Similarly with Newton's own alchemy. The information we expect to find here is biographical, not scientific. We have no need to 'save the appearances' from such a representational world, since we have abandoned it. And we now seem happy to accept that light entered one of Newton's prisms as particle and exited the other as wave.

MYSTICAL NUMBERS.

DOES THE TRUTH arrive in words or numbers? Those who are numerate are normally literate too, but there are many highly literate people who close the book on encountering a single equation. For these, according to certain accounts, there can be no precise apprehension of the nature of physical reality; merely a discursive approximation, a fumble of words and phrases, a lexicon of imprecisions. The case of Galileo might seem exemplary here. He argued that God had spoken through the Bible, but that he had also spoken through nature, and the language he spoke there was mathematical and geometrical. Cézanne appears to have been thinking on similar lines when he said: 'Render Nature by Means of the Cylinder, the Sphere, the Cone, all Placed in Perspective.' Galileo had specified triangles, squares, circles, spheres, cones and pyramids.

The Bible might tell you how to get to heaven, but it couldn't tell you how the heavens worked: for that you needed science. Here is an example of complementarity, in this case between scripture, astronomical observation and experiment. Richard Dawkins would say this is a false complementarity. If we interrogate it with sufficient vigour we shall find mere contradiction. So how much intellectual heterogeneity, we ask, is possible under the rubric of complementarity?

The argument can hardly be said to have softened. Is our fate ultimately expressed in numbers? The numbers that calculate whether the universe will die a cold death, dispersing forever into space, or a heat death, contracting backwards through the force of gravity, do of course express 'our' ultimate fates, or at least the ultimate fate of our habitat. Roger Penrose and Stephen Hawking also appear to be saying something like this: the calculations which we have applied to work our way back to the Big Bang are the most meaningful forms in which we can talk about creation. From the equations it appears that the universe could have been created *ex nihilo*, with no matter to start with. We start, in effect, with the equations. Plato's academy had a sign over its door advising those ignorant of geometry to stay outside. And Pythagoras, it is said, visited many sects and religious leaders in his early life in an attempt to glean any knowledge he could. He was on a quest for the truth of things. Then it was back once more to a serious study of numbers. The most noble pursuit was to understand how nature expressed itself in mathematical form, in uttering itself through the relations inherent in a triangle, or in the intervals discoverable in musical scales. Number was a sacred category. Those ignorant of the knowledge it divulged were doomed to remain outside the brotherhood.

The largest leap is always to get from one to two. Once we have accepted that all is not a singularity of consciousness, in which no laws apply except hunger and desire, a random motion of excitement beyond the trackings of any rationality, but that there is here before us subject and object, and that I cannot include all that exists in the *unum mundum* of my consciousness, or pre-consciousness, or unconscious, then I have ventured into the perilous realm of plurality. And once I accept that A is not the alphabetic totality, the undifferentiated kingdom of the Alpha King, but that alpha is in a dialectic marriage with beta, then logically this relation between two ones can only be perceived from a third position, even if that triangulation is achieved by apperception. Apperception, after all, is not mere self-communing, but announces a fracture of perception into self-consciousness.

And if there are three, then why not four? A trinity presupposes some sort of quanternion, if only to locate it in space and time, or at least in eternity. If one can look in from outside to see how alpha and beta might link in a copula that issues in gamma, then why cannot the observer of such configurations also be observed?

Even in number mysticism, the trinity can be a form of self-completion, but once we have progressed to quadrilaterals, we have surely entered the multitude of numbers. Once you have counted up to four, you are pointing towards infinity. Infinity (whichever one) can never be specified, because you can always add another digit to the specified figure. Even worse, as Cantor noted with rising mania, some infinities are bigger than others.

Anyone devoted to astrology, in whatever form (and a remarkable number of people are), is ultimately committed to the idea that it is number, in the form of planetary positions and relations, which governs the individual life. And there is a persisting fondness for the idea of mystical numbers with supernatural or magical properties, numbers which could unlock the nature of things.

One number has been obsessing us for thousands of years. At its most banal it is merely π, the number by which you need to multiply the diameter of a circle so as to get the extent of the circumference. It is a transcendental number, which is to say that the line of digits behind the decimal point outcompasses our measurements. Computers have now got into the act: the calculations were last seen at five trillion digits and rising. There is a compelling film by Darren Aronofsky called *Pi*. In this, Max, a tormented mathematician, believes that numbers control reality, and that even the movements on the stock exchange should be deducible in mathematical form, perhaps as a series of algorithms. A group of Kabbalists is also searching for a number, a number which spells out the secret name of God, and thereby inaugurates the Messianic Era. The number they are looking for consists of 216 digits, and is an application of the Jewish mystical practice known as *gematria*. Max's computer Euclid discovers this number and starts to secrete an organic substance, which gives the impression that it could be a form of semen. Max is pursued and harassed by people from the world of finance too: they think he could help them get rich by predicting the daily movements of stocks and shares. Finally, tortured beyond endurance by these numerical and numerological obsessions, Max trepans himself with an electric drill. Only after this neurological DIY does he begin to smile.

The notion of a number which might somehow break open reality, decode it, appears in various forms of religious literature. It is there in the Book of Revelation, which is strewn with examples of the mystical significance of the number seven, as a register of completion, fullness, *pleroma*; and in the number 666, which was thought to be the number of the beast, the signature in numerological form of the Antichrist. These numerological clues have caused much mischief amongst the inhabitants of this planet. They are still calculated and re-calculated so as to work out when this particular period of history will end, in great tribulation and catastrophe, inaugurating the millennium. When the Great Fire occurred in London in 1666, there was no shortage of pamphleteers explaining that the devil's hour was at last arriving. The number of the beast was announcing itself through chronology. In an intriguing gloss on this tradition, Arthur C. Clarke wrote a story called 'The Nine Billion Names of God', in which a lamasery in Tibet has been working its way through its special alphabet to spell out the nine billion names of the Creator. Once this task is completed the world will end. It would have taken another fifteen thousand years to complete the calculation manually. But the redemptive arrival of computers allows the process to be speeded up. Computer programmers are shipped in from New York, and set to work. At the end of the story, having completed their task, the computer men watch astounded as the stars begin to go out, one by one.

And of course there is Arthur Dent and *The Hitchhiker's Guide to the Galaxy*. There the ultimate computer brain is encountered, which finally spews out the answer to life, the universe, and everything: it is, bafflingly, forty-two. (And we have still not fathomed the significance of the magic square in the upper-right corner of Dürer's engraving 'Melencolia I' in which every line adds up to thirty-four.)

As if to alert us to the danger of mystical numbers, and the decoding of life according to their lights, the earliest papyrus containing a version of the Book of Revelation in Greek was recently discovered. It dates back to the third century. Here the number of the beast is clearly written as 616. So many calculations over two thousand years might have been based upon a misconstrued digit. The number, in any case, appears to have been used to avoid using the name Nero: it is a form of samizdat communication. Those obsessed with applying this number to calculations involving the nature of reality seem to want to find the secret hidden away in the fabric of things, without doing the necessary maths first.

But back to numbers versus words. Niels Bohr was aware of the necessity of both. 'We are suspended in language,' he said more than once. On the other hand, in speaking of what quantum mechanics had achieved he wrote: 'Such an interpretation of the properties of matter appeared as a realisation, even surpassing the dreams of the Pythagoreans, of the ancient ideal of reducing the formulation of the laws of nature to considerations of pure numbers.' And he is reputed to have said to Heisenberg: 'When it comes to atoms, language can be used only as in poetry. The poet, too, is not nearly so concerned with describing facts as with creating images.' This beguiling statement leaves us with a lot to think about regarding the relationship between poetry and 'fact'. The formulation of the 'laws of nature' would undoubtedly appear to be a matter of numbers. And yet poetry and mathematics appear to be portrayed as complementary representational worlds.

SECRETS.

WHEN ISAAC NEWTON was not formulating the universal law of gravitation or writing *Principia Mathematica*, he was engaged in alchemical experiment, or trying to fathom the clues provided by scripture for the duration of history. In all of these activities he was pursuing secrets, and secrets need to be first detected then decoded. The principle of gravitation did not disclose itself readily: it took a long time and a lot of mathematics to arrive at the discovery, and yet the evidence was always there before our eyes, at least in the form of heavenly bodies and their motions. The inverse square law itself follows from Kepler's Third Law. The word *clue* takes us back to the labyrinth. What Ariadne gives Theseus is a clue, a *clew*, a thread, to take him into the darkness and then find his way out again (the original meaning of clew was a ball of thread or yarn). While in there he would kill her half-brother, the minotaur, whose demand for youthful flesh from Athens represented a recurrent terror to the inhabitants of Crete. Ariadne's reward for this act of sisterly betrayal is to be betrayed in her turn: Theseus dumps her on Naxos. Then, approaching home, he forgets to change the black sail to a white one. His father reads this as an announcement of his son's death, and throws himself into the sea, thereby giving his name Aegeus to the Aegean. Gaining entry to labyrinths, following the clues, would appear to be a tricky business.

Sigmund Freud certainly thought so. He had a ring made for his close associates: it showed Oedipus answering the Sphinx's riddle. This for Freud represented the activity of the psychoanalyst, peering into the darkness and bringing light out of it. At the beginning of *Oedipus Rex*, Oedipus is presented as the saviour of Thebes; he had removed the curse the Sphinx had imposed. He was rewarded with the hand of Jocasta. Here the plot, the machinery of the narrative, conceals a terrible secret. Jocasta's hand is available only because her husband Laius was killed. As the plot unfolds we have the secret revealed to us: Oedipus kills Laius, his own father, then he marries his own mother and begets children on her. And all of this occurs because the oracle had declared at the boy's birth that he would grow up to do these things. And so they had him taken up into the hills, to be exposed, so as to die. The real 'chronological action' of the play, the fable from which the complications of the plot are constructed, begins with an attempted infanticide. Infanticide in legend always represents the attempted refusal of the future. Unfortunately, the future cannot be refused. It is like the force of a mighty river: dam it up here, and it will find another way through, somewhere else. In a sense, the death of Laius can be seen as time's revenge upon the attempt to thwart its scheme. You were told that this boy would grow to kill you, and look, he has. All your attempts to escape the oracle's force have led you to this lethal moment.

Freud's appropriation of the image of Oedipus seems fraught with danger. After all, the original action being alluded to does not end well. But of course Freud believed he had discovered in the figure of Oedipus a secret so terrible that humanity had collectively agreed to forget it for ever, through the process Freud called repression. It was the end of the nineteenth century and he attended two performances of the play. He asked himself how events so occult and remote in time could have such a profound effect on a modern audience. His conclusion was that it was because a deeply hidden universal truth was being enacted in the form of a literary allegory. All male children want in infancy to kill their fathers so as to possess their mothers entirely. Oedipus actually does it. Immediately after this reading of the play in *The Interpretation of Dreams*, Freud discusses *Hamlet*. The main character here, he believes, is implicated in the same sexual labyrinth: he cannot kill Claudius because Claudius has done what he himself secretly wanted to do: kill his father so as to possess his mother. When he does finally kill Claudius, it is as though he were killing his own desires, since he himself dies a few moments later. The action is less explicit than in *Oedipus Rex*. The forces of repression have grown stronger over two thousand years.

Freud's reading of *Oedipus* is possibly the most radical re-reading in history. What he effectively says, and it is a shocking thing to say, is that the whole of modern science knows less than the knowledge secreted in occult form in an ancient play.

He is saying that the most important knowledge we can have about ourselves is there to be detected, just as the data regarding the universal law of gravitation was there before our eyes, but it presents itself to us in the form of a secret, and it is a secret because of the dark antagonisms within our own psyches. We cannot own up to our own desires and cravings; civilization imposes its necessary discontents upon us in the form of repression, and repression makes us ill and miserable. Freud's is in effect a Gnostic creed: the real truth is hidden, and only initiates have the means to discover it.

When John Maynard Keynes read through the writings of Newton concerned with alchemy and Biblical cryptanalysis, he was appalled. Here was the greatest scientist of all time immured in the murkiest intellectual activities. He was looking for secrets in the wrong place. As a scientist he should surely have been dedicated to reputable practice and experiment, but instead he was just as involved in the disreputable practices associated with alchemy and Biblical numerology – not that Newton found them disreputable. The curious thing is that Newton never seems to have drawn any distinction at all between his different forms of activity: they all allowed for a search, an enquiry into the secrets embedded in the fabric of nature or history or scripture. One entrance was as good as another. One representational world as valid as another. His beliefs about many things – his Arianism for example – would have classified him as intellectually disreputable in any case, so he kept quiet.

NARRATIVE AND PLOT.

IN THE NARRATIVE of attempts to understand why an apple falls from a tree to the ground, Newton's perceptions and calculations represent the moment of *anagnorisis,* that point in a story when the information arrives via a messenger; when we realise that Oedipus is the slayer of his father, the husband of his mother, the brother of his own children, the cause of the curse that lies upon the land, rendering it sterile. And in the narrative of attempts to understand why the neurotic becomes ill, Freud's self-imputed revelation about the nature of *Oedipus Rex*, and the desires it reveals, if only obliquely, claims to be a moment of *anagnorisis* in psychology; in our collective understanding of ourselves.

In both these cases something has to be painfully discovered, a secret has to be analysed and decoded. The effort is all in the disentanglement, so that we can proceed to the *dénouement*, which in French means unknotting: we are back with those clues which were originally clews, threads or ropes, which lead us in and out of the darkness. A lot of energy and ingenuity must go into understanding the clues which nature presents to us. But why should we expend seemingly as much energy in actually *creating* secrets? Why should we construct plots in plays and novels and stories, whose complexity lets the secret be fully revealed only at the end? Why do we need to create innovative contexts for secrecy, as though there weren't more than enough of it around already? Should we not be sufficiently exhausted by the attempt to decode the secrets already contained in our world without having to create secondary worlds in which conundrums once more taunt us beguilingly to solve them? Why are we so in love with narratives that we continue to construct them with such an expenditure of effort? What is the nature of our need for secrecy and the divulging of it?

Is it possible that we create our artificial worlds in art and literature, filling them with clues as to the secrets that need uncovering, the riddles that need solving, because we never feel we really can solve them so effectively in life itself? In other words, might our fiction be a way of assuaging our torment in the domain of fact? And if that is so, we then have to ask another question: to what extent does knowledge claiming to decode secrets about nature, what we normally call science, enact (knowingly or not) the manoeuvres which characterise fiction? To what extent does our addiction to narrative shape even scientific thought? This might be one way to describe the work of Nietzsche: when we imagine we are uncontaminated with fiction, it may actually be dominating our thought.

Freud himself believed that the ontogenetic recapitulates the phylogenetic, which is to say that the life of the individual and his psyche mirrors that larger narrative in which we as a race came to have these particular psyches. Thus does the Oedipus complex re-enact the killing of the primal father, to enable the frustrated sons to enjoy the womenfolk whom the primal father had kept for his own pleasure and procreation. These arguments have not withstood much serious historical scrutiny, but it is intriguing how frequently they seem applicable to art, for there one can see a constant rehearsal of our oldest themes, a return to our earliest and most unyielding preoccupations, whether enacted in history or not. In art, said Picasso, one must kill the father.

The etymology of 'secret' takes us back through Latin to the notion of separation, setting something aside. *Cernere* has the sense of distinguishing and secreting. There is an interesting parallel here with the Hebrew word for creation, *bara;* this also means a cutting, a separation. That which is holy is set aside, where the etymology of 'profane' means 'open to all viewers' – in other words, not set aside. The sacred, the hallowed, needs to be cut off from the profane, and yet it can only be arrived at (in narrative anyway) through it. It is a great mistake to assume that the secret is in effect secret from the text in which it is embedded; it is instead secreted within it, part of its integral fabric. Only the full understanding of the text, in all its profanity, can lead to the hallowed secret. Another way to put this is to say that we can only arrive at the latent meaning through a scrupulous journey through the manifest one. The sacred element of the text must be discovered as a separation from, a creation set apart from, the profane availability to all which is the published manifest text. Even if the latency (the secret) can only be obtained through the profanity, it still exalts itself above and beyond such profanity, as the narrative completes its journey.

There are other ways of announcing the secret. 'Riddle' takes us back to the Old English word for a dark utterance. As for 'parable', that takes us to the Greek word for an allegory, analogy or similitude. All three have one thing in common: they devise various means of utterance whose function is to delay or thwart comprehension. They are not straightforward; the meaning is bent into an unfamiliar shape; it is defamiliarized. It is not to be distributed freely to the profane. Or perhaps more subtly, if the profane wish to understand, they will have to set aside a part of their profane mind, dedicating it to the sacred. That will only be possible after the narrative journey. Any narrative involving the sacred and the profane is as much 'both/and' as 'either/or'.

ART, MODEL, TOY.

ART ABBREVIATES AND miniaturises. It functions through formal compression. It is like a child's toy; it gives us the illusion of possessing a larger reality, which is actually beyond our reach. Compressed into art we find what most obsesses us, even when, as in the Oedipus plays or *Hamlet*, we can't consciously acknowledge what that obsession might be or how it came into being. In other words, art allows for expression which in another context the psychic censor inside us could negate. It permits the creation of parallels, the inauguration of secondary worlds. It was this facility for bypassing the conventions of expression, for evading the protocol which governed the interior dialectic of disclosure and repression, that made art such a valuable resource for Freud. Here were the clues that led in and out of the labyrinth. They were also to be found in the realm of dream, and Freud spoke of the process of artistic creation as akin to that of daydreaming. When not entirely governed by the conscious ego, the mind lets slip its primeval enchantments and demoniacal possessions. Art facilitates the exposure of the primitive within us, and its entanglement with the discontents of civilization. What we bury deeper and deeper inside ourselves does not thereby get left behind.

One of Freud's observations of childhood behaviour was watching a little boy engaged in the *fort-da* game, whereby he threw something away from himself and then pulled it back. This, Freud concluded, was a way of mimicking the 'control' of a reality which was in truth beyond his control. His mother went away from him when he didn't wish her to do so, and the repetitive game was a way of exercising control over things, so that they would seem to come and go at his bidding.

A toy has many similarities with a model in the scientific sense. The child's little town, in which he can move the figures and animals around, bears a striking resemblance to an orrery, an elaborate model of the solar system, in which, by turning the right handles, the planets actually move around the sun. This is a model, a miniaturization of observable nature so that it can be operated, observed and studied in an abbreviated shape, in a compact form in which all noise, in the cybernetic sense, is excluded; all the data presented is in the form of information.

Is it possible that we take such delight in complex narrative structures whose sequentiality ultimately discloses their secrets because they present us with a kind of model, a microcosm of the process of understanding itself? We see how the evidence, the data, can amass beyond our comprehension; but once the terms of understanding, the agency of translation, has appeared, then all the data is promptly transmuted into information. We are attending to the process of our own understanding; we observe the progress of a specific enlightenment in microcosmic or abbreviated form.

So toys have much in common with both scientific models and works of art as comprehensible abbreviations of reality, or miniaturizations of experience. By so modelling the world we make it manageable for comprehension. We like to read texts that only reveal their secrets after the pleasure of painful scrutiny, after a fastidious negotiation between intellect and the density of material presented for its perusal, because we suspect that this echoes the larger and longer procedures of the history of our understanding. The drama with its occulted aetiology, the novel with its core of revelation that must be lengthily won: these represent a mimesis of our ongoing battle with the data life presents to us.

Why does the apple fall from the tree to the earth rather than flying off towards the moon? This is part of the narrative of human understanding whose secret, when satisfactorily revealed, we call 'science'. Newton, to make his discovery, had to employ the principle of uniformitarianism, a word he could not have used because it was not yet invented. This principle insists that the same laws apply throughout the universe; that what is valid here is also valid there. The implication of the Ptolemaic system was that universal space was not isotropic; that the universe did not extend homogeneously in all directions, but that nature was centred upon us, our planet, sitting at the centre of a created reality which had in its turn centred itself on humanity. The heavens were immutable, while we lived in the sublunar realm governed by change and decay. Now we assume that we are far from the centre of things, indeed that there is no 'centre of things', that the universe is like that legendary circle whose circumference is everywhere, whose centre is nowhere. Space turned out to be isotropic, after all, if not homogeneous; it goes off similarly in all directions but lumpily. The heavens were not the region of perfection; things change as much out there as they do down here.

If we journey back to the 1660s, we find Isaac Newton in his rooms in Trinity experimenting with light and what happens when you pass it first through one prism then through two. The assumption he is working on is what we have just called uniformitarianism. Newton is assuming that light will behave the same way inside his room as it does outside. This is a large assumption, and it is one that can only be endlessly tested rather than proven. It was Galileo's assumption; it is the assumption of all experimental science. Without that notion we have magic, the notion that universal laws can be suspended by discrete occult operations. Or we have miracles, which presuppose that universal laws can be suspended at the behest of their creator.

What Newton discovers here is that white light contains colours which can be separated by a prism. He has made a fundamental discovery about the nature of light, and he will announce the fact in his *Opticks*. It is a curiosity worthy of remark that Newton didn't want an edition of his greatest work *Principia Mathematica* to be published in English in his lifetime. The book, already formidably difficult, was made a little more difficult by existing only in Latin until the time of his death. This was, so he said, to avoid 'smatterers'. In other words, he wanted to keep the matter secret, to restrict access to it to those in a position to fully understand, of whom there were remarkably few. He did with *Principia* what Mark tells us (4:11-12) Jesus did with his teachings about the kingdom: made them a matter of restricted access, lest those not actually chosen for salvation should achieve it anyway. He did not want these hallowed truths made available too readily to the profane.

Two centuries later Freud sat in his consulting rooms at Berggasse 19 in Vienna, having created for himself a space which he believed to be as much a scientific space as Newton's Trinity rooms, or the laboratory he had built outside. If Newton needed prisms and telescopes, Freud needed his images from antiquity, those sculptures and reliefs and engravings which so cluttered this Viennese space that it often startled his analysands. Yet what this space was proclaiming was another form of uniformitarianism: that of the psyche. The forces which had driven us in the earliest period of our history are still potent. They might be hidden in the darkest, most repressed depths, but they are still there, as Oedipus and his dreadful secret still lurk murderously inside the male psyche.

Freud surrounded himself with models of the human psyche in operation, shapings of the drives that populate us with their contrarian desires; creatures of heaven and hell, supernatural messengers, gods, goddesses and minor demons. If their first encounter with this anthropological menagerie frequently startled his patients, the objects expressed their own vivid logic: the dark forces configured by the statuary inside his glass cases remained potent agents in the contemporary psyche. The unconscious does not acknowledge time; no drive, no terror or desire, is ever superannuated so long as it lodges in the dark labyrinth of the mind.

MYTH.

WE OFTEN DESCRIBE models of the world as either myth or science; they are frequently combinations of both. Like the minotaur we are hybrid creatures, made half of science, half of myth. We are therianthropic, and it can be hard to distinguish where the two hemispheres actually meet. All too often, when we look back in time, we discover that much of what we thought science turned out to be myth after all. To use the word with something like neutrality, we could say that a myth is a structured world of perception and experience which can be observed externally; it is an inhabited world of meaning, a system of representations, however loosely organized. In which case, we might well be inhabiting a myth ourselves, but because our myth appears to us to be no more than a transparency onto the fabric of reality, we perceive it as science rather than myth. We cannot then see it externally; our structure of thought and the realities it perceives are connected by a transparent filament, invisible to our own eyes. Once such a transparency is superseded, once we can see how seemingly neutral scientific perception was in fact implicated in a set of cultural assumptions, structured if not necessarily contaminated by the fictions of the time, then we can start to make out the lineaments of a myth.

We do not have to travel back far in time to see such operations at work. For example, positivism in the second half of the nineteenth century regarded itself as the least mythic form of thought that had ever existed. Now we can see how its confident scientism, its commitment to a notion of history that was techno-progressive, was about to blow up in its own face in the form of the new century and its quantum mechanics, the Great War, the rise of fascism. Its notion of science was altogether too unproblematical, its notion of history likewise: what appeared to be the transparency of science turned out to involve the motivated operations of fiction, which is to say the non-transparency of the age's specific configuration of myths. The infinite attenuations of classical physics were about to be broken by the scandal of quantum discontinuity.

Isaac Newton in his laboratory, the fires kept alight day and night, was not attempting to explore the 'myth of alchemy'; on the contrary, he was engaging in what he believed to be science. It is not time that has rendered Newton's activity mythic rather than scientific. A hundred years before, Ben Jonson in *The Alchemist* was already viewing alchemists as creatures of myth in the invidious sense of charlatans committed to untruth, whether wittingly or not. Jonson's alchemists are the chapmen of wonders, the mountebanks of hermetic lore, but then Keynes came to a not dissimilar conclusion about Newton, having read his secret papers:

> *Newton was not the first of the age of reason. He was the last of the magicians, the last of the Babylonians and Sumerians, the last great mind which looked out on the visible and intellectual world with the same eyes as those who began to build our intellectual inheritance rather less than 10,000 years ago. Isaac Newton, a posthumous child born with no father on Christmas Day, 1642, was the last wonder-child to whom the Magi could do sincere and appropriate homage.*

He was looking for the wrong secrets in the wrong place, it would appear, as well as discovering the right secrets in the right places, employing the correct methods.

He was yet another hybrid, a species of intellectual chimera, and he still puzzles us. He inhabits several worlds of representation so radically at odds with one another that we must find him guilty not of intellectual complementarity, but of a pluralism so capacious as to amount to eccentric eclecticism.

MYTH AND REPRESENTATION.

REPRESENTATIONS FIND THEIR meaning inside myths, inside the field of mythic discourse, but they find them inside science too. The difficulty as always is disentangling one from the other. We can never do this entirely for ourselves, because it is always too early to judge. By the time a coherent judgment arrives, we shall be dead. We must wait for other generations to do the judging, to work out how much of our science was really a myth so integral to our way of inhabiting the cosmos that it was invisible to us. An image of an auroch on a Palaeolithic cave wall, a chart of the stars in a lab in the astronomy department, a drawing of a proposed new building in the council offices – all of these might have more in common than at first appears. They are all what we might call, with caution, 'models of reality', using different technologies to present images which convey information. Which is to say, they are all representations, and like all representations they take their place inside a larger world of meaning which grants them their significance. That significance can change if the representation is extracted from its original position and placed inside a different intellectual context. If the Palaeolithic images had some magical or sacred character, guaranteeing the hunt, or even making reparation for it, then the representation takes on a different function when placed in an analytical context in modernity. Now it is not guaranteeing the hunt but disclosing information about an early society, its beliefs and practices. The image in the council building is printed on paper and uses the current convention of groundplan and elevation. In two hundred years time its main function could well be as an example of our quaint technology of reproduction, or even the bizarre protocol of our optics; it would have been removed from its original function and significance, just as a medieval altarpiece, placed inside an art gallery, has had its function utterly transformed by its change of context.

In his book *Mythologies* Roland Barthes argues that a myth is a way of rendering natural that which is in fact historical, cultural or political. It can be a narrative, but does not need to be: it can be a picture, a song, even a gesture, as long as it articulates itself as mythic sign. Another way of putting this could be to say that myth appears to render scientific, as a fact of nature, that which is in fact culturally and historically contingent.

Let us take the moment in the church wedding ceremony when the father of the bride 'gives her away'. No one gives the groom away. So, if we use Barthes' categories here, what we see is a ceremonial gesture in which the patriarchal myth expresses itself. A woman is always possessed by a man, father or husband, unless she chooses the identity of spinster, which is to say one who must now provide for herself at her spinning-wheel; one who remains self-sufficient (and childless) at her loom. The bride to be did once have an actual price on her head in the form of a dowry.

Freud believed himself to be a mythographer; we now think of him as being at least as much a mythologist. He created a world of meaning which has never been underpinned, as he had initially dreamt it would be, by the rigorous techniques of science. What is of value in his work is not his discovery of a universal principle in the infant psyche called the Oedipus Complex. The conflicts he might have been observing here were surely far more localised than he ever imagined. What is of value is his elaboration of the nature of narrative. What Freud came to believe about the psychoanalytic space and dynamic was that there was no immediately disclosable truth; that the truth could only tell itself through the procedure of its own self-discovered enunciation. There was no short-cut into this. The narrative would form itself through encounters with occlusions and repressions. The narrative must inevitably encounter these; it cannot evade them. Encountering the repressions, and seeing how they were enacted – this is an integral part of the improvised narrative. The sinuousness of this manoeuvre has of course led to accusations of the whole procedure being unscientific. Psychoanalysis is certainly not scientific, in the sense of obeying the protocol of experimental science as practised since Galileo. It is unable to provide evidences of its own falsifiability, a failure which, according to Popper, made it spurious. Einstein could provide such evidences. He predicted precisely to what extent light from distant stars would bend around the sun in the event of a solar eclipse. A solar eclipse provided the opportunity for the measurements to be made, as they duly were by Arthur Eddington, and they showed Einstein's theory to be in accordance with scientific observations. Had they not done, his theory would have been shown to be untenable. But if there is any 'scientific truth' in Freud then it is in the older sense of *scientia*, of the accumulated body of knowledge of different sorts. Narratives are more flexible, more freely exploratory, than mathematical proofs.

Not all truths can disclose themselves with the clarity of an equation. Wittgenstein distinguished between truths that could be told and those that could only be shown. The example he gave was the height of Mont Blanc. If I know this, then it is meaningless to say that I cannot tell you what it is. But what of the sound of a clarinet? I might know this very well, but I cannot 'tell' you; I can only show it. Language breaks down here. Language cannot convey the sound a clarinet makes.

Let us consider two types of map: the London Underground map devised by Harry Beck, and the ones that preceded it. The earlier ones tended to be topographical, which is to say they situated the railway lines in the actual landscape of London. Beck's map is topological: it ignores all relationships except those between stations and lines. It is not interested in real distances, or the actual trajectory (topographically speaking) of any of the lines. It is a brilliant map because it presents with great lucidity the interconnecting system of the railway. It maximises signal and minimises noise. The topographical maps, by contrast, retained much of the noise of the actual topography of London to such an extent that it was hard work discerning the searched-for signal: how do I get from here to there by the most economical means on this railway system?

We must always beware, however, in so fine-tuning the signal-to-noise ratio. By effectively excluding so much noise, might we exclude some information which should have been included? By banishing topographic information, Beck's map might mislead us into imagining that the outlying stations on the longest lines will be reached much more quickly than is actually the case. The map presents the whole railway system as a convenient village of communications. It is no such thing. It takes hours to get from one side of the Underground to the other. The furthest reaches of the London Underground map are not underground; nor are they even in London.

A famous example of the dangers inherent in tuning our signal-to-noise ratio too fiercely is the discovery of the background radiation of the universe. In 1964 in New Jersey, Arno Penzias and Robert Wilson were working on radio waves. They were picking up interference, noise. They tried to get rid of it. They even removed some nesting pigeons, which they assumed had been 'causing the problem'. Fortunately, something transmuted this noise into a signal; interference suddenly became information. Astrophysicists at Princeton had predicted that the Big Bang must have been accompanied by a mighty radiation blast. Look in the right place, they said, and you would surely find it. Wilson and Penzias had found it, in fact, but they hadn't been looking, and therefore hadn't been seeing. Because of the topological map in their minds, they were trying to lose it again. Fortunately the two sources of information joined up and we discovered and measured background radiation. Had we not evolved the theory of the Big Bang, that background radiation would still be noise. We would have had no topological schema in which to situate the data, and find the pattern meaningful.

We know that myth functions like a topological map: it transforms the topography into a specific shape of perception. It appears to have a palpable agenda, but it cannot be analysed merely in terms of its manifest content. Freud understood how psychic significance, investment of energy or *cathexis*, is frequently in inverse proportion to self-disclosure through manifest content. It is the latent content which must reveal the real significance for the psyche of this particular mythic site. It is often harder to see how science sometimes functions in the same way. We can perhaps see it most clearly when we look at the Ptolemaic system. It seemed not merely natural but proveable that we were situated at the centre of the universe; that everything revolved around us. It was a battle to retrieve enough of the actual topographical information so that this dogmatic topology might be superseded. Science needed to transcend itself, so as to become more scientific. Perhaps we might come to feel that the topological exclusion principle of our times is our metaphysic of things. We talk of electrons and protons and neutrons, but are nouns really the best way to classify these phenomena? Even ascribing nouns to them might betray our hidden topological agenda, as David Bohm has pointed out. Bohm was intrigued by the way that certain Native American languages are verb-based, so that sentences in them can have no nouns at all; instead, they convey an unmediated dynamic process. Underlying all our microcosmic realities are not minute 'things', but processes and forces, which cannot properly be specified into objects. And yet the unspoken epistemology of our naming of objects and particles subliminally suggests that all moving things must come to rest at some point, and can then be turned through three hundred and sixty degrees for scrupulous examination. Our nominal assumptions here seem to be radically misrepresenting nature. The word particle itself carries an implication of solidity, of thingness or quiddity. If you treat an electron like an object and try to get it to sit still so as to have its portrait taken, the electron disappears. 'We are suspended in language,' said Bohr, and the terms of that suspension can easily mislead.

We might elaborate the distinction between topography and topology a little more extravagantly. Topography, we could say, is realism and metonymy; it represents that horizontal line along which we describe historic occurrence with, we hope, forensic exactitude. Topology by contrast is vertical, connecting discrete intellectual regions, delighting in a riot of categories. So to which realm does the algebraic equation belong? The most famous equation of all time is Einstein's. It brings together energy, mass, and light in its immaterial speediness. No metaphor ever moved more swiftly than this through heterogenous realms.

While Freud was elaborating his notion of myth, Sir James Frazer was writing *The Golden Bough*. The fundamental assumption behind that work was that myth was an early and erroneous attempt at science, a primitive and bungled description of reality which science would subsequently supersede. There was not enough reality in myth. Freud's argument was pretty much the opposite: the reason something becomes mythic is because there is too much reality in it. It cannot be contained in the normal discourse of existence; cannot be held steadily in consciousness; it becomes cathected, which is to say that an investment of energy beyond conscious control exaggerates the dynamic of the mythic representation. Myths are dangerous because they gather such a vortex of psychic energy around them, while never fully disclosing even to themselves the original motivation. Art does something similar, but without any requirement for credal subscription. Aby Warburg believed that art stood midway between the primacy of unmediated perception and the ultimate distancing of conceptual rationality. It inhabited a vortex in which contrary forces could be expressed without either being diminished. There is a similar perception in Lévi-Strauss's notion of the working of the *bricoleur*, that poet of the mythic mode: between the perception and the sign, he says, is the image. Art then can function as a representational space in which contradictory forces are momentarily reconciled as complementary. This makes it culturally essential. Art permits a negotiation between forces which must otherwise war upon one another. Contradiction appears under the aspect of complementarity: Newton's light enters one prism as particle, exits the second as wave. Either/or becomes both/and.

There is one last aspect to our topological formations which Barthes does not explore: it is a species of myth to imagine that culture can always be read back into history; identity into nativity; artistic form into social form. This is an expression of the myth, once scientifically credible, that all of the contingency encountered in life can necessarily be translated into causality. Quantum physics and chaos theory between them should have done away with this particular manoeuvre for ever, but it constantly re-appears. The anti-Stratfordian position regarding Shakespeare's work is an expression of such a mythology. The great unexpected potency of Shakespeare's writing, its unprecedented exploratory manoeuvres, its sudden and astounding heuristic autonomy, cannot be accepted. Since the universality of this work can never be explained by the background, education and occupation of William Shakespeare of Stratford, we must choose instead another historical figure, an aristocrat and courtier, who would have been knowledgeable in precisely those areas where Shakespeare was not. The fact is (and here we encounter the mythology with force) Shakespeare's work cannot be 'read back' into the biography of any historical figure at all. It can be historically situated, but not historically explained. It outruns its explanations. That is the source of the intellectual exhilaration it generates. This is work of such richness that it still situates us more than we can situate those plays. Hamlet is still sounding us more thoroughly than we sound him in return

There is always a dissonance between social existence and any serious artistic achievement, whatever consonance there might also be. If it is good enough, it always comes as a surprise. Shakespeare is still surprising us four hundred years on. We find ourselves in a world of representation at least as vivid as our own. No one has ever written anything more intelligent than *Hamlet*, a fact as shocking in its way as Freud's belief that *Oedipus Rex* contained an ancient allegorical truth, of which contemporary science had remained entirely oblivious.

V

THE SELF-SUBVERSION OF THE BOOK.

IN THE YEAR of Shakespeare's death, 1616, Ben Jonson collected and published his own works. Such an edition was novel; it treated a living writer's work as though it had the status of a classic. The *imprimatur* of such a 'definitive edition' announced that contemporary writing for the stage could be laid side by side with the works of the ancients, without embarrassment. Then 1623 saw the publication of the Folio of Shakespeare's works. The playwright had now been dead for seven years. The work had been assembled by Heminges and Condell, his companions in the world of the theatre.

Once again, contemporary work was presented as having sufficient authority to be printed in a substantial edition. Both the edition of Jonson and that of Shakespeare announce that contemporary literature of the highest calibre had true authority, and therefore should be published authoritatively.

Just over one century later, Alexander Pope would be working on *The Dunciad*. This work would accrue, agglomerate, grab everything of interest in the London of its time; a London, intellectually speaking, of inversion and degradation, at least if the poet is to be believed. It would, initially at Swift's prompting, begin to gather footnotes about it, until their gargantuan proportions competed with the lines of the verse; cod scholarship threatened to inundate the text for which it supposedly provided a glossary.

And now, in our own time, the glossary itself has come to require a further glossary; the annotations now need themselves to be annotated. The gesture involved in the publication of the Folio is here being subverted from every direction. This definitive edition has, in effect, become a mockery of itself. The epic of dullness must be provided with a scholarly machinery which is itself an exercise in pedantic dementia.

THREE DECADES EARLIER, Swift had written *A Tale of a Tub*. This work too provides its own scholarly machinery of footnotes, prefaces, glosses, explications – all of which are in effect decorations for the Bedlam walls of its literary madhouse. The footnotes put into question the veracity of the text, but then the text, left to its own devices, was already chewing up any evidence of its own veracity. Even Martin, who is presumably meant to exemplify at least the possibility of an intermediate sanity between Peter and Jack, appears to be only fractionally less demented than they are. Extremity here runs its course; the centre cannot hold. We seem quickly to be approaching that condition philosophers refer to as 'infinitized irony'. The subversive voice ceases to have a dialectical effect, prompting its necessary reply from the margins of sanity, and becomes instead the dominant note of a chorus. There is no one voice we are hearing: the voices instead are legion. And no one voice, it appears, can secure the wayward energy of so many competing voices; the hydra's heads all have a tongue apiece. And the pit from which they sing is a vortex.

What *A Tale of A Tub* and *The Dunciad* have in common is a radical self-consciousness in regard to themselves as books, not merely compositions but books, and this self-consciousness is employed to subvert the status of the book itself; to foreground the question of its authority. Both books mock the pretensions of any book to assert the truth; both ridicule what Walter Benjamin would call the book's 'universal gesture'. In arriving at the moment of their own belatedness in the tradition, they assume the role of commentary upon a pre-existing text. Here they link with the strategy of Borges, who was clearly aware of the precedents of Swift and Pope, and of what such precedence might represent. As Italo Calvino says of the Argentinian writer:

> *What helped him overcome the block that had prevented him, almost until he was forty, from moving from essays to narrative prose was to pretend that the book he wanted to write had already been written, written by someone else, by an unknown invented author, an author from another language, another culture, and then to describe, summarise or review that hypothetical book.*

One immediate effect of this strategy is to abolish the illusion that there is a single plane of text, one into which the reader's consciousness might enter unproblematically, and remain there for the duration of the narrative. A footnote alerts the critical consciousness to the existence of a region beyond one plane of reading.[1] An ellipsis marked in the text (a favourite technique in *A Tale of Tub*) informs us that the text itself cannot be assumed to vouch for its own complete integrity, since the rats of entropy and misprision have already been chewing away, even during the act of writing. Prefaces and introductions, which distance the author as editor from the actual authorship of the text to follow, insert a question-filled distance between author and text, text and reader. In other words, that very gesture of guaranteed authenticity (*videlicet*, guaranteed authorship), which the edi-

---

[1]   So that one must flick back and forth between textual planes, like this.

tions of Jonson and Shakespeare sought to claim and proclaim for themselves, is here being deliberately undermined, not by the pirates and plagiarists of Grub Street, but by the authors themselves.

A text can be imbued with every narrative and rhetorical device so as to assert its authority as that single plane of reality which, once entered, proclaims its supremacy over all competing forms of consciousness until the narrative rite of passage is complete; or it can, on the contrary, draw attention to its own rhetoric, its devices either overt or covert – in a word, to its artfulness. In not merely employing its art but also foregrounding such an art's devices, it must inevitably draw attention to itself as an expression not of unironized sincerity, but instead of skilful construction. This leads, not necessarily to the abolition of sincerity, but certainly to its self-questioning as a form of rhetorical expression. The modes and manners of sincerity are themselves asked to prove themselves as amounting to more than a congeries of rhetorical manoeuvres. The 'page-turner' must at least admit its identity as a sequence of pages.

IN THE FIRST lines of Nabokov's *Despair* we are told 'If I were not perfectly sure of my power to write and of my marvellous ability to express ideas with the utmost grace and vividness…So, more or less, I had thought of beginning my tale.' But this strategy is abandoned. In the explanation as to why, the reader is apostrophized as 'gentle reader'. A somewhat elaborate simile is attempted, comparing the narrative to a bus, but it is abandoned: 'Rather bulky imagery, this.' Then we revert to the traditional narrative device of genealogy: 'My father was a Russian-speaking German from Reval, where he went to a famous agricultural college. My mother, a pure Russian, came from an old princely stock.' A few lines later, we are told: 'A slight digression: that bit about my mother was a deliberate lie. In reality, she was a woman of the people, simple and coarse, sordidly dressed in a kind of blouse hanging loose at the waist.' So why does the author contradict himself? Why does he not cross out the previous description? He leaves it in 'as a sample of one of my essential traits: my light-hearted inspired lying.' The information is put into parenthetical question, so that another type of information might accrue: information about the identity of the narrator, and necessary data about the way fiction itself is 'put together'.

The phrase 'in reality' had pointed us, of course, to the dimensions of reality which are available within the book, its planar perspectives. And in terms of the 'slight digression', all fiction is a digression from the serious business of acting. All writing that analyses human motivation or describes the psychological condition of its characters is to some degree recapitulating the fable of Achilles and the tortoise: to the extent that every distance is infinitely divisible into more and more minute units of description, writing is a series of parentheses within parentheses. Its very nature is to be digressive. We are in one sense getting nowhere. The kind of writing we are examining here does not exist simply to 'get on with things', in the manner of a John Buchan story. It translates such 'things' into modes of understanding, so that the constellations of consciousness might be delineated a little more brightly.

And here the fictiveness of fiction has surely grown ever-more aware of its distantiation from 'scientific writing'. Six years before the edition of Jonson and thirteen before the Shakespeare Folio, a book was published which offered not the planar perspectives of epistemological self-questioning, but a new description of 'the facts' of our situation here in the universe. The book was Galileo's *Sidereus Nuncius* of 1610. As a result of his development of the telescope, Galileo could see the pockmarked surface of the moon; the four circumjovial planets; something of the vastness of the Milky Way. His book gave testimony to this new evidence. It is simultaneously a celebration of ocular discovery and a series of scientific assertions. Pirated copies were soon being sold across Europe. Everyone with any interest in the scientific dimensions of reality wanted a copy of this book, and a telescope to accompany it, where possible.

NOW WE MUST confront a dilemma which has never since been resolved. What nature of truth might books offer us, if any? Swift's patron Sir William Temple was explicit: truth lay in the ancient texts, the new ones having added nothing of any significance. At Moor Park in Surrey he wrote in 1692 'Upon the Ancient and the Modern Learning', the gist of which can be conveyed thus: nothing new in the way of discovery or science has in any way displaced the great philosophical tradition. Nothing substantial has been *added*. And Swift went along with this, being entirely dependent upon Temple's good will. And it this Swift, at the same intellectual moment, who in *A Tale of A Tub* effectively despairs of detecting any voice which might tell an indisputable truth about the world we inhabit. None of the voices in *A Tale* is really striving for truth; they are all rhetoricians in Nietzsche's sense, employing the arts of language and persuasion to increase their power and indulge their appetites. If ancient wisdom obtains, it is in its hard-bitten ability to perceive and articulate the corruption of humanity. Three decades before *A Tale* Thomas Sprat had written his *History of the Royal Society*. There he had pleaded for a new language, a language of plain description which would declare war upon a certain 'vicious abundance of phrase' – i.e. metaphor. It sometimes seems as though Swift is exemplifying the Bishop's execration. The hideous fecundity of metaphor, the nightmarish generative prolixity of language, is here proclaimed: '...whereas, *Wisdom* is a *Fox*, who after long hunting, will at last cost you the pains to dig out: 'Tis a *Cheese*, which by how much the richer, has the thicker, the homelier, and the courser Coat; and whereof to a judicious Palate, the *Maggots* are the best. 'Tis a *Sack-Posset*, wherein the deeper you go, you will find it the sweeter. *Wisdom* is a *Hen*, whose *Cackling* we must value and consider, because it is attended with an *Egg*; But then, lastly, 'tis a *Nut*, which unless you chuse with Judgment, may cost you a Tooth, and pay you with nothing but a *Worm*.'

It is surely hard not to hear in this engulfing of judgment by the rich suggestiveness of language a specific precedent:

> *Hamlet: Do you see yonder cloud that's almost in shape of a camel?*
>
> *Polonius: By th'mass and 'tis – like a camel indeed.*
>
> *Hamlet: Methinks it is like a weasel.*
>
> *Polonius: It is backed like a weasel.*
>
> *Hamlet: Or like a whale.*
>
> *Polonius: Very like a whale.*

Hamlet's point of course is the infinite tractability of the courtier before a royal will, but in making his point he has employed the infinite productivity of language in figuring the world; and this is Swift's device too. Once the coinages begin then, like a corrupt mint (another of Swift's many obsessions) there is no necessary end to the debasement of the currency, and therefore the debasement of the realm. Where has the authority of the book disappeared to, given such a 'vicious abundance of phrase'? And what in any case, Swift seems to ask, is the purpose of any narrative? The vulgar pleasantries they might afford are eschewed thus in *A Tale*:

> *I shall not trouble you with recounting what Adventures they met for the first seven Years, any farther than by taking notice, that they carefully observed their Father's Will, and kept their Coats in very good Order; That they travelled thro' several Countries, encountered a reasonable Quantity of Gyants, and slew certain Dragons.*

So much for enfolding the reader in the narrative adventure. Given the profound alienation of Gulliver from his human fellows on his return from his travels, so that he finds his wife repellent, and sleeps in the stable with his horses, one can't help wondering whether Swift regarded the hunt for the exotic in the form of fiction – whether writing it or reading it – as a straight-forward degradation of the moral faculties; which would, in effect, make it one more severe questioning of the authority of 'the book', the sort of book in which metaphor runs riot; in which the referent grows smaller and smaller, like figures out of Lilliput.

BY THE TIME Nabokov comes to write *Pale Fire*, the notion of the text accompanied by its necessary commentary has become an institutional aspect of the late European intellectual tradition. Nabokov made his living for many years as an academic teaching literature, and was as aware as anyone can be of the necessity of producing interpretation and analysis; that after all is the nature of the job. The setting of most of the novel is a university; the poet is tied to the university; the critic teaches at the university. And if the latter is mildly more demented than most of the characters who occupy such posts, this, it is implied, is surely a matter only of degree. Kinbote claims to come from Zembla, an emblem of impossibly distant places, taken from Pope's *Dunciad*. Kinbote's commentary on John Shade's poem functions in the way an anti-Stratfordian's commentary on the works of Shakespeare might do: to show what an infinity of interpretation is possible for any text, and to show too how much the reader's desire inevitably commands the textual truth. It shows Sprat's 'vicious abundance of phrase' to have had a point, and it demonstrates how, in a world of proliferating titles, 'the authority of the book' is hard to find. It is necessary for Kinbote's intellectual survival that he should find Shade's poem to be preoccupied with himself; consequently, he does so find it, even though other interpreters can see no such textual evidence themselves.

And here we must remind ourselves of Francis Bacon, who wrote:

All depends on keeping the eye steadily fixed on the facts of nature, and so receiving their images as they are. For God forbid that we should give out a dream of our own imagination for a pattern of the world.

And yet isn't this precisely the space fiction creates for itself, and the freedom it allows itself? What then is it that fiction is permitting itself to discover? The constellations of consciousness, the way we arrange and re-arrange reality so that it might function for us, and we might find a functional relationship with it; in portraying a bottle, we are not trying to find the chemical composition of the bottle, but rather the way such a bottle is arranged in the spectrum of perception, as in a Cubist painting. We are examining how we all of us, to some degree, give out a dream of our own imagination for a pattern of the world. Wordsworth in 'Tintern Abbey' speaks of 'both what they half create, and what perceive.' To the extent that the modernists deliberately elected 'primitive' modes and forms, they were rejecting the realist notion of 'receiving images as they are', in favour of the radical interplay between imagination and reality, which generates its own 'pattern of the world'.

THE MOTTO OF the Royal Society whose virtue and whose precision of language Sprat was extolling was: *Nullius in Verba*, a contraction from the line of Horace: *Nullius addictus iurare in verba magistri*, translated by Freeman Dyson as 'Sworn to follow the words of no master'. That is surely another way of saying that knowledge and wisdom cannot be assumed to lie in books, however ancient, however sanctioned by tradition. In other words, Sir William Temple was wrong, and Swift along with him: the only way to find out about reality was to go and test it for yourself. This was the new science, devoted to experiment, calculation and measurement. What Aristotle said was not the truth: there was not a celestial realm of perfection, where nothing ever changes. The pockmarked face of the moon seen through Galileo's telescope proved this. He had seen imperfection in the heavens, and he used his book *Sidereus Nuncius* to prove the fact. The authority of one book was here dislodging the authority of another. This is the real battle of the books.

Donne is much preoccupied in his writings with how the new philosophy is destabilising the realm of learning and tradition; how it 'puts all in doubt'. And a fracture begins to open up at this point between writing which, in the words of Bacon quoted earlier, is 'keeping the eye steadily fixed on the facts of nature, and so receiving their images as they are' and that other species of writing which Bacon deprecates, which 'should give out a dream of our own imagination for a pattern of the world'. The receiving of images starts to come into conflict with their autonomous generation. Out of this conflict will be generated the notion and the image of the Romantic artist.

There were two contradictory versions of light extant until Newton resolved the matter in his *Optics*. One tradition, the *lux* version, held that light shone from within us outwards; selected its object and focused the inner light upon it. The other spoke of *lumen*, the notion that light falls upon the object, is reflected and then enters our vision, so that we might receive the images 'as they really are'. If the latter is the modern scientific description of the operation of light, the former has continued its hermetic tradition as the iconography of genius. Picasso painting with light, Einstein with the electrodes fastened to his head while he was instructed to 'think about relativity' – these images surely hang on to that notion that the light shines from within, and spreads its illumination outwards. This is the work of the artist or the writer who has shaken free from the constrictions of a scientific tradition which will only let us describe the world as the reception of a series of 'images as they are'.

In Borges this conundrum re-iterates itself as one of textuality: there is always a text before us. Our imagination, and for that matter our rationality, can only function by acknowledging that between us and 'the world' lies the text, whether it is that of a medieval cabbalist, or that of a natural philosopher who assembles the data, the taxonomies, the genealogies and the laws, and then attempts to construct a meaningful world from the assembly. So what is it then that the imagination can do in the face of such a text? It can only re-create it in the terms of possibility and imagination available to the writer now. The ultimate extremity of this gambit is 'Pierre Menard: Author of the Quixote'. Here the text, in its inescapability, its canonic immovability, cannot be changed; it can only be re-written, word for word, line by line. Once the new text is assembled, however, it will be seen to be entirely different from the old one, since the reality to which the words are pointing us has changed so irrefutably in the intervening centuries. Signifier and signified now have a different relationship.

This version of the book, which accepts its own subversion of knowledge, claims that it compensates for its deviation from the received images as we know 'they really are', by its exploration instead of the realm of understanding. This distinction is one which Wittgenstein used in a different area, but it might be useful here. Philosophy, he said, does not advance knowledge. That is why ancient philosophy can still tell us modern truths, whereas ancient science can only provide data about the history of itself. It is why, in one sense, Wittgenstein instructs us at the end of the *Tractatus*, to accept the dubiousness of the passage through which the book has directed us, if we accept the truth it is edging towards. A Borges story is helping us understand how the mind arranges and re-arranges the world so that it might inhabit it. It is not then giving us 'knowledge', which it has abandoned as belonging to the realm of science, but 'understanding', which is the way in which the intellect makes the world and society habitable for itself.

BUT BACK TO *The Dunciad*, a precursor of so much that was to come. In his essay 'The Literature of Exhaustion' John Barth described a condition where one arrives at the end of the tradition, to find literature completed: everything worth doing has effectively been done. This is the condition Harold Bloom refers to as belatedness. It is the literary equivalent of the situation Jackson Pollock found himself in, when he lay in bed one morning reading a large book on Picasso. On finishing it, he threw the book at the wall, and said, 'The bastard's already done everything'. Jackson Pollock's answer to this state of encyclopædic completion was what came to be called action painting. And the literary equivalent, the escape from such belatedness, would be what exactly? Barth speaks of the concept of the artist as 'the Aristotelian conscious agent who achieves with technique and cunning the artistic effect'. This notion that the creation of art involves impeccable technique combined with spiritual acceleration still haunts us, but we often seem to find it easier to apply such categories to the past, rather than the present. There's no doubt the two factors are there in Rembrandt, but in Damien Hirst? Technique he often leaves to others, and the notion of spiritual acceleration would presumably do little more than raise a snigger at the Groucho Club. This older concept of the artist is under attack, Barth reckons, because it is not thought to be democratic enough. He himself still likes it, all the same.

Barth reminds us that in the great story of Borges, 'Tlön, Uqbar, Orbis Tertius', no book is thought to be complete in Tlön which does not contain the terms of its own refutation. This is how we escape the Panglossian fatuity, the pseudo-mystical winsomeness that no serious person truly believes a word of in any case: we include the negative equivalent for every positive term. Thus do we supply the terms of refutation of the book itself. So, in the case of *The Dunciad*, we supply the Variorum Edition, where no one can come along in our wake and footnote us into dullness or idiocy, since we have already done that ourselves, at the inception of the text. In their vivid self-consciousness as books, as rhetorical manœuvres which are always vulnerable to being out-manoeuvred by subsequent texts, both *A Tale of A Tub* and *The Dunciad* announce a species of modernity. Only a century has passed since the publication of the First Folio, but we are living in another age. The Gutenberg Revolution has now passed through three hundred and sixty degrees. The authority of the book is being flatly contradicted by the book itself. No idiot, however egregious, can degrade any further by coarse interpretation a text which already adumbrates this supreme good, to be achieved by the employment of philosophy: 'The Serene Peaceful State of being a Fool among Knaves.'

The self-subverting book gets over its resentment at its inadequate reception before it is even published. Anticipating stupidity and mendacity in equal measure it builds them into itself beforehand, often as a form of textual machinery. Like Prospero looking upon Caliban, it declares: 'This thing of darkness I acknowledge mine.' It advertises its resentment through its own annotations on itself. Pope had no illusions about what awaited him out there in the world of the great and the good. Pamphlets were published against him monthly for the last three decades of his life. Here is a characteristic example from 1728: 'The *Frame and make of Pope's Body* is thrown into the favourable Scale, and inclines People to excuse and forgive him; for it is generally remark'd, that crooked, minute, and deform'd People, are peevish, quarrelsome, waspish, and ill-natur'd; and the Reason is, the *Soul* has not Room enough to pervade and expand itself thro' all their nibbed, tiney Parts, and this makes it press sorely on the Brain, which is of a yielding Substance; and this *Pressure* again causes frequent Irritations and *Twinges on the Nerves*, which makes the crooked Person exert his Hands, his Feet, and his Tongue, in sudden *Starts* and *Fits*, which are very uneasy to himself, and which prove disagreeable and outragious [sic], often, to others.'

SO THERE WE have it. Pope was as nasty as he was because he was a crippled dwarf. As the Randy Newman song regarding small people announces, you'd have to pick him up just to say hello. Out of such a wretched and deformed body, together with its concomitant deformation of spirit, you can't expect much, other than poison and bile, and you most certainly won't be disappointed. *The Dunciad* might be the greatest work of resentment to achieve the status of great art. The textual machinery of *The Dunciad* is a device for containing the world's witlessness while simultaneously exemplifying it; the commentary on John Shade's poem in Nabokov's *Pale Fire* does exactly the same thing. Here the world's dementia is localized in the monomaniacal mind of Charles Kinbote. Pope's main target famously shifted from Lewis Theobald to Colley Cibber, but the real target is larger. The real target did not have only one name; its name was legion.

The self-subverting book says this: you are surrounded by the products of dullness and meretricious self-applause, but here is a book which has mocked itself before you could even read it, and understands entirely the terms that will be provided for its own destruction. It is a tribute to the poem's modernity that it contains within itself the terms of its own negation; it understands the manner of its own anticipated cancellation. It is, as it were, pre-mocked. It certainly does not confine itself to the affirmative, and any writing that does now surely risks appearing as a form of sentimentality. At such a belated moment in culture, the affirmative mood unalloyed can seem perilously close to kitsch. The affirmative faced with modernity is a mood that tends to modulate swiftly into the subjunctive, since our affirmations can only be local, never universal.

In his essay on *The Dunciad,* written to mark the publication of the Twickenham edition, F. R. Leavis insisted the notes were not needed: '…notes are not necessary: the poetry doesn't depend upon them in any essential respect.' But then we would inevitably be confined to the one plane of the verse. So much exquisite versification, examples of which Leavis quotes, is not diminished by being surrounded by the unceasing clatter of dullness in the form of the textual machinery; on the contrary, it is enhanced. The footnoted dullness is a foil upon which the verse might glitter all the more brightly. *The Dunciad* represents the midnight of the sublime; this is the darkest voicing of lyric exactitude before Paul Celan.

Can any genuinely modern work afford to be entirely without irony? Irony constitutes the book's anti-self; the condition of its non-being. From the looking-glass world of negation, every value the book represents is threatened constantly with extinction. By acknowledging this threat in the texture of its own writing, the book at least inoculates itself against any bogus innocence, that *gestus* of theatrical wonder with which the insincere like to put a broad smile upon their insincerity. The self-subverting book instead says this: you are surrounded by the products of dullness, mendacity and self-applause. Here is a book which has mocked itself before you could even read it, and understands entirely the terms of its own demolition. Pre-mocked already, it knows what is at stake.

VI

SCIENCE AND DISENCHANTMENT.

1

GALILEO HAD A plank down which he rolled different-sized metal balls. He was questioning Aristotle, according to whom bigger balls should have reached the ground first. But they didn't. All the balls, whatever their size, arrived at the same time. This was the plank of disenchantment, of measurement and close observation. When the balls reached the bottom of the plank, two thousand years of Aristotelianism died there and then, and ever since, experiment has taken over from scripture. Don't take anyone's word for it: *Nullius in verba* became the motto of the Royal Society later in that century, the seventeeth.

2

ACCORDING TO MIRCEA Eliade, in shamanistic communities, the shaman's home has a pole (sometimes a tree) which goes through the roof. During the ceremonies of initiation the shaman climbs to the end of this pole, thus establishing that he has journeyed to the extremities of perception, travelled where the non-initiated members of the community cannot go. He returns with a different level of consciousness, an ability to perceive and heal illness, an awareness of the realm of the spirits. He is now fully initiated.

Must we chose one or the other of these as our *axis mundi*? We live, it seems, between the pole and the plank; between our continuing wish to be enchanted and our eagerness to disenchant the world through science (to know it as it really is, not as we would wish it to be). The question is put to us daily: which is it to be? But is it possible that the choice is a false one, like being asked to choose your left mental hemisphere or your right? Are we being told we must choose one side of the paper or the other? Maybe the pole and the plank represent complementary aspects of the human condition. Could they both be the expression of fundamental needs?

WHY DO WE REPRESENT?

TO REPRESENT THE world is to absent ourselves temporarily from it. We cannot be seamlessly situated in the present moment, and also be simultaneously situated so as to create a representation. The creation of a representation requires a separation from that which is represented; we cannot simply merge into the perception. We disengage from the present and absorb ourselves instead in what Max Raphael called 'the means of figuration'.[1] Here then the scientific and the artistic moments share at least one condition of existence: displacement from utter absorption in the sensuous moment.

Were our earliest intellectual acts in fact moments of orientation? Did we have to remove ourselves from the sensuous continuum in order to situate ourselves intellectually in the world? Constellations may well have been the first moment of art and the first moment of science too. At that stage in human history there was no distinction between the two. What is interesting about the constellations is that they are both there and not there. It is our moment of perception, linking up the light of different stars from different times, which creates the constellations; and yet our astronomical charts are still filled with them. These gods, goddesses and mythical hunters populate the heavens. In constellations, the past and the present co-exist; different planes of reality are brought together to form mythic shapes. There is only one single plane upon which these realities co-exist, and that is the plane of perception.

A representation is an exteriorization of perception, but also its negotiation into form; we make our marks upon the cave wall, and thereby project the perceptions we have of the world back on to the exterior world from which they came. In the process, they metamorphose.

SCIENCE AND MAGIC.

OUR FIRST ATTEMPTS at science appear to have been primarily magical. There was no distinction as yet between the scientific and the manipulative impulse. We placed ourselves in a relation with nature where rain could be summoned, fecundity guaranteed, sickness and death averted, or wishes fulfilled. There was often built into these procedures and ceremonies an acknowledgment of the nature of reality, even where the impulse was to overcome it. For example, the rain dance demonstrates an awareness that rain is a necessity if crops are to flourish. Therianthropic masks worn by spiritual agents of various sorts acknowledge a physical strength in animals which is not present to anything like the same degree in humans. Herbs initially used for their magical properties proved themselves efficacious in some cases; ineffective in others. So through experiment a therapy began to take shape, even an effective one. Magic can measure itself by results, just as experimental science can. We can, if we look hard enough, find the rudiments of some of our present practices there: a doctor still takes something from the earth and gives it to the patient for ingestion into the body, so as to avert or palliate illness. Drugs go 'on trial', and when they are deemed efficacious enough we call them 'wonder drugs'. We have undoubtedly shifted the nature of the correspondences, and their alignments one to another. With the demise of alchemy, we have looked increasingly to experiment and measurable results to dictate the nature of our science. Alchemy is the last moment when the magical is still permitted as a licit element of the genuinely scientific enterprise, and it is a moment that has a sort of afterlife in Newton, who would appear to have regarded force at a distance as an occult power, and who never gave up his alchemical experiments to the end of his life.

Already the plank and the pole no longer seem so far apart. What is it that the shaman is doing when he climbs his pole? The word *shaman* is derived from the word sorcerer in the Tungus language. A shaman could visit the land of the dead; bilocate; assume an animal form. A shaman would undergo a psychic vastation, a journey across the valley of death, and only after that would his control of the spirit world enable him to perform curative acts. Like Dante, he must first undergo the terrors of the Inferno before the paradisal state might be witnessed and vouchsafed.

THE CONTRADICTION OF THE SENSES
AND DISENCHANTMENT.

NULLIUS IN VERBA: don't take anyone's word for it. Examine it; observe it; record it; experiment. Modern science tells us that what we perceive is untrue. It frequently contradicts common sense. It is obvious that a heavy object will fall to the earth faster than a lighter one, so obvious that Aristotle stated the fact and its factuality was accepted for two thousand years. Galileo showed 'the fact' to be untrue by experiment and measured observation, science's techniques of disenchantment. We do not sit on a stationary earth at the centre of the universe. This appears to be the case to our unexperimental senses, certainly. But science has established that we inhabit a tiny space inside an unimaginably vast one; that we spin around, although we do not appear to be doing so to ourselves; that the sun does not rise above our settled selves and then set later in the day, while our point of observation remains unmoving. The old perceptions that this is precisely what does happen continue their afterlives in our use of the words 'sunrise' and 'sunset'.

And then science really gets started in earnest. Not only are we not at the centre of our universe, but we are not even separated by the act of creation from the realm of the animals. We all have a common ancestor, so Darwin assures us. We name the animals, after all, they don't name us, but it still turns out that we have all emerged from the same struggle for existence. And our sacred texts (such as the Bible) turn out not to be dependable accounts of how we got here, certainly not in 'the literal sense'. Bishop Ussher in the seventeenth century famously used the Old Testament to calculate the age of the earth. 4004 BCE was his confident assessment. But along came disenchanting science to assert that there was not enough time given to us here; the Book of Genesis was seriously short of time to get us to our destination, if what Lyell was asserting in *Principles of Geology* was to be believed. Once again the perceptions we have so carefully grouped into beliefs, the narratives we have created to account for our position in the scheme of things, find themselves contradicted by the juggernaut of enquiry we have come to call science, an activity that appears to move along in its progress without either taboo or sentiment, though it can certainly be abused, as it was in the Third Reich and Stalin's USSR.

THE MOMENT OF RECONCILIATION.

THERE WAS A moment between the end of the eighteenth and the beginning of the nineteenth century when 'the truths of religion' and 'the truths of science' seemed to have found a possibility of merging. The one word which conjures this world most economically is 'Unitarian'. The belief in a Creator and the belief in the truths revealed by science were not incompatible; indeed they would prove to be mutually self-supportive. Joseph Priestley's experimentalism, or the combination of religious zeal and technological assiduity of some members of the Lunar Society, all seemed to confirm the possibility of a scientifically informed Christian religion. When Laplace asserted that he could 'now dispense with this hypothesis' (i.e. God) others were still holding on to the notion that they could now establish that same hypothesis as a founding truth for all scientific explorations.

A commitment to determinism and causality meant that all phenomena, including the mental variety, would have to extend back in a logical and explicable chain to the Almighty's originations; hence the burden of Hartley's associationism. It is significant that Coleridge espoused both Hartley and Priestley and very nearly became a Unitarian minister at Shrewsbury. At that moment his radicalism in politics was matched by a radicalism in religion and philosophy. Unitarianism seemed to provide a deistic framework for belief which, by dispensing with miracles and the notion of Jesus of Nazareth as in some way supernatural, allowed for the free play of scientific enquiry. This moment of apparent reconciliation passed in a matter of decades, and has never returned.

SCIENCE AS DISENCHANTMENT.

INSTEAD, AS THE nineteenth century wore on, science seemed to deliver blow after blow to the cynosure of religious belief. Strauss's *Leben Jesu* in 1835 effectively argued that all the supernatural elements accruing to the historical Jesus's life, including the miracles and the virgin birth, were mythic additions, signs of respect inscribed upon the record of the life from worshipful disciples who came later. This did not need to trouble the Unitarians who had already arrived at their own similar conclusions. Lyell's time-scheme for the geological formation of the earth made Bishop Ussher's dating of creation risible. Darwin then came along to assert that there was no individual creation of species. Man was not shaped by Godly fingers, separately in the fastness of Eden, any more than the different species of finches on each separate island of the Galapagos had been made one by one, by a Creator finessing each of his makings in turn. The process of speciation through evolution meant that humankind did not have a privileged place in the scheme of things, except insofar as it had achieved this through a history of cunning and rapacity. We live not at the tip of a providential pyramid of blessings and provisions, but at the top of an invisible mountain of savagery and extinction. Fossils were starting to make this mountain more visible with every day that passed.

By the time Einstein described himself as 'a deeply religious unbeliever' he was effectively saying that his commitment to scientific thought made it impossible for him to subscribe to any known religion; that what was asked of him in terms of credal subscription was not compatible with his intellectual integrity as a scientist. And yet. Why is this unbeliever 'deeply religious'? Is Galileo's plank once more asserting a certain identity with that other carboniferous axis, the shaman's pole?

IN THE CAVE OF SHADOWS.

WE ARE PERMANENTLY negotiating with our own representations. In fact, any representation is a negotiation. Even those who believe Moses wrote the Pentateuch at God's dictation must still acknowledge that a human hand was needed for the transcription. What is at stake is the ability of our representations to yield some kind of truth; or alternatively their potency to provoke falsehood and superstition.

Some of the earliest known makings of humankind are the paintings on the walls of the Palaeolithic caves. These are undoubtedly representations, even if their purpose remains in dispute. Are they emblems of a form of enchantment? There is a kind of measurement going on, or we would not recognise today the shapes of the auroch and the bison. But the measurement is almost certainly instinctive.

We know there were no aurochs or bison down there, so far underground, so our forebears were carrying an impression away and then setting it down; separating themselves from the sensuous moment. They (we?) were in one sense inventing a kind of history, if only a history of perceptions. Variegated perceptions have focused themselves into single images; we have resolved a complex of experiences into a single representation. We have negotiated ourselves out of immersion in the sensuous present.

David Lewis-Williams speculates in *The Mind in the Cave*[2] that these images are the results of shamanic trances, possibly drug-induced, certainly ritualistic. He also alludes to the moment in Plato's *Republic* when Socrates tells Glaucon of the allegory of the prisoners in the cave and the shadows upon the cave wall. How do we know how much reality there is in representation? And if we absorb ourselves sufficiently in representation, does the primary reality from which our imagery is meant to arise diminish in consequence.? Yeats lamented such a state late in his life:

> *Players and painted stage took all my love,*
> *And not those things that they were emblems of.*

The cave-dwellers in Plato's allegory do not realise that the light is projecting images of themselves on to a wall; they take their own secondary shapes as primary realities. They have generated their own phantasmagoria, then subscribed to it as a representation of reality. This will be known at a later date in history as ideology. An unbeliever faced with the Pentateuch and its supposedly divine authorship would have to say something similar: we mistake our own creations for Creation itself. We fetishize the making of our hands as gods. We worship what we ourselves have first brought into being.

ART'S ENCHANTMENT.

DO GALILEO'S PLANK and the shaman's pole represent different and irreconcilable worlds of experience? Are they both the totems at the centre of such different intellectual frameworks that they are frankly incompatible? One world represents itself through the Palaeolithic cave-paintings; and the other through a book like *Sidereus Nuncius*, which Galileo had printed in 1610, to demonstrate the discoveries about the stars and planets he had made through his telescope. Are these two modes of experiencing, observing, measuring and representing the universe and the life contained within it utterly incompatible, or might we perhaps try to think of them instead as complementary?

Let us present ourselves with a melodramatic contrast. How can we reconcile the account of creation in Genesis with Lyell's *Principles of Geology*? How could we reconcile the text that prompted Ussher's dating of the world (using Genesis) to 4004 BCE, and Lyell's requirement of vast periods of time for the terrestrial geological formations to have shaped themselves into their present forms? There could only be one possible reconciliation, and that is through a notion of form, and the specific creativity of form; a sense of the appositeness of types of representation to their specific functions.

In speaking of cinema, Jean-Luc Godard likes to refer to 'forms that think'. Each form, if it has any vitality, thinks in its own specific way. Genesis seen as what it is, a primitive cosmology expressed through Hebrew poetry, works very well. It can even be read as allegory. It cannot, however, be read as modern science. There was no modern science when it was written. To write or think as though Genesis could be 'scientific' in this way is an impossibility founded on a misunderstanding.

BAD READING HABITS.

THE FACT IS that Bishop Ussher had bad reading habits. He had insufficient respect for the *formal* nature of the book before him, Genesis. He at least had some excuse, even though he did live in the same century which was later to create the Royal Society.

Those who read that book today, and then create Creationist Museums in which life-size figures of Adam and Eve go walking in the garden with dinosaurs, have no such excuse. The development of modern science should at least have taught them that, whatever else Genesis is, it is most certainly not a record of 'scientific' observation or enquiry. How could it have been?

Only if we do not understand that the Book of Genesis is magnificent Hebrew poetry, employing metaphor and parataxis, might we make the mistake of thinking it an alternative to modern science. If we do not realise that the Book of Revelation is a samizdat text, using symbols to express the oppression of the early Christian community beleaguered by a Roman hegemony, and expecting the end of the world at any moment, then we might start imagining that it gives an encoded version of our present reality, and permits us to predict forthcoming political events, including the terminus of history. If we can read Genesis and see it, in Godard's phrase, as a form that thinks, and thinks very effectively within the terms of its own formality, then we have solved at least part of the problem. Such a reading cannot settle the matter of whether or not you believe in God, but it might at least solve the problem of what different sorts of writing are for; what sort of performances they enact as we read them.

When Galileo went to see Cardinal Bellarmine, the Cardinal directed him to what we would call the text of Psalm 19, in which the sun is described as rising at one end of the heavens and travelling to the other. So Holy Writ had already established that it was the sun that moved about the sky, while earth remained stationary. The geocentric model must be true; the heliocentric one, false. None of Galileo's experiments or observations with his telescope could disprove this, for a simple reason: if something is 'holy' in the Cardinal's sense, then it is beyond proof or question. All contingency has passed from it. It inhabits an intellectual realm of pure and unassailable causality. It has become a different sort of narrative, a narrative that is beyond intelligent enquiry.[3] The truth is, as Galileo was aware, his eminence the Cardinal had bad reading habits too; these extended in one direction to the Book of Psalms, and in another to Aristotle.

Similarly, when a particular sort of reader points to the opening of Genesis and says that the earth was made in 'six days', that person has bad reading habits too. This, as we have noted, is Hebrew sacred poetry, not a treatise devoted to scientific measurement. Numbers and days are characteristically used to punctuate such a text, not to provide data for an experiment. And in any case what does 'a day' mean here? The Hebrew *yom* is flexible; it is a period of time. It can hardly be held to be twenty-four hours, for that would require the Almighty to be inhabiting the earth while He is actually engaged in the process of creating it. If He were gazing at the matter from Pluto, for example, then a day would be six and a half times the length of our own. But since He is presumably inhabiting the vault of heaven, then each day could take billions of years. This is how Jewish scholars have reconciled the account of creation in Genesis with Lyell's geological time and Darwin's biological long perspectives.

Galileo was surely entitled, had he been feeling frisky, to explain to the Cardinal that if we have become so literal that every figure of speech loses its figurativeness, then God, according to the evidence of the Psalms themselves, would appear to be some sort of fowl, though an oddly martial one: 'He shall cover thee with his feathers, and under his wings shalt thou trust: his truth shall be thy shield and buckler.' Thus what we call Psalm 91. God is an armed dove. All methods of representation are formally shaped, and every mode of representation inevitably shapes and distorts according to the laws of its medium. Language, and in particular poetry, uses metaphor to convey as much information as possible as vividly as possible. But it is an act of illiteracy to expect every metaphor to 'literalise itself' through 360 degrees. Marianne Moore informs us that the swan 'turns and reconnoitres like a battleship'. So where are the guns on its wings then, the naval crew, the living quarters? A metaphor finds its point of focus, a moment of similarity, between two objects, two beings, two realms, and discovers there a source of vivid imagery. The keels plough the waves. Why? Because keels and ploughs (both made out of wood in those days) enter the medium beneath them at an angle, cut through it, and leave a trace – either a wake or a furrow. And the men who stand above earth or sea direct the implement, as they go about their business: farming or warfare.

Galileo's plea was that the Bible was not the only book which was relevant, and that all books perform a particular function in language. The universe, according to Galileo's *The Assayer,* was 'written in a mathematical language', which should be seen as being just as sacred as the sacred text.

COMPLEMENTARITY.

GALILEO WAS ARGUING for the principle of complementarity, three hundred years before that principle was formulated by Niels Bohr. This is the greatest principle of modern physics, whereby the wave and particle characteristics of light ceased to be two warring principles involved in a zero-sum fight to the death, and became instead two aspects of the same reality.

It is characteristic of a form of thought known as positivism, and sometimes scientism, to assert that all truths must be translatable into the terms of modern science; that anything encountered or recorded on journeys along the shaman's pole must be translatable to, and testable upon, Galileo's plank. We should at least note a curious dissonance here: Galileo himself did not believe this. The Bible might tell you how to get to heaven, he said, but it could not thereby tell you how the heavens work. Different 'thinking forms' think in different ways.

Different forms provide different sorts of information. Their difference should not, however, be necessarily read as contradiction, but as a species of complementarity. If I ask you for a picture of your friend and you give me an X-ray, you are in one sense fulfilling my request. You are providing me with a truthful visual account of the person concerned, but you are being insensitive about types of information, and their thinking forms. You are simply not thinking enough about the way in which forms think.

A JOURNEY, NOT JUST A MEASUREMENT.

MIRCEA ELIADE, IN *Shamanism: Archaic Techniques of Ecstasy*,[4] talks at length about the *axis mundi*, the sacred pole which, as we have seen, certain sorts of communities place at the centre of their villages, the centre of their world. It connects the highest and the lowest, connects up the realm of heaven with that of the underworld, humankind's habitation being usually placed somewhere midway between them. This axis locates the community in cosmic space, situates it in what is otherwise a homeless homogeneity. Eliade discusses many different manifestations of this pole, employed to centre existence in the vastness of unwelcoming space. In certain villages, as we have seen, the pole goes right through the centre of the ceremonial house, exiting through the roof. The shamanistic figure, dedicated to the furthest explorations possible in the most far-flung realms, climbs the pole. This spiritual journeyer is then gifted with the ability to connect up heaven and hell; he can now make the ultimate journeys that the rest of the community is unprepared for, but needs to have made nevertheless – for solace, healing and spiritual information.

It is an instructive and intriguing image, and a psychic pattern that recurs in many different forms in many times and cultures. We have noted how, in one sense, what the shaman does in climbing the pole, in the trance-like state of his initiation, is parallel to what Dante the poet does through his dream vision in the *Divine Comedy*: he visits heaven and hell and the regions between. He makes the ultimate journey and returns with the necessary images and information for the rest of the community to locate itself, to orientate itself within the totality of existence. Those Palaeolithic cave-painters must have been doing something like this.

Poetry has often performed the same function. In Book VI of the *Aeneid* we have a descent to the underworld, and much Romantic and post-Romantic poetry involves visits to one sort of hell or another, counterpointed by just the occasional glimpse of paradise. Coleridge's 'caverns measureless to man' recur with continued hallucinatory force in Baudelaire and Rimbaud. The earliest epic we have, *Gilgamesh*, contains a journey to the underworld. Human curiosity must touch the extremities of perception, even when they lie beyond death.

The *axis mundi* locates the centre of existence, its truth. It places us at the still point at the centre of our phenomenological vortex. In comparison, Galileo's plank can never offer anything other than observation and close measurement. It lets us conclude that $F=ma$, which is to say that any force can be calculated by multiplying the mass of the body by its acceleration, or the other way about. Watch closely and you will discover that gravity is evidently a uniform force, since objects fall at the same rate, whatever their size. If Galileo's plank is about to become the new *axis mundi*, and so the centre of the world, so that all the central perceptions about the world are about to become scientific, subject to such forensic scrutiny and measurement, does this new scientific world of perception then constitute a replacement of myth, or does the myth simply evacuate itself to other, more welcoming, homes? What we are asking effectively is, what's the story, since the Greek word *mythos* originally meant story. The world is about to grow larger, whichever *axis mundi* you employ. Galileo is about to look through his telescope and see an unimagined vastness. At that moment the *axis mundi* is his 'optic tube'. It will soon enlarge and inform Milton's imagination.

But you cannot derive *Paradise Lost* from Galileo's plank. Nor can you test its truth on that wooden surface. So, unless we are to dispense with *Paradise Lost*, we have to accept a fundamental difference between the plank and the pole.

THE MODERN SHAMAN'S JOURNEY.

THE SHAMAN'S JOURNEY repeats itself over and over again, in many different cultural forms, and well into the age of modern science. Why does realism, having attempted to formulate itself as science in the form of Zola's naturalism, then need to re-introduce the enchantment of the earlier narratives, and become 'magic realism'? Perhaps we are continually exploring an essential aspect of our humanity, going back, as Lewis-Williams appears to imply, to our earliest psychic and cultural requirements.

In the recorded accounts of his journey, the shaman, we have been told, mentally disintegrates. He undergoes a catastrophic collapse of identity. Another way of putting this is to say that the pre-existing structure of the psyche proves inadequate to withstand the destructive forces which are arraigned against it. Consequently, it must re-form and re-structure itself to accommodate the darkness of the quest's encounter; thus will it achieve a kind of enlightenment. Enlightenment here involves not the exclusion of the dark forces, but their inclusion within the psyche's economy. We incorporate the deadly powers. The plunge into the destructive element is liberating, as long as we survive the experience.

We might mention two shamanic journeys, which have certainly not taken place in 'primitive' societies. Arthur Rimbaud, in a letter to Paul Demeny, wrote of the poet: 'He makes himself a visionary, by a long immense and reasoned derangement of all the senses. He seeks in himself every kind of love, of suffering, of madness, he exhausts all the poisons in himself in order to keep only their quintessences. Unspeakable torment, in which he has need of all faith, all super-human power, in which he becomes among all the great Sick Men, the great Criminal, the great Damned – the supreme Scholar! – For he comes to the unknown! Since he has cultivated his soul, already more rich than anyone else's! He comes to the visions, he has seen them! Though he collapses in his leaping among things unheard-of and nameless, other horrific labourers will come; they will begin at the horizons where the other sank.'[2]

This is shamanism, alive and well in nineteenth-century France. The dreadful journey will be made so that the shaman can return with news from the land of the unknown. He will bring the hidden treasure of occult knowledge. Rimbaud, as we know, was soon to abandon all this, and devote himself instead to a disenchanted life of trade. The fact is that, as a shaman, he was unemployable; which might make us pause when uttering the word 'primitive' about different sorts of societies. Bob Dylan, that life-long devotee of Rimbaud, has enacted his own shamanic journey in songs like *Desolation Row* and *Isis*. The world re-arranges itself amidst surrealist scenes of a nightmarish intensity. When the traveller returns to the world he left, its meanings have changed irrevocably. And so has he.

LET THE PLANK BE THE POLE, AND VICE VERSA.

LET US TRY an experiment then. Let the plank be the pole. Let it be the *axis mundi*. The silver balls may continue to roll down it, but it must also receive the shaman climbing up and down on the ladder of his dreadful journey. We live in an age of modern science, but Rimbaud's poetic journey, or Dylan's musical journey for that matter, cannot be discarded without a dreadful cost to our mind and our culture. (Einstein actually makes an appearance in Dylan's *Desolation Row* – he is disguised as Robin Hood. Perhaps he intends to steal their preconceptions from those who find themselves all too richly endowed with them.) Let all of the knowledge of modern science branch out from this new trunk, but let us not pretend that the shamanic journey has somehow been superseded or rendered irrelevant. No one is disparaging the luminous equations, or doubting their efficacy, but one is entitled to point out that the entirety of human experience cannot be translated into mathematics.

If I can respect the Book of Genesis and *Sidereus Nuncius;* see the point of both the *Divine Comedy* and Lyell's *Principles of Geology;* if I can acknowledge the necessity for complementarity in physics, while realising that *Desolation Row* is a work as astoundingly potent as Robert Browning's 'Childe Roland' (they in fact have many points of similarity), then it is because I acknowledge that each of these works constitutes a 'form that thinks'. They are radically different forms, admittedly, and they have therefore done their thinking in radically different ways. The world requires of me at any moment a plurality of readings, readings that must be informed by the history of beliefs as well as the present state of science. But I do not have to believe Dante's cosmology in order to acknowledge the immense potency of Dante's poetry; I am surely permitted to make that adjustment. There is still sufficient play in the subtlety of the mind and its reception of forms for that. Different types of writing offer different types of truth. The Book of Genesis does not present me with a scientific problem, any more than Dante does; and the psyche still experiences the privation of its shamanic journey, even in our age of science; perhaps, particularly in this age. Time does not, in fact, make ancient good uncouth, despite the assertion of the famous hymn to the contrary. Truth comes in many different forms. One is entitled to celebrate these forms for the richness of their variety, the way in which they 'think', rather than merely engage in the usual exhausted routines of disparagement.

CHAPTER NOTES

1. See Max Raphael, *The Demands of Art* (London: Routledge, 1968)."

2. David Lewis-Williams, *The Mind in the Cave* (London: Thames and Hudson, 2002).

3. It is the argument of these pages that no text, however hallowed, should ever be placed beyond intelligent enquiry.

4. Mircea Eliade, *Shamanism: Archaic Techniques of Ecstasy* (New York: Princeton University Press, 2007).

5. Translation taken from Edgell Rickword, *Essays & Opinions 1921-31* (Manchester: Carcanet, 1974), p. 126.

VII

DEMOTIC RITUAL.

1

'A CONFUSION OF familiarities.' Thus did Constantin Brancusi describe the ceaseless accrual of detail in the realist tradition in its terminal phases, immediately before its fracture by the movement that has come to be called modernism. So what was the alternative to such unfocusing proliferations? 'Simplicity,' said the Romanian sculptor, 'is complexity resolved'. Not evaded then, but resolved. Such resolution required dynamic and expressive form, a form that could cut through the infinite attenuation of detail of late realism and naturalism. It occurred to the most radical artists of modernity that there was a precedent here: not their immediate precursors in the western artistic tradition, but those from ages before, who had not even been known as artists. The 'primitives', whose vision was unconstrained by any protocols involving single vanishing-point perspective or three-dimensional illusionism. All those fellows had wanted was an image potent enough to convey a god, goddess, demon or figure of fecundity. Realism and its expectations was something still to come; immediate perception of expressive form was for them the sole requirement. Votive offerings were presented before the gods, not a Parisian salon.

Time had been arriving at one of its crescendos; that at least could not be doubted. But time had also been stopped in its tracks by photography, and it was now being archived by film. And this was entirely new. The surface of modernity fractures: it has no alternative. So great are the forces pounding upon it, from the past and the present simultaneously, that it breaks up. What we find beneath this fracturing surface is not more modernity, but the seemingly archaic forms of an archetypal potency. The sky-blue surface of Picasso's *Les Demoiselles D'Avignon* shatters, the background becomes indistinguishable from the foreground, whatever depth there is can be found only on the surface itself, and what reveals itself through that surface are two women with tribalized heads. They need not acknowledge time; they might have re-surfaced through time, but modernity certainly did not facilitate their appearance. They had been there all along. 'Progress' would be a meaningless term, applied here. Modernism in the arts has simply re-discovered them, and it was to engage in such re-discoveries over and over again, in its unrelenting search for form.

In the killing fields of the Great War, David Jones finds the Queen of the Forest numbering the men she is re-gathering (*In Parenthesis*); in the streets of London in 1921, T. S. Eliot finds the blind seer Tiresias from millennia before foreseeing the contemporary futility, and also inevitability, of casual coition (*The Waste Land*); on the streets of Dublin in 1904 James Joyce sees the Homeric epic playing itself out once more, finding new urban forms for the journey (*Ulysses*); Ezra Pound begins his epic of modernity with a classical god in a boat, amidst a confusion of Homeric mythic detail (*The Cantos*). The surface of the present breaks up, and archaic form asserts its longevity; perhaps even its agelessness. It cannot however be presented 'steadily and whole'; it must be presented instead in a montage sequence, so as to preserve the truth of the form and the requirements of its representation, in the ceaseless speeding sequence of the modern; framed in the context of fragmentation that the modern requires. The windows of the train speed by, as do the individual images of the moving picture, frozen spots of time soon to move at twenty-four frames per second.

It is significant that the one newly-invented modern form is cinema, since that is constituted entirely by montage. A sequence of images speeds up; out of the differences between the images, combined with persistence of vision, emerges apparent motion and fluency. Speed is inseparable from this form's effect: take away the speed and there is no cinema, only a sequence of stills. But both Eisenstein and Hitchcock were equally lucid about exploiting montage rather than disguising it: montage is cinema's strength, not its weakness. And a part of that strength comes from its truthfulness to modern experience. Things break up; the train keeps moving past unknown faces; we pass by those whom we have never met and will never encounter again. It is instructive to see how many of the earliest films were fascinated with trains and speed. Cameras attached to the engine were capturing the fastest motion possible on earth at the time. Cinema is the first visual medium dependent on speed or its perception

This urban contingency was appreciated by Baudelaire, one of the first clear-eyed modernists. The contingency was the other half, the modern half, of art – so he argued in 'The Painter of Modern Life'. What separates the cantos in Dante's *Commedia* is a silent continuity of direction and purpose; what separates the cantos in Pound's *Cantos* are silent, and unexplained, discontinuities. We could call this 'the modern'. It certainly corresponds to the montage-effect of living in modernity. We hear different voices; see different visions from one moment to the next. This experiential heterogeneity finally overwhelmed Pound, in more ways than one, and in his last fragmented cantos he laments: 'I cannot make it cohere'. *The Waste Land* is a collage of voices appearing without introduction in the kaleidoscopic modern city.

THE MEANING OF time (then as now) was problematic. For the artist at least it had come to seem that temporal progression had not transcended the primitive, merely occluded it. Realism in its refinements and attenuations had ceased to deliver the reality it had once so confidently promised, and was now seen to be merely fulfilling conventions and the appetites attached to them – Brancusi's familiarities. But since the new technologies of photography and cinema could between them reproduce the image in all its surface verisimilitude, why then should the other arts continue to compete on this terrain? Likeness could now be delivered mechanically. So the modernists would replace realism by an art of dynamic form, which frequently found inspiration in the primitive. When Picasso emerged from his trip below ground to see the cave paintings created by the remarkable artists of the Upper Palaeolithic, he stepped back into the sunlight to say, 'We have invented nothing'. The 'we' here is almost certainly meant to signify modern artists. So what might once have appeared to be the belated inventiveness of the modern, its unaccountable fracturing of the realist surface, in fact consisted of a return to the unhampered expressiveness of the primitive, the formal clarity of prehistoric art. The latest extravagant wildness, mocked in the journals, in fact constituted the most radical conservatism. And this had further implications: the originary forms, modern art proclaimed, had never in truth been superseded, so that when they returned, they returned in glory; they reclaimed their territory. They shifted from museums of anthropology and ethnography to museums of modern art. The forms thus re-discovered, it seemed, were not regressive after all but transcendent. Time had not surpassed these early forms, as the Renaissance or the Enlightenment might have thought; on the contrary, it was the early forms which had transcended time, scattered around on distant islands, or kept in cupboards in city museums. They had retained an urgency and a vitality which had finally become recursive. The implications of this were myriad, and we are still negotiating them to this day.

We could call the period 1890 to 1930 the era of high modernism. All periodizations are inane and simplistic, but this one has a certain purpose. A number of developments took place in this period, in vastly different intellectual regions, which inter-connected in a way that demands some kind of description, even where definition itself is impossible. In the visual arts, expressive form disrupted the surface of classical realism. The infinite attenuation of concordant detail was challenged and fractured by the visual insistence on a formal coherence whose expressiveness was more than happy to dispense with any 'surface exactitude'. This was a mimesis of essential form, not of superficial resemblance. Its emergence can be charted in the career of a single artist. In 1896 the youthful Picasso painted *Science and Charity*. The painting observes realistic criteria; we even have a narrative content: a modern doctor sits at the bed of a sick girl. The conventions of western realism remain unperturbed. But by 1907, a little more than a decade later, Picasso has managed to create *Les Demoiselles D'Avignon*. Here the formal inquiry is so insistent and ruthless that the heads of two of the women have been replaced by masks, and those masks might well be from the Ethnographical Wing of the Anthropology Museum at the Trocadéro. Which is another way of saying, that the mode of seeing found in these 'primitive expressions' is employed as having a truthfulness at least as great as the 'realistic' truthfulness of the western post-Renaissance tradition. We didn't, it would appear, leave the past behind us after all: it has been travelling with us all along, effectively concealed within our psyche as well as the museum. So in discovering the new, in the simplified forms of modern art, we are simultaneously re-discovering the ancient. The recent ocular tyranny that made a fetish of surface resemblance has been abolished. The image is no longer obsessing over topographical detail; it has the courage to be topological, which is to say, to find the essential elements of the image, and dispense with the rest.

This seeming co-existence of post-Enlightenment intellectual scrutiny and image-making from a cave wall has, of course, an intriguing parallel. In the same years that Picasso was scavenging amongst the detritus of history and pre-history for clues as to the future of art, Sigmund Freud was practising his new talking-cure at Berggasse 19 in Vienna. And what did the good doctor surround himself with, as he attempted to peer into the psyches of his very modern patients with their contemporary neuroses? Gods and goddesses, sphinxes, fertility emblems, the creatures and monsters of ancient drama. Why? For the same reason that Picasso spent so much of his early time in Paris in the ethnographic wing of the Trocadéro: they were both in search of forms, forms which transcended history, forms which had not become cluttered with the mere accruals of chronology; forms, in other words, which eluded Brancusi's 'confusion of familiarities', some of which might even by now have become 'scientific familiarities'. In Freud's case, the forms he sought were those that shape the soul or the psyche, since *psyche* is the Greek form of that Germanic *Seele* which subsequently Englished itself to soul. In the proto-Germanic *saiwalo*, from which both *Seele* and *soul* derive, there is the clear meaning of coming from the sea or belonging to the sea, the home of the soul before and after death. The return of Viking warriors to the waves, the return of Arthur to the lake, are returns themselves upon this theme. Freud was well aware that in iconography and in etymology, our psychological history can be mapped and traced. The fossils of our consciousness are embodied in our languages, both verbal and visual. His fellow Viennese, Ludwig Wittgenstein, described the English language as a graveyard of metaphors. It's not a quiet place, though: this is a graveyard where many revenants arise and talk.

In 1938 Paul Engelman took a series of remarkable photographs of Freud's apartment. What we see, in rich concentration, are Buddhas and Egyptian gods; a torso of Aphrodite; the print of Oedipus and the Sphinx by Ingres; Michaelangelo's

Moses: it appears as though the fragments and the emblems of the past surrounded and confronted him at every turn. He had transformed his home and his consulting rooms into a cave, crammed with the *memento mori* of ancient talismans. In seizing upon a notion like 'the Oedipus Complex' he is, in effect, saying that the underlying form was there all along; it merely needed decoding into the language of modernity. The present here is a palimpsest beneath which lies a constellation of primary forms. These forms have potency because of what psychoanalysis came to call *cathexis*: i.e. the investment of energy by the psyche in a specific psychic object, image or configuration of memory.

We might look at the operation of *cathexis* when Picasso stared at the Ethnographic Wing of the Trocadéro in Paris. 'The masks weren't just like any other pieces of sculpture. Not at all. They were magic things...we hadn't realized it. The Negro pieces were *intercesseurs*, mediators; ever since then I've known the word in French. They were against everything. I too believe that everything is unknown, that everything is an enemy! Everything! I understood what the Negroes used their sculpture for....The fetishes were...weapons. To help people avoid coming under the influence of spirits again, to help them become independent. Spirits, the unconscious (people still weren't talking about that very much), emotion – they're all the same thing. I understood why I was a painter. All alone in that awful museum, with masks, dolls made by the redskins, dusty manikins. *Les Demoiselles d'Avignon* must have come to me that very day, but not at all because of the forms; because it was my first exorcism painting – yes absolutely.'[1] In the Catholic Spain of his youth, Picasso had been surrounded by images for veneration, as well as *ex voto* offerings to keep the evil spirit away. He had been brought up in a culture where images had a potency which Enlightenment thought would have deemed superstitious.

In *Les Demoiselles d'Avignon* space has risen to the surface of the painting, so that 'background' and 'foreground' lose their separation. In principle a section of female body does not appear to occupy a different space from a section of lighted background. The painting is self-consciously a painting; it is not offering us the kind of illusionism which *Science and Charity* did a decade before. We are not being offered the substance of illusory space. Nor are we offered narrative or allegorical content, though in the first sketches Picasso had retained some: a sailor, a medical student with a skull. But he cut them out. Here he is discovering the new formality of modernism, which does not provide itself as a window on to something else, either a realistic vista or an allegorical grounding, but instead proclaims itself as what it is: a material form, with formal limitations and formal possibilities. These figures have a terrifying force: masked or not, they represent an undisguised sexuality, as though the materiality of the painting and the materiality of its subject have both emerged after a lengthy hibernation, a hibernation which has been going on, in one form or another, since the Renaissance.

The surface is now the actuality of the medium, and it has gained a ritualistic force through its divestment of surface detail. It is precisely the ritualistic use of the masks that attracts and fascinates Picasso. What the images have lost in urbanity they have gained in psychic resonance. When in 1913 the first performance of Stravinsky's *Rite of Spring* was performed in Paris, the same principle could be observed: the violent formality of the music had undoubtedly dispensed with Brancusi's 'confusion of familiarities', and the dance of the girl enacted a form (human immolation to guarantee fertility) which was age-old. From the bassoon's first startling statement of the theme, all artistic *politesse* had been dispensed with. The form in both cases amounted to a simplification, which is another way of saying that there was an underlying form to be discovered, once the clutter of recent tradition had been dispensed with. The product of that dispensation, what emerges from the wreckage of late 'realism', is what we call modernism.

Contemporary reality, it appears, can be conveyed more effectively by the employment of 'primitive' forms than by the employment of post-Renaissance realism. Here we should perhaps pause and think about this word 'primitive'. What does it actually mean? What does it mean in the historical context of the modernist moment? Another way to pt this is to ask simply: where did all the fetishes and masks in the Trocadéro actually come from, and how were they being read? They were read, at least to some degree, through a set of assumptions, and an economic and political power, which brought 'the savage' into existence. The savage as a concept and a perception can only exist by way of comparison; in the very act of calling this group savage I identify myself as being evidently otherwise.

Anthropological fieldwork had created its own object of study, 'the primitive', a mode of being which had, by definition, escaped the transformations of modern European history. Like Freud's Unconscious, 'the primitive' did not acknowledge time; and in another parallel, it appeared to foreground desire over all other competing forces. It appeared then to offer a gallery of archetypes, a set of forms uncorrupted by post-Renaissance illusionism, or the nagging conventions of social propriety. Here surely was an escape from Brancusi's ubiquitous 'confusion of familiarities'. The realm of the fetish and the *intercesseur* is the realm without restriction; here Coleridge's 'shaping spirit of imagination' simply wishes into being whatever it momentarily desires. Here the projection of classical Freudian theory and the projection inside a cinema coincide.

And yet the modernists, Picasso amongst them, lived in modernity. Their forms, their aesthetic rituals, might be primitivist but the goings-on in the street outside the window were not. There were motor cars. If such art was to be not merely ritualistic but also demotic, then it had to incorporate the contemporary life by which it was surrounded. How could it do this? The most immediately available technique was montage, since montage in painting is a structural expression of the juxtaposition of dissimilarity within a single framing manoeuvre. Moreover, montage not only finds dissimilarity in juxtaposition, but similarity too, a similarity which requires an enlargement of the original terms to make it perceptually possible.

What is the actual effect of cinematic montage? A series of still images is sped into sequence at the rate of 'X per second'. The viewer sees movement where there is in fact a reel of discrete and static images. In this sense, montage and juxtaposition are the very essence of cinema. But the word has, of course, come to have a different, more elaborate meaning, too. By sequencing one image after another we thereby create a more radical juxtaposition which elicits an interpretative response. A much-quoted instance is the sequence in Eisenstein's *Battleship Potempkin* when the stone lion couchant rises and finally becomes a stone lion rampant. This is stone statuary: the observing eye knows this. And yet, inserted into an account of the oppression of the Russian poor, these images transmute into an emblem of the people's rising. The montage here permits a gap between two sequences of images, so that through the gap, between the poles of juxtaposition, meaning will be produced. Montage insists upon the generation of interstitial interpretation. All montage posits a certain imagistic dissonance which, in ultimate combination, goes on to suggest an overall consonance; a certain radical pattern-recognition is demanded of the viewer. The minute we see the rising stone lion as emblematic of the revolting Russian proletariat and peasantry, the dissonance between actual historical people and stone statue is re-harmonised into two expressions of one theme: insurrection against oppression and a dormant strength which, should it be roused, will soon enough demonstrate its potency and menace.

How did montage work in Cubism? In its synthetic phase, by grafting different aspects of representational reality onto one another as collage. A musical instrument is represented by cut-out portions of coloured paper; a section of a newspaper is pasted on to the same space and drawn upon. There is here a collation of representational spheres and surfaces which is insolent in its audacity. The conflation of radically different modes of representation – music, drawing, the written word now printed and distributed as newsprint, linoleum employed to represent the wickerwork of a chair – forces us to confront the materiality of any representational mode, just as the analytic Cubist technique of approaching an object simultaneously from different angles in space-time, constructing and reconstructing the visual object, forced us to see how we build reality optically: how it is not simply 'given', but exists in the multi-dimensionality which is space-time. What Stephen Dedalus in *Ulysses* calls the 'ineluctable modality of the visible', the formal thusness or quiddity of any mode of representation or perception, is here presented to us as a collage of possibilities. Each mode to some degree subverts its alternatives; though from another angle, it also confirms them. Since they are all provisional and partial, each must accept its fragmentary part in the whole.

The word 'fragmentary' alerts us to the fact that the realities of modernity (one can hardly speak of *a* reality, since the singular would be misleading) are inherently fragmentary. Speed of communication and transport, the conveyance of ever-increasing amounts of information, and the incessant contingency of urban life, between them mean that all the fragmentary parts never can add up to one single stationary whole. A wholeness here would have to be chosen or willed, by subscription. Aesthetically at least, it would appear to be an option, rather than an ontological ordination. Cinema is the new artistic form of this new period of history, and it depends on speed for all its discrete images to cohere into narrative.

In painting and sculpture, the primitive at least appears to provide a certain wholeness; it dramatises reality into a singularity of form. Against this form the scattered contingency of our everyday, modern, demotic reality can be juxtaposed. And juxtaposition allows for the portrayal of the luminous object, whose foil can be an urban incoherence. André Breton's Surrealist manifestos make it plain that he saw Freud's Unconscious as the home of the imagination. Once again we have dispensed with Brancusi's 'confusion of familiarities'. Instead we have a realm of luminous juxtaposition in which desire, untrammelled by propriety or the requirements of chronology and scale, places side by side whatever it chooses to retrieve from the old mansion of perception and memory. How often in Surrealist scenes the dream-landscape is littered with incongruous but luminous objects. In their synchronicity, Surrealist panoramas share something with the interior space of the museum, without which they could not have existed.

This primitive form is often ritualistic, irrational, 'savage' perhaps; it does not acknowledge the constraints of civilisation, nor, in Freud's phrase, its discontents. But it can have no life, this ritualistic, even fetishistic form, if it is being employed in the context of modernity, without the demotic bustle which provides the contemporary energy for any form of art. However atavistic some of the archetypal forms in *The Waste Land* might be, the poem has a vivid and contingent immediacy because of the dialogues in pubs and bedsits: 'When Lil's husband got demobbed, I said/ I didn't mince my words, I said…' Part of the demotic immediacy here was provided by Pound, who inserted the word 'demobbed'. But it is undoubtedly this demotic energy tied to the ritualistic longing represented by the final words 'Shantih shantih shantih' which illuminates and electrifies the language of that poem in a way that was never to happen in *Four Quartets*. In a parallel of which Eliot was only too aware, the form provided by Homer in Joyce's *Ulysses* allows the linguistic exuberance of the demotic life on the streets of Dublin to articulate itself within a formal shaping those streets could not themselves provide.

What is still so intriguing about the war-time paintings of Paul Nash and Nevinson is the conflict between abstraction and the documentary impulse. A painting like *Flooded Trench on the Yser, 1915*, could easily be (in effect *is*) an exercise in Vorticist jagged abstractionism, except for one thing: the title. All that is left out of the visual field of information rushes back in through the words on the frame. The surface of European reality, its actual terrain, has been shattered by the forces of modern technology in conflict. Nash was quite explicit in his letters about what he saw there: a vision of the inferno. Modernity had invented (or re-invented) hell. Once again the surface of modernity breaks up to reveal archaic form immediately beneath it.

Of the two great pioneer Cubists, Braque went to the war and had to be trepanned for his injuries. Picasso characteristically managed to stay out of the fighting, but when he saw French armoured vehicles rumbling through the streets, he realised that they had been painted with Cubist camouflage devices; he knew then that he had made his contribution to the war effort after all. Could aesthetics and economy, aesthetics and politics, even aesthetics and war, actually be separated any more? Have they ever been, in truth?

Art, however ritualistic, cannot live for long without the demotic. Rouault's whores forever rebuke his judges. David Jones's *In Parenthesis* is the great modernist work it surely is partly because of the ceaseless cross-over between mythic and ritualistic pattern, and the demotic life and talk of infantrymen. Joyce moved his epiphanies from inside the Roman Catholic churches to the Dublin streets outside, even the red light district, in a quintessential modernist manoeuvre, though one that has plenty of precedents in literature and art: in Caravaggio, Shakespeare and Browning, for example. We still return so frequently to the plays of Shakespeare and Jonson because the language of the streets lives on so vividly inside them. But Shakespeare, like the modernists, was also in pursuit of the marvellous; the last plays are full of that elusive category. The voices in the street must be turned into ritual, and such ritual can only be achieved through form.

AT THE SAME time that the Cubists were discovering a form of greater primacy than any which realism or naturalism could afford them, modern physics was making its own discovery that reality is not an arena of infinite attenuation either: it is dictated ultimately by form. The quantum states tell us that nature itself is formally shaped. Between one quantum state and the next there is nothing, except that 'nothing' here is a logical illusion, seeming to make intellectually palpable an absence which is mere impossibility. Faced with the dereliction of description at this point one can only echo Wittgenstein: 'Whereof one cannot speak, thereof one must be silent'. The book in which this statement occurs was published in the same year as *The Waste Land*.

When in 1913 James Franck and Gustav Hertz conducted some experiments to find out if they could change the planetary orbits of atoms, what they discovered was that atoms didn't have planetary orbits, at least not in the sense that classical physics would have predicted for a Newtonian planetary system. A considerable amount of energy was required to make *any* difference at all to the atoms and the orbits of their electrons. Although they couldn't formulate it in this way at the time, what had been discovered was that there is a threshold of energy between the ground state and the first excited state. Such a scandal of discontinuity appalled many scientists, since it contradicted everything they had believed up to now. An electron can either remain in the ground state or receive sufficient charge to jump to the next state up, one of the states of excitement, but it can't go anywhere in between. Which is another way of saying that there *is* nowhere in between. There is no formless place, no no-man's-land between one form and another. There are forms and no forms. Energy simply can't leak out of one form on its way to another. No intermediate non-formality obtains. Form and energy are indivisible in science, just as form and content are indivisible in the arts.

What E.H.Gombrich has called 'a preference for the primitive' in the arts of modernity has been in truth a preference for form over surface detail, for radical pattern-recognition over the accrual of realistic minutiae, for an economised formal dynamic over 'a confusion of familiarities'. These artists were choosing formal supremacy over a ceaseless amassing of agglomerated detail. They were saying that the imagination too has quantum states, forms and shapes which in the focus of their patterning show forth reality.

There is something uncanny about the parallel and the simultaneity. As the surface of modernity shattered, the modernists found form (ancient, primeval or timeless, but assertive and vigorous) beneath the breaking surface. Starting with Planck's discoveries in 1900, quantum mechanics discovered that underlying everything is form, form which can never be negotiated away: the form of the quantum states. Energy can take one form or another, but it cannot negotiate anything in between; there is no 'in-between' to be negotiated. The shift in the arts known as the modern movement and the movement of the modern mind in physics coincide. The discovery here too was that reality is not a vast system of infinite attenuation, a seamless continuity of negotiation, but a series of radical shifts and breaks called quantum states. Reality at its heart is not liquidly fluent, but granular; it arrives in discrete packets of energy. The energetic form is always either thus or thus; it either takes this form or that – there is no in-between, no attenuation between one quantum state and another.

This might provide us with a clue in regard to what is going on when we look at the disintegrating surface of *Les Demoiselles d'Avignon*: form is breaking through, a form of ruthless assertiveness, with no soft edges, and no readiness to be attenuated into a negotiated shape. Here form is meaning; decorative detail a distraction. Adolf Loos, the modernist architect, declared decoration a crime.

3

IN THE PREFACE to *The Anathemata*, David Jones quoted Nennius: 'I have made a heap of all that I could find.' One cannot read the phrase without thinking of Eliot in *The Waste Land*: 'These fragments I have shored against my ruins'. The narrative has broken down; in fact the narrative has now become an account of its own fragmentation. In which case, it is a question of selecting the fragments that are most effective; that have the strongest form in chaotic circumstances. Perhaps even the fragments that might be expected to function as *intercesseurs* in Picasso's sense; or at least to have some liturgical validity.

Jones speaks of making a work from 'mixed data'. His sources were made available to him 'by accident'. Contingency is inescapable, given his modern condition. The title page itself describes the work as 'fragments of an attempted writing'. And the structural modes of *The Anathemata*, alternating prose and poetry, acknowledge shifting differentiations in the register of modern experience which can only be expressed formally. A homogeneity of tone and structure would amount to a misrepresentation: it would be a mendacious mimesis. To capture the fragmented reality, form itself must share in the fragmentation, not by breaking up in itself, but by accepting heterogeneity and dissonance as its context: there is not necessarily any negotiation between these strong forms, any more than there is a mediation between the quantum states. We either have this form or that one. They co-exist as contrasts not reconciliations. Hence the appropriateness of juxtaposition and montage.

Montage here is expressed as shuffling. Here is Jones again: 'I find, for instance, that what is now sheet 166 of my written MS has at different times been sheet 75 and sheet 7. What is now printed represents parts, dislocated attempts, reshuffled and again rewritten intermittently between 1946 and 1951.' In *The Communist Manifesto* Marx and Engels wrote of the era of modernity: 'All that is solid melts into air'. Jones says something remarkably similar: 'The times are late and get later, not by decades but by years and months. This tempo of change, which in the world of affairs and in the physical sciences makes schemes and data out-moded and irrelevant overnight, presents peculiar and phenomenal difficulties to the making of certain kinds of works...' The reason for these 'phenomenal difficulties' is that the artist works with signs, and we have to ask, as more fortunate artists did not: from what do signs gain their validity? These signs cannot work without what Jones calls 'a requisite now-ness'; this we might call the demotic aspect of all demotic ritual. It is hard now for the artist to employ signs which have genuine validity, and also the 'now-ness' that the demotic ensures. He and his friends had begun to refer to this dilemma as 'the Break'. He is frank in saying that he does not know whether there is a fundamental conflict or incompatibility between the world of the 'myths' and the world of the 'formulae', or if there is only a temporary one, brought about by specific historic conditions. If myth can contain modernity, then there is no ultimate incompatibility; if, however there is such an incompatibility, then myth, if used in art to shape contemporary experience, must be doing it a disservice: it is being untrue to that 'now-ness' which is purports to represent. Myth here seems to represent a wholeness of vision, that unity of experience and perception indicated by the old Doctrine of Signatures, or hoped for in Coleridge's coinage 'esemplastic' – the imaginative force that shapes dissimilarities into unity.

Jones, in one sense the most traditionalist of writers, acknowledges that the tradition as perceived from modernity cannot be made whole: 'I regard my book more as a series of fragments, fragmented bits, chance scraps really, of records of things, vestiges of sorts and kinds of *disciplinae*, that have come my way by this channel or that influence. Pieces of stuffs that happen to mean something to me and which I see as perhaps making a kind of coat of many colours such as belonged to "that dreamer" in the Hebrew myth…You use things that are yours to use because they happen to be lying about the place or site or lying within the orbit of your "tradition".'

The surface of modernity breaks up and we perceive archaic form beneath it. The notes to *The Anathemata* are disruptions of the text; the surface of the contemporary language must snap to allow more archaic forms through, to facilitate the form of words which misuse or oblivion has effectively rendered a palimpsest. So, lest the smooth surface hide too easily the occulted forces trying to find their way through, we find 'lattices' in the text immediately footnoted: 'Cf. the derivation of the word chancel, from *cancelli*, lattice bars'.'

4

IN THE REMARKABLE story entitled 'The Unknown Masterpiece' Balzac anticipated modernism and its dilemmas many decades before they actually happened. His fictional painter Frenhofer is visited by the unfictional painters Poussin and Porbus. The studio is in the rue des Grands Augustins in Paris, where Picasso was later to have a studio himself, even insisting that its spiral staircase must mean it was the same apartment as that of Porbus. Picasso was obsessed by this story and produced engravings and etchings for a special edition commissioned by Vollard; it continued to preoccupy him throughout his life.

Frenhofer is a master, the only student Mabuse ever had. He has learnt all the great techniques of the western tradition and can deploy them to remarkable effect. And yet he seems contemptuous of his own achievement here. For ten years he has been working on his portrait of Catherine Lescault. No one has seen this portrait, which has replaced any actual relationship in the aged artist's affections. So desperately do Poussin and

Porbus wish to see the painting that Poussin talks his youthful mistress Gillette into being a model for Frenhofer. So great is her beauty that she is used as a means of bargaining with him, so that the two painters might have sight of the 'unknown masterpiece'. When finally they come to see it, they can see only incoherence, an anarchy of lines and form, except for a radiant foot emerging from the morass. 'They stood petrified with admiration before this fragment which had somehow managed to escape from an unbelievable, slow and progressive destruction. The foot seemed to them like the torso of some Venus in Parian marble rising from the ruins of a city destroyed by fire.'[2]

This fragment of modernity is escaping the 'fire' of Frenhofer's unremitting concentration. He will have nothing to do with the superficialities of illusionistic art: 'To be a great poet it is not enough to know your syntax to perfection and to avoid grammatical errors'. It is not the copying of the superficialities of nature that he pursues, but the search for essential form: 'The mission of art is not to copy nature but to express it! You're a poet, not some paltry copyist!'

He is surrounded by the tradition which he is in the process of transcending: 'Anatomical statuettes in plaster, fragments and torsos of antique goddesses, lovingly polished by the kisses of time over the centuries, lay strewn about the consoles and shelves'. Like Freud, then, at Berggasse 19, tradition surrounds him as fragmented clutter. It becomes clear that the painting is no longer a painting of the mistress (if she ever existed); she now is the mistress. She has become one with artistic form, the ultimately longed-for object: 'You do not go intimately or deeply enough into form, you do not pursue it – through all its flights and detours – with enough love and perseverance. Beauty is a thing severe and difficult of access which does not allow itself to be attained in that way. You have to await the right moment, spy her out, press her and grasp her tightly to force her to surrender'. This is the true pursuit of art: 'Undefeated painters do not allow themselves to be fooled by all those shifts; they persevere until nature is forced to lay herself bare and stand revealed in her truest spirit'.

Cézanne was also obsessed with this story, and at times Frenhofer speaks as though he were quoting that most dogged of painters: 'Nature consists of a succession of rounded forms enveloping each other. Strictly speaking drawing does not exist!'. Cézanne too attempted to reduce nature as perceived and portrayed to a series of geometric inter-relationships. He too was an embodiment of the wish to seize form, rather than dally with superficial appearance. There is also what appears to be an allusion to the Impressionist principle of optical combination: 'From close up the work seems fuzzy and lacking definition, but take two steps back and the whole thing consolidates itself, acquires its own space and stands out…'

In Frenhofter Balzac created a remarkable prolepsis of the modernist artist.

Picasso (who insisted that all the important early modernist work started with Cézanne) illustrated the story with etchings and engravings in which the painted image becomes an apparent chaos of unintelligible lines, which is what both Poussin and Porbus see when Frenhofer's canvas is finally revealed to them. Picasso seems to be at the very least doodling with the idea that there was a fair amount of Frenhofer in himself, though the notion of Picasso devoting ten years to a single painting, while creating nothing else, does not bear examination. What does bear examination, of course, is the crisis of representation which modernism both expressed and initiated. In the engravings and etchings generated by the Balzac story Picasso exemplifies the crisis: he portrays both painter and model in a traditional, visually intelligible form. It is the activity on the canvas that has become unintelligible. See, I can function both in and out of the tradition, Picasso seems to be saying; out of the tradition here means that rectangle of 'art' in the centre of the representation. Frenhofer has concentrated all his energies here. The response of his devotees is to call it unintelligible. But then Picasso had to roll up *Les Demoiselles* and put it under his bed for many years. Even his faithful *bande-à-Picasso* – Apollinaire, Salmon and Jacob – simply didn't get it.

5

THE IMAGE IN modernism's most extreme expression becomes an image of itself; it is the mimesis of its own process of creation. It has absorbed its original referent into the boundaries of its own signification. The background and foreground merge in *Les Demoiselles* so that form can be fully expressive. The object is approached from all angles in Cubism so that the painting itself, as constructed representation, can show itself to be the ultimate object of its own inquiry. A series of optical possibilities converge one upon another. All the demotic elements - newspapers, bottles, wickerwork chairs, linoleum, love notes - are assembled into this ritualistic object, within whose 'sacred space' only the rules of art apply. Within these borders, the work proclaims, a festival of perception is now possible. The work has become entirely itself. Its demotic aspect is the montage of 'now-ness' which it represents; one half of what Baudelaire insisted the authentically modern work had to be. It has transmuted, in its autonomy from what Jones called 'the utile', into its own sacred space; its own ritual.

CHAPTER NOTES

1. John Richardson, *A Life of Picasso:1907-19177* (London: Jonathan Cape, 1996), p.24.

2. Text from 'Gillette or the Unknown Masterpiece', by Honoré de Balzac, translated and introduced by Anthony Rudolf. Menard Press, 1999.

VIII

EXTREMITIES OF PERCEPTION IN AN AGE OF LENSES.

1

LUKA ROCCO MAGNOTTA killed and dismembered Jun Lin. He videotaped the process, and posted it online. He then left Montreal and was spotted at the Helin internet café in Berlin, where he was surfing the internet. The police raided his hotel room, where they found a stash of pornographic magazines. Everything here was done with the aid of lenses, perhaps for the benefit of lenses. Life was seen through lenses, as was death. Magnotta was a man living through lenses.

The Jerry Springer Show was performed before lenses, of course, in the form of ranks of television cameras, and because of those shiny Cyclops eyes, whole families turned themselves inside out, humiliated one another, even hit one another in the face, all for the sake of those who would see on their television sets what lenses might now provide in the way of entertainment. The cisatlantic version of this ritual of lensed humiliation was the emotional pornography of Big Brother, whose sole purpose was to show how wretched, mean-spirited, foul-mouthed and vacuous human beings can be, when they are confined in a space with one another. All while being stared at unrelentingly by cameras.

Truly we live in an age of lenses. Photography has now been with us for nearly two hundred years, and cinema for well over a century. We do not have separate compartments in our minds into which we can insert photographic images, as opposed to those we first encountered with the lenses of our own eyes. So, many of us are unable to sift and separate what only ever entered our mind through photography or film. I never saw Elvis Presley in the flesh, and yet the image of him in my mind is more vividly present than the physiognomies of people I went to school with. I am unable to recall the features of my first girlfriend, and yet the Kennedy assassination sometimes plays and replays in my mind, not that I was in Dallas on that day, or any other. Muhammed Ali is in my mind; I can still see the sweat glistening on his torso, though I doubt I have ever come within two hundred miles of his actual person.

Does this constitute a separation from reality as fissiparous as that which once came from reading romances, and then subsequently interpreting reality through them? Is this the lensed equivalent of mad old Don Quixote, intellectually ruined by his addiction to the romance narratives, or Madame Bovary, training herself for a life of emotional mendacity by mentally devouring the cheap fiction of her time?

We smile before lenses; we point them; we post the images around. We switch on Skype to see our nephew on the screen in New Zealand. We watch men dancing around in moondust, and we often view these images in the corner of our living rooms, more clearly than we see the neighbour outside mowing his lawn. Our memories have been converted into photographic museums, and we have never even asked who is responsible for the curation. How can we really distinguish between primary and secondary experience, between what is known and what imagined, even though that distinction still lies at the root of our notion of what segregates the psychotic from the functional (if melancholy) ordinary soul?

2

SO WHEN DID all this start? When did our reality begin to depend so much on lenses? This is one of those rare occasions when we can be utterly specific. The process began on 7 January 1610 when Galileo Galilei, having fashioned himself a telescope more powerful than any used on earth before, stared out into the skies. With this new instrument, he could see things in the heavens no one had ever seen before. He published *Sidereus Nuncius* that year. His book first explained how lenses had changed for ever our perception of reality, and our understanding of our place in space.

When in 1665 Robert Hooke published *Micrographia*, together with its remarkable microscopic illustrations, the extremities of human perception had been enlarged to an unprecedented degree. In forty-five years we had left one scheme of reality, and been lensed into another one entirely. We could now begin to see the vastness of space out there, and observe the tiny creatures we are obliged to live amongst down here. The age of lenses had now truly begun; we have been situated inside it ever since.

In 1656, a decade before the publication of *Micrographia* in London, Baruch Spinoza was excommunicated from the Jewish community in Amsterdam. He was to spend the rest of his days philosophizing, and making lenses for telescopes and microscopes. He could only do this because he was living in the middle of the new century of optical instruments. Human perception had now been extended in a manner previously unknown, and it was those humble lenses of his that were making it all possible. Stars became nearer, moons became bigger, reality was changing decade by decade as it was viewed through these lenses. *Gulliver's Travels* is an acknowledgment of that change. It is a meditation upon the shifts in reality that lenses had now brought about. Seven years after the publication of that book, Jonathan Swift was still pondering the vertiginous effects of scalar perspectivism:

> *So nat'ralists observe, a flea*
> *Hath smaller fleas that on him prey,*
> *And these have smaller fleas that bite 'em,*
> *And so proceed ad infinitum.*

In the seventeenth century the development of the telescope and the microscope expanded the human imagination at both the macro and the micro level. The great vision of falling bodies which opens *Paradise Lost* would not have been possible without Galileo's development of the telescope, and Milton himself pays tribute to Galileo in various places. He was aware of the vast implications of the telescope and the 'optic glass', as he called it, appears in the first book of *Paradise Lost*:

> *He scarce had ceased when the superior fiend*
> *Was moving toward the shore; his ponderous shield*
> *Ethereal temper, massy, large, and round,*
> *Behind him cast; the broad circumference*
> *Hung on his shoulders like the moon, whose orb*
> *Through optic glass the Tuscan artist views*
> *At evening from the top of Fesole,*
> *Or in Valdarno, to descry new lands,*
> *Rivers or mountains in her spotty globe.*

Here we seem to be peering back to the beginning of time through a telescope. This of course is precisely what the Hubble

Telescope now does. Einstein's physics has taught us that there is no space that is separate from time, and no time separate from space. When we look at the sun we are seeing it as it was eight and a half minutes previously, since that is the time it takes for its light to reach us. When we stare at other galaxies we are seeing them sometimes as they were millions of years ago. Having introduced the telescope at the beginning of his poem, Milton contrived to bring in the microscope in the last book of *Paradise Regained*, but he didn't appear to understand what it was for. He does not in fact appear to have looked through one, and he was of course blind by then; he seems to have assumed that this particular optical device was designed for peering into houses from the outside.

As Marjorie Hope Nicholson points out in *Science and Imagination*, we don't actually know how far back in history the invention of the telescope goes. We're not sure what the *merkhet* of the Egyptians was; or the 'queynte mirours' and 'perspectives' mentioned in Chaucer. Roger Bacon's 'glasses or diaphanous bodies' were evidently optical devices, and in the sixteenth century Thomas Digges and John Dee both appear to have made use of 'optic tubes' of some sort, but as far as we know they employed them solely for the magnification of terrestrial objects, to bring faraway visions closer to the eye.

The truly momentous occasion in the history of this device, the one which made its use obligatory and shifted the perceptions of humankind irrevocably, redefining in the process the extremities of perception, occurred on that night in January in 1610, when Galileo stared through the latest telescope he had made for himself. In a matter of hours he saw that the Milky Way was more crammed with stars than anyone had previously imagined, and that Jupiter had planets. He could see a covering of earthshine on the moon's surface, our own sunny reflection handed back into the darkness of space, but he noted also our moon's asperities, its ragged, pockmarked surface, its irregularities and protruberances. Aristotelianism, except as a form of superannuated antiquarianism, and a pretext for Vatican torture, died that night, for there was not, as the Greek philosopher had asserted and the European intellectual tradition had maintained for nearly two thousand years, perfection in the celestial sphere. It would still take some time to fully realise that the same laws applied up there as apply down here. What could be observed fitted in nicely with Galileo's previous discoveries: he had noticed that bodies in the sublunar sphere fall, all bodies fall, unless a force acts upon them with sufficient potency to prevent them from so doing. This would be encoded by Newton in three laws before the end of the century. Soon enough everyone would have to accept that the planets didn't move in the celestial perfection of circles either, but described instead a circuit of imperfection, the gravitationally-distorted ellipse. But all this was still to come.

Soon everyone in Europe who could afford it wanted to have one of these telescopes. Galileo tried to make sure he had a few spares with him whenever he performed his demonstrations before princes, since even scientific geniuses need to make a living. And later that year when Galileo's book *Sidereus Nuncius* was printed, every fellow of means had to get hold of a copy. Sir Henry Wotton wrote a letter to the Earl of Salisbury on March 13th 1610, in which he said the work 'is come abroad this very day'. Pirated editions were soon far more numerous than the authorised imprints. The heavens were at last yielding their secrets, though some of the defenders of heaven itself weren't best pleased at this turn of events. After all, Dante had represented the regions of hell as circles, not ellipses; and everyone knew that the trinity was a perfect equilateral triangle. Eternity was an ouroboros, a snake swallowing its own tail. And, whatever Giordano Bruno might have preached, there could be no plurality of worlds: Jesus had come here directly from heaven, and then gone straight back there, after a brief detour in hell. He had not called in on any other spatial colonies.

So it was that the vast space of the Baroque entered Milton's mind through a telescope, though by the time he came to portray that vastness, he was himself already blind. He had looked through one though, and he describes a visit to Galileo in *Areopagitica*. Though the words of *Paradise Lost* were written by a man without physical vision, they seem to see the vast spaces more vividly than even the most apocalyptic of its nineteenth-century illustrators, John Martin. And what they see is the demolition of boundaries; hence the negatives in so many of the descriptions:

> *Before their eyes in sudden view appear*
> *The secrets of the hoary Deep – a dark*
> *Illimitable ocean, without bound,*
> *Without dimension; where length, breadth, and highth,*
> *And time, and place, are lost.*

Thus did the telescope start to habituate the mind to a vastness previously unconceived. And not long after, the microscope was busily extending perception in the other directions, prompting Pope's plaintive request to remain, perceptually, where we had been first and properly planted:

> *Why has not man a miscroscopic eye?*
> *For this plain reason: man is not a fly.*

Thus did Pope, in the *Essay on Man,* look askance at the newly magnified world, though he used it to delightful effect in *The Rape of the Lock.* It is not possible to ask why man does not have a microscopic eye, unless you live in a world filled with microscopes, any more than it is possible to identify a plough in the night skies before you have undergone a Neolithic Revolution here on earth. Robert Hooke's *Micrographia* had become a famous book after its publication in 1665, and soon after it was to feed directly into the literary imagination.

Here, for example, is Gulliver in Brobdingnag:

The Kingdom is much pestered with Flies in Summer;
and these odious Insects, each of them as big as a
Dunstable Lark, hardly gave me any Rest while I sat
at Dinner, with their continual Humming and Buzzing
about mine Ears. They would sometimes alight upon
my Victuals, and leave their loathsome Excrement or
Spawn behind, which to me was very visible, although
not to the Natives of that Country, whose large Opticks
were not so acute as mine in viewing smaller Objects.

This passage simply could not have been written without the publication of *Micrographia*, with its superb illustrations of the large grey drone-fly and the flea. When Pepys collected his copy of this book soon after its publication in 1665, he sat up until two in the morning reading it, and described it as 'the most ingenious book that ever I read in my life.' As with *Sidereus Nuncius*, this was one of the rare occasions where one can point to a publication and announce that this one book has extended the extremities of perception overnight. It furnished for the first time unseen realms, and alternative dimensions. It is his awareness of telescopic vision and microscopic vision which enables Swift to meditate on larger and smaller 'Opticks' and their appropriateness for the worlds they view.

Now what Pope's lines indicate is that our optics are appropriate to our functions, and in a sense both the telescope and the microscope had confused the issue, to the mildly theatrical distress of Pope. The fact is that Gulliver's eye in Brobdingnag is a microscope, and much pain it causes him as he gazes on human lice making their way over the human body. The most famous of the illustrations in *Micrographia* had been a sixteen-inch fold-out of a louse. The genius of *Gulliver's Travels* was to understand that perception had been altered for ever by the introduction of the telescope and the microscope. The discovery, however, is not an altogether happy one. The engravings of lice and fleas which Robert Hooke had engaged in had been of non-human creatures. So what happened when one transferred such perceptions to our own realm, the realm of humanity? This is what happened. Here is Gulliver in Brobdingnag:

> *There was a fellow with a wen in his neck, larger than five woolpacks, and another with a couple of wooden legs, each about twenty foot high. But, the most hateful sight of all was the lice crawling on their clothes. I could see distinctly the limbs of these vermin with my naked eye, much better than those of an European louse through a microscope, and their snouts with which they rooted like swine. They were the first I had ever beheld, and I should have been curious enough to dissect one of them, if I had proper instruments (which I unluckily left behind me in the ship) although indeed the sight was so nauseous, that it perfectly turned my stomach.*

Despite his sensation of nausea, Gulliver cannot resist his scientific impulse: he thinks of dissecting a louse. He knows he is in a great age of dissection. The famous painting by Rembrandt, The Anatomy Lesson of Dr Tulp, shows a cadaver being dissected in a theatre. The avid spectators look on as a dead human being is turned inside out, to demonstrate the organs, intestines etc., that reside within. The corpse is that of an executed criminal. This was an arrangement made to the benefit of medicine: those who had passed beyond the stage of shame, whose criminality had already disgraced them in the public eye, underwent a further humiliation posthumously by being dissected. Wordsworth was to complain two centuries later: 'We murder to dissect'. Already there was a new fad: the écorché painting or sculpture, in which the human being is presented flayed. These images had moved out of the anatomy theatre and into the gallery. Swift might have thought that the flaying of a woman altered her person for the worse, but many stately spectators seemed to differ. Quite a lot of the écorché figures of the time were of pregnant women. Our fondness for turning ourselves inside out in public is not new, though registering the progress from Titian's The Flaying of Marsyas to the Jerry Springer Show does make one ponder the significance of that word 'progress'.

Gulliver is very much a man in a scientific world. He is extremely practical about such matters as navigation, warfare, architecture and engineering. We might remember that, when that other great novelistic victim of shipwreck, Robinson Crusoe, finds himself on his island, the first thing he does at night is to find a tree to sleep in, from which he also cuts himself a branch as a weapon to ward off attackers. The function of nature is to provide resources for resourceful men. It is not there to be worshipped, or to provide a gateway to heaven; it is there to be exploited. It provides a home and a weapon; this is nature as the zone of resourcefulness and exploitation. This is nature as the object of reason. Robinson Crusoe was published only seven years before Gulliver's Travels.

Gulliver is of a most practical cast of mind, however bizarre and unaccountable his voyages. Here is his account of how he came to enter into the holy estate of matrimony: 'I took part of a small house in the Old Jury; and being advised to alter my condition, I married Mrs Mary Burton, second daughter to Mr Edmond Burton hosier in Newgate Street, with whom I received four hundred pounds for a portion.' He does not remark upon her beauty, her accomplishments, her conversation, or her skill at playing the virginals; no, he tells us that she provided him with four hundred pounds for a dowry upon their union. Even Jane Austen was never less sentimental than this. But it is precisely such a lack of sentimentality which facilitates the achievement of the book. Gulliver's practical eye, his attention to detail, his forensic calculation, are the attributes that permit him to convey to us the extraordinary, which he describes in the practical prose of a builder's manual. The unflustered descriptiveness of his prose is what makes his account of marvels so compelling.

SWIFT WAS FASCINATED by the goings-on in the scientific world. The Royal Society had been founded in 1660, and its *Transactions* were to be avidly read by Swift. To some degree, *Gulliver's Travels* is a parody of those pages of the *Transactions* which were often filled with wondrous journeys affording new discoveries about the flora and fauna of newly discovered parts of the world. And here we need to situate Swift in regard to this new scientific temper, one which he regarded with the gravest suspicion.

In the 1690s Swift's patron at Moor Park in Surrey was Sir William Temple. Temple was handsome, powerful and opinionated. He believed, as did many others at the time, that all true learning came from the classics; that insofar as modern learning presumed to surpass the classics, it was being impertinent. In 1692 he wrote 'Upon the Ancient and the Modern Learning', the gist of which can be conveyed thus: all wisdom lies with the ancients. Nothing new in the way of discovery or science has in any way displaced the great philosophical tradition.

Swift went along with this. We can only speculate as to why. Swift was so entirely dependent upon Temple's good will. He functioned as his secretary, and it was in Temple's power to make or break this young man upon whom he was lavishing his largesse. We might speculate that, if Sir William had been of a more scientific temper himself, then Swift might have written differently. Whatever the personal motivation, Swift followed his master in his prejudices. Later in the same decade he wrote *The Battle of the Books*, and in that work the ancients are compared to bees, busily about their honeyed task of sweetness and light, whereas the spiders, which is to say the moderns, think that they can weave all knowledge and learning out of their own guts, as a spider does its web. It is a curiosity worthy of remark that in Bacon's essays, the imagery had been reversed: the spiders are the ancients, who think all discoveries can come out of the innards of tradition, which is to say, ancient learning. The bees go off in search of fresh nectar, which is to say modern experimental knowledge.

Let us remind ourselves here of the momentous nature of this conflict. In Marlowe's *Doctor Faustus*, Faustus says:

> *Having commenc'd, be a divine in show,*
> *Yet level at the end of every art,*
> *And live and die in Aristotle's work…*

'And live and die in Aristotle's work…' We in fact know remarkably little of Aristotle's work, since almost everything that has come down to us through history with his name attached was in the form of reconstruction by his students. But what came to be called Aristotelianism in the Middle Ages had an enormous authority, an authority to be consolidated by both church and state. And this authority had tremendous implications for the new science. One of its implications was to set the empirical evidence of the new lenses against the body of traditional learning. What was being delivered through the new lenses in the form of information appeared to contradict the great tradition. There were those who simply would not look through Galileo's telescope, as there are those now who will not read *The Origin of Species*.

Aristotle asserts that the sublunar realm, our realm, is the region of imperfection. Here we find change and mutability. The celestial realm, being the realm of perfection, is unchanging. So when Galileo looked through his uniquely powerful telescope on that night in January 1610 and saw the pockmarked surface of the moon, he was observing the flat contradiction of the Aristotelian world. This was evidently not the realm of perfection, and some said that, because of this, the evidence being thereby gleaned could not possibly be true. Here we are seeing in conflict the contrast between the new experimental method, the inductive method, based on observation and measurement, and a mode of thought based upon the appeal to tradition and textual authority. When Galileo was condemned for his insistence that the earth moved around the sun, the condemnation was based on the fact that this contradicted the tenets of both scripture and tradition, and the tradition in this instance had been derived from Aristotle, as well as certain references in the Bible. This was why Francis Bacon portrayed the traditionalists as spiders, imagining that the gut of tradition can provide an endless amount of gossamer for our intricate invention, without the input of any new science. And this, he asserted vehemently in *The Advancement of Learning*, is surely an absurdity.

Temple was already seriously outdated in his defence of the classics against the new learning, and Swift in following him did himself no favours in terms of the history of thought, though he might have sharpened his own skills as a satirist. That aristocratic disdain for the learning of merchants and seamen, that dyspeptic attitude to all that made the modern world possible, might well have given Swift an advantage as a writer of satire. Satire functions best when it stares through the lens and notices something the age appears to have missed. Look, it says: there it was before your eyes all the time.

Irony in Swift can be looked at as the adoption of an optic, one that always reveals the extremities of perception. We have already seen this at work in *Gulliver's Travels*. And another classic example is *A Modest Proposal*. Here the irony begins with the title itself, for what the writer of this document is recommending is a solution to the problems of poverty and starvation in the Ireland of Swift's time, which is in fact far from modest: the solution is the cooking and eating of the children of the Irish poor. This legendary piece of writing is ironic from beginning to end, and the irony permits a silent cry of pain at the wickedness humans can inflict on one another. One of the advantages of his recommended scheme, our proposer writes, is as follows:

Men would become as fond of their wives during the time of their pregnancy as they are now of their mares in foal, their cows in calf, or sows when they are ready to farrow; nor offer to beat or kick them (as is too frequent a practice) for fear of a miscarriage.

4

CURIOUS HOW THE effect here is like watching an ancient silent film. And the distancing effect such irony generates can also induce a kind of vertigo. We find ourselves staring down at the gap opening between surface meaning and its tonal contradiction, and wondering if we might be about to fall in. What size of flea are we exactly, and are we being preyed upon, or preying, or both? Can this really go on *ad infinitum*?

Back to *Gulliver's Travels*. In Section Three, Gulliver travels to the Academy at Lagado. Here he discovers many extraordinary things going on. The people dreaming up their schemes are known as projectors. One of them has spent eight years attempting to extract sunbeams from cucumbers, which he then intends to put into hermetically sealed vials, which can be released to provide sunshine at a later date. Another projector wishes to find the original elements of human food in excrement, so as to arrive once more at the rudiments of nourishing material. Feculent this may be, but it is certainly holistic. Such projects undoubtedly parody the wilder schemes of the Royal Society, but in Chapter Six of Section Three we have this piece of sustained irony:

> *In the school of political projectors I was but ill entertained, the professors appearing in my judgement wholly out of their senses, which is a scene that never fails to make me melancholy. These unhappy people were proposing schemes for persuading monarchs to choose upon the score of their wisdom, capacity and virtue; of teaching ministers to consult the public*

*good; of rewarding merit, great abilities and eminent
services; of instructing princes to know their true
interest by placing it on the same foundation with that
of their people: of choosing for employments persons qualified to exercise them; with many other wild
impossible chimeras, that never entered before into the
heart of man to conceive, and confirmed in me the old
observation, that there is nothing so extravagant and
irrational which some philosophers have not maintained for truth.*

Here the irony is deliberated and extensive. Every sensible
and prudent scheme – 'of choosing for employments persons
qualified to exercise them' for example – is described as extravagant and irrational. The camera angle is like those floor-shots
in *Citizen Kane*, when normality suddenly looms so large and
weirdly above us. The point being, of course, to make us think
of how decisions actually are made in institutions and political
life, how favourites are put forward not because of ability but
because of their fawning upon power, how those who grease
their inside leg so that they might the more fluently slide up the
pole of preferment, have a hideous tendency to be promoted.

5

SO WE HAVE in *Gulliver's Travels* a parody of the modern
travelogue, a satire upon the *Transactions of the Royal Society*,
an ironic meditation on the organisation of human society in
comparison with some other invented ones, and an employment
in fiction of the latest optical devices, both telescopic and microscopic, to see how differently we might look to ourselves, if
we could turn the lenses around and stare, not out into space,
but back into ourselves; not at the magnified louse, but at a magnified version of ourselves. We would see, as the Gospels put
it, not the mote in our neighbour's eye, but the beam in our

own. Gulliver normally reports with a tone of mild incredulity whatever he discovers of indisputable wisdom in other lands. He says of the King of Brobdingnag:

> *He confined the knowledge of governing within very narrow bounds; to common sense and reason, to justice and lenity, to the speedy determination of civil and criminal causes; with some other obvious topics which are not worth considering. And, he gave it for his opinion, that whoever could make two ears of corn, or two blades of grass to grow upon a spot of ground where only one grew before, would deserve better of mankind, and do more essential service to his country, than the whole race of politicians put together.*

Irony expresses amazement at that which is blatantly true; by this means it alerts us to how frequently the blatantly true is flatly contradicted by the monochrome falsehood we see all around us. This becomes pronounced in the final section where the Houyhnhnms are contrasted with the Yahoos; the Yahoos are sadly nearer to humanity than the horse-like creatures they confront. Indeed the horses are so rational that their reasonableness can seem forbidding. F. R. Leavis complained in a famous essay that if the Houyhnhnms had all the intelligence, the Yahoos appeared to have all the life. In their statuary ethical stillness, the Houyhnhnms can seem to present us with a species of intellectual *dressage*. And like the dwarfs in Terry Pratchett's *Discworld*, they are not very good at metaphors. Doubleness in language (and its brother mendacity) seems to them to be an altogether too-Yahoo-like linguistic gift. It is significant nonetheless that the word Yahoo has entered our lexicon along with hooligan as representing a form of human behaviour we recognise as characteristic and frequent.

It is the optical dimension of Swift's book which has made it the centre of a certain sort of modern criticism: its employment of defamiliarization. This is not a term which would have been known to Swift, since it was only invented in the twentieth century by the Russian Formalists; it is in fact a translation of their word *ostranenie*. It means seeing something anew; seeing it not with the eyes but through them; abandoning a conventional view and seeing instead from an unanticipated one. It involves, in other words, a change of optic.

A great deal of defamiliarization in fiction comes from displacement; this is often a displacement in location or time, but there are other types too, and these usually take the form of a reconfiguring of our five senses. *Robinson Crusoe* and *Lord of the Flies* both have this much in common with *Gulliver's Travels*. In all three books our protagonists are taken away from the normal rules and expectations of society, to islands where they must survive as best they can. When Thomas More wrote *Utopia*, providing us with the name we have used ever since, he employed a similar device. If you shift your characters in this manner, then all of their normal preconceptions might be challenged. They might, for example, start to wonder why we think so highly of gold – not a useful element on an island if you are trying to work out how to survive. Why then would people kill one another to acquire it? Ruskin was to ask the same question in his lecture 'In Praise of Rust.' Displacement, as one of the devices of defamiliarization, allows for the re-assessment of prejudices and preconceptions.

In the instances we've mentioned the displacement is a literal one – there is a place at the heart of the word dis*place*ment, and we have been removed from it, to somewhere strange and unpredictable, where our perceptions might suffer a sea-change. The foundations of our life are thereby put into question. This is still a much-used device of adventure fiction and cinema. The plane-crash or the shipwreck deliver our fates to a new place, stripped of our normal expectations.

Now think of what goes on in SF writing. Here we often have a more complex, even more elusive, form of displacement.

Gulliver's Travels can be regarded as one of the founding texts of SF. In *Robinson Crusoe* we are transported elsewhere, but the normal rules of perception continue to apply; reality has grown lonelier, but it hasn't re-arranged itself entirely. Our central optic remains domesticated. But think of Gulliver in Lilliput or Brobdingnag. Here reality *has* re-arranged itself. In one place Gulliver becomes a giant surrounded by tiny people; this gives him a different vantage-point on reality. Perception has been radically re-routed. Gulliver is looking through a telescope at reality. Then in Brobdingnag it is he who is the midget, gazing up at the monsters all about him. His vision has become a microscope. He sees with vivid detail the coarse details of the life presented to him, and he finds it grotesque.

Good SF writers keep their eye on what is going on in the world of science and technology; often they have some training in science, like Isaac Asimov or Arthur C. Clarke. The fact is, as we have already remarked, that some of the passages above simply could not have been written without the publication of Robert Hooke's *Micrographia*, with its illustrations of the large grey drone-fly and the flea.

Defamiliarization shows us things as we had not previously thought to consider them. In Lilliput the Lilliputians examine all the goods which Gulliver keeps about his person, and make an inventory of them. Here is their description of his pocket watch:

> *We directed him to draw out whatever was at the end of that chain; which appeared to be a globe, half silver, and half of some transparent metal: for on the transparent side we saw certain strange figures circularly drawn, and thought we could touch them, till we found our fingers stopped with that lucid substance. He put this engine to our ears, which made an incessant noise like that of a watermill. And we conjecture it is either some unknown animal, or the god that he worships: but we are more inclined to the latter opinion, because*

he assured us (if we understood him right, for he expressed himself very imperfectly), that he seldom did anything without consulting it. He called it his oracle, and said it pointed out the time for every action in his life.

They are tiny, of course, but they have noticed the vast importance of mechanical time in the life of the west. Gulliver himself had never noticed. He had been more than ready to discount the significance of the endless ticking that controlled his existence.

6

THE PHILOSOPHER NIETZSCHE often spoke of resentment. He thought it typical of the slave mentality. Those who accept a life of passivity and obedience are filled with resentment for those who are more powerful than they. But there is at work in Swift a kind of reverse resentment. It would appear from the biographical data we have that his *Tale of A Tub* might have satirised a little too effectively the idiocies not merely of the Church of Rome and the world of the conventicles, but seemingly of the Established Church itself, in the favoured form current in England during his lifetime. Swift's great gift was to be able to mock the pretensions, vacuity and mendacity of our species, by employing the same precise vocabularies under which we so often bury our customary contortions in pious prattle. He was never to be forgiven for such satirical exactitude. The curious scene in Part Two of *Gulliver's Travels* where he puts out the fire in the Queen's Palace by urination, thereby provoking her unyielding wrath, is often thought to refer to Queen Anne's dislike of the vulgarity of much of the goings-on in *A Tale of A Tub*. Swift probably came to feel that he had not received the attention he had hoped for because of this dislike. Then, with her death in 1714, he was to be politically out of favour for the rest of his life.

And so we witness his distinctive form of resentment. This is not the resentment of the mean towards the mighty, but the resentment of the gifted and articulate writer towards the toadying journeyman who creeps ever onwards towards the enhancements of his pension. It is the same sort of contempt Thomas More felt towards Richard Rich, one of his more loathsome betrayers. Swift takes his fictional revenge on all those he had seen promoted beyond his sphere in the final part of *Gulliver's Travels*. The loathed creature of privilege is, of course, a Yahoo: 'That this *leader* had usually a favourite as *like himself* as he could get, whose employment was to *lick his master's feet and posteriors, and drive the female Yahoos to his kennel*; for which he was now and then rewarded with a piece of ass's flesh. This *favourite* is hated by the whole herd, and therefore to protect himself, keeps always *near the person of his leader*. He usually continues in office till a worse can be found; but the very moment he is discarded, his successor, at the head of all the Yahoos in that district, young and old, male and female, come in a body, and discharge their excrements upon him from head to foot.' The images succeed one another, as in an anthropologist's film of a distant land and its inhabitants. We are being presented, seemingly, with an early documentary, which was precisely what some of its first readers took it to be. We seem to be looking backwards in time through a mighty telescope.

'Satire,' Swift wrote, 'is a sort of glass wherein beholders do generally discover everybody's face but their own, which is the chief reason for that kind of reception it meets in the world, and that so very few are offended with it.' We are back once more with optics. Hamlet urged the players to hold the mirror up to nature. As Roland Mushat Frye points out in *The Renaissance Hamlet*, the only mirrors the Globe audience knew were small, probably not more than a few inches across, convex and imperfect. Such a mirror would be held up to the face at an angle, so as to find blemishes. We need to understand something of the optics of the time to understand what the line actually means. Just as we need to beware when we gaze upon the technicolor splendours of the Hubble images, presenting us with the latest extremities of perception. At least Galileo actually saw through his telescope what he subsequently drew and published in *Sidereus Nuncius*. No one has ever 'seen' the Hubble images, which are in fact constructed out of data no human eye *in situ* ever could perceive. And in a final interaction between art and science, we might note that Galileo could only make such immediate sense of the images of the moon he saw through his *ochiale* because of his previous studies of chiaroscuro. He realised that the lunar shadows could only be cast by protruberances occluding the light source. Thomas Hariot in England had been staring at the moon through his own (weaker) telescope throughout the whole of 1609, but he had never realised the significance of what he called those 'spottie' patches of dark. The techniques of art here facilitated the discoveries of science.

We cannot escape the world of lenses we now live inside, but we can at least try to be alert to some of the ways in which it functions. *The Project for a New American Century* in 2001 announced that the aim of modern American foreign policy had to be 'full-spectrum dominance'. Is that merely in the visible spectrum then, or are we also heading off into the realms of the gamma ray and the infra-red? No problems seeing in the dark these days. One thing is for sure: our new drones, currently named Predators and Reapers, will be bombing away. No human eyes inside them, of course, but many miles away in Nevada a fellow will be staring at a screen, and believing his own eyes, even as he so swiftly closes the eyes of others, in a faraway land of which he almost certainly knows nothing. Swift would have taken note. Here, he would have said, we have entered the world of a new optic. How exactly does a whole culture present itself to you when you only ever see it through a drone's sensors? Now at last Achilles can choose to be the greatest warrior on earth, while also staying home to till his father's fields, and living to a grand old age.

IX

PATTERN RECOGNITION AND THE PERIODIC TABLE.

WE FIND OUR way through complication, or even apparent chaos, by pattern recognition. If we are working according to tradition, then it will be routine pattern recognition. If we are involved in discovery, then it is radical pattern recognition. We are finding something new, rather than merely confirming something old. We creatures of modernity are painfully aware that the paradigm structuring our perceptions can facilitate discovery, but can also prevent it.

The Ptolemaic system in its latter stages had to complicate itself to a remarkable degree (with additional epicycles and such-like) in order to save the appearances while holding on to the paradigm. Once the paradigm shifted to a heliocentric one, there was a radical simplification. The epicycles disappeared. This was an example of how the paradigm can block pattern recognition by falsifying the actual significance of the patterns being observed. But the paradigm can also release knowledge of phenomena that have never yet been observed at all.

Dmitri Mendelyeev predicted the existence of new elements (including germanium) and he also predicted their characteristics; he was right, and it was the architectonics of his own system which facilitated the discovery. He located unknown phenomena through the interstices, the symmetric patterns, of his model. The Dirac equation predicted the existence of anti-matter, and Dirac's maths were proved right when a positron was detected some years later.

Does literary and artistic form allow such discoveries? Or to put the matter another way, does the artistic representation ever cease being instrumentally representative, and become instead autonomously heuristic? Can its architectonics allow discoveries produced out of its own form, the same way that Mendelyeev encountered the reality of his own new elements, before anyone had ever actually encountered such elements in nature? By examining the construction of the periodic table by Mendelyeev, and the writing of *The Periodic Table* by Primo Levi, I will try to explore some of the implications of these questions.

PATTERN RECOGNITION IS most easily detectable in aberration. King Lear on encountering Mad Tom, naked and raving, asks if his daughters have brought him to this pass; in other words, he now sees reality as so irredeemably patterned by filial ingratitude and viciousness that the whole world simply presents itself to him in such a guise. There is a South Sea cargo cult that still worships Prince Philip, the Duke of Edinburgh, and awaits his second coming. The logic of the pattern recognition here is impeccable: out of the sky came a great metal bird; out of that stepped a man taller than any of them, and with a far fairer skin, wearing an immaculate white suit that blazed in the sun. During his sojourn from heaven he distributed gifts among them here on earth. Then the great metal bird took him back to that heaven where he lives with the most powerful queen ever known. Since then, they have awaited the blessing of his return, and the cornucopia of good things he will doubtless once more distribute amongst them during that wished-for millennium.

Patterns can be delusive, then. But the total absence of pattern means chaos; we cannot find our way about. What mythology shows us is that we have always provided ourselves with patterns; as a species we have a genius for mapping ourselves on to the cosmos. And what religion and politics show us is that when observed reality contradicts scripture, tradition or ideology, we are usually as ready to re-arrange our observations as we are to question the credal patterns of our sanctioned taxonomies.

The periodic table is a luminous example of how we observe nature through our own modelling of it. After all, there is no such 'table' to be observed in nature, and no one has ever thought there was. This diagrammatic symbolization of the inter-relations between different aspects of matter presents us with a representation of the fundamental elements we can detect in nature. Why such radically different elements as neon and sodium should sit next to each other in such a table was inexplicable at the time the table was being constructed; it took the discoveries of quantum physics to establish how the constellations of particles inside the atom, their ordering in certain groupings and in certain orbits, bestow on them either stability or instability. They are either avid for union with other elements or compounds, which is to say lively and active, or they are inert, noble even, not to be tempted into any easy marriage, certainly not a morganatic one. It is impossible to describe such atomic situations without metaphor.

The seven groups into which Mendelyeev arranged the elements, on cards pinned to his wall, allowed for the perception of pattern; individual patterns and overall patterns. Active metals like sodium, rubidium and potassium belonged to one group, the first; active non-metals like iodine and chlorine could be seen to belong to another group entirely, the seventh.

A pattern is a kind of rhyme. Or to turn the perception around, rhyming itself is a species of pattern recognition, and Dryden was explicit in saying that he had often found the idea while hunting for the rhyme; so here we have one of those paradigmatic generations: out of the model itself and its exploration comes the unanticipated discovery. Routine rhyming, as with all routine pattern recognition, simply confirms what we already knew. Trite verse is all too good at reminding us that moon rhymes with June and both of them with soon. At the radical edge of the activity we have a poet like Paul Muldoon, a rhymer of genius, who produces the frisson of registering in our minds that ankle rhymes with tranquil. Bob Dylan also had this uncanny gift for aural pattern recognition, rhyming 'Let the boys in' with 'It's not poison'. His pronunciation helps. At the beginning of the Book of Genesis in the Hebrew we are told that there was waste and darkness over the deep, and the words used to convey that patternless chaos actually rhyme: *tohu wabohu*. Out of such coherent incoherence God sees patterns arising, and makes them emerge with his breath, his *ruah*, his spirit of order and redemption. Light is summoned, and then it is divided from darkness; heaven is divided from earth; the land from the ocean. God had seen the order inherent in the *tohu wabohu*, as Michelangelo told us the sculptor sees the shape inherent in the marble.

Until a few hundred years ago, the usual means of diagnosing the personality was by mapping how the elements of the macrocosm, earth, water, fire and air, expressed themselves in the microcosm of the human mind and body. The balances or imbalances between these fundamentals dictated the balance of your humours, which is to say whether you were phlegmatic, choleric, sanguine or melancholy. But modern science has discovered that these 'elements' were not in fact elemental. We now have Mendelyeev's periodic table instead, to direct us to what the truly elemental components of nature are. In employing the periodic table as a grid in which to locate all matter, including human personality and historic context, Levi found a formal device which is creatively generative; all artistic and literary form – unless it is moribund – should be creatively generative to one degree or another. In the 1960s Dylan found that the form of the popular song, allied to the riches of the folk tradition, and crossed with literature as diverse as Shakespeare and Rimbaud, opened up for him a space in which to work, a space which no one had ever opened up in that way before. The songs permitted the discovery of surrealistic symmetries.

So Levi behaves as though he were a sixteenth-century physician and astrologer, employing the humours in the analysis of humanity and its discontents, except that it is our modern understanding of the elements out of which he constructs his metaphoric grid. One of the things that is so extraordinary about *The Periodic Table* is the way in which Levi could construct such a delightful taxonomy of human morphology during a period in history when his place in the human (or inhuman) taxonomies of Europe was actually destining him for extermination.

Levi started writing the full version of *The Periodic Table* in 1973, though he had published a section of it long before in 1948 – this was the titanium chapter. The book covered the years 1935 to 1967, and the knowledge transmuted and structured into it covered the whole of Levi's life. It was finally published as a book in 1975.

SCIENCE, METAPHOR AND THE
'FREEDOM OF THE WRITER'

WHAT IS THE relationship of the writing of science to the writing of fiction and poetry? We can see that the first books of *Paradise Lost* could not have been written as they are without the work of Galileo in establishing the vastness of space. We can see that certain lines of Alexander Pope could not have been written without Newton's work on optics. But what is the relation between that which is discovered in science and what is written on the page by someone called a novelist or poet? If a contemporary poet writes of his woman as the only fixed star in his firmament, I am entitled to respond by saying that this would not be difficult, since there are no actual fixed stars out there for the beloved to compete with.

Hamlet and *King Lear* are both about heroes who are trying to get to the heart of things; to find out what's what. Hamlet wants to know what it is to be a man, and a son, since these two conditions are for him inseparable. Lear wants to know what nature is; he had thought nature was that all-controlling power which guaranteed the loyalty of children to their parents. He finds that this is not the case. Nature begins to seem much more like Edmund's goddess: brutal, rapacious, quite unsentimental about custom and tradition, closer to Darwin's nature than Hooker's. Legitimacy here is not about which womb you were conceived in or when, but the extent of your power and cunning. Hamlet's father comes from another world, since he comes out of Purgatory, which had been abolished in England over half a century before. But he also comes from another world in the sense that he is an emissary from a revenge tragedy, and Hamlet does not live in such a world of vengeance and vendetta. His Renaissance humanism cannot be dovetailed into that earlier world in which act is cancelled so symmetrically by counter-act.

At the same moment that these explorations of the nature of things were proceeding, Francis Bacon was also trying to get to the heart of things, and to express his discoveries in the plainest possible language, but he was aware that nature is a labyrinth, and that it does not readily disclose its secrets, but needs to be interrogated with vigour. The forensic metaphor is apt; Bacon was a lawyer, indeed for a while he was the highest lawyer in the land. He also fell foul of the law, in circumstances which are disputed to this day. Are Bacon's exploration into the nature of things comparable to Shakespeare's? Are Primo Levi's exploration into the nature of things in *The Periodic Table* comparable to Mendelyeev's in constructing the periodic table? We are suspended in language, according to Niels Bohr, but are we also suspended in form? Is the nature of reality perceived in *Hamlet* or *Lear* different in kind from that in Bacon's *Essays*? Is the language doing something fundamentally different?

There is no mention of the works of Shakespeare in Bacon; nor any reference to Bacon in Shakespeare. For Baconians this is simply explained: they were one and the same person. For the rest of us, it is not so straightforward. Would Shakespeare have been interested in Bacon's essays? Would Bacon have been interested in Shakespeare's plays? It is chastening to remember that after his return from the Galapagos, Darwin soon found that he couldn't read poetry any more, even though *Paradise Lost* had once been one of his favourite books, and had accompanied him on the Beagle voyage, along with Lyell's *Principles of Geology*. The work we are obliged to do in language sometimes precludes certain usages of language still open to others.

ADORNO FAMOUSLY ANNOUNCED that there could be no lyric poetry after Auschwitz. What he meant was that the spirit of lyric celebration, the litany of luminous delight at the heart of the lyric impulse, had been cancelled by the goings-on inside the camps. Humanity could never sing so freely again. One form of literary language was no longer available to anyone with a remaining shred of respect for the intelligent use of words; it would be like playing the banjo at the deathbed of a child. But then Adorno encountered the poetry of Paul Celan, and he changed his mind. What happened here was that Celan redefined lyric poetry for Adorno; it was no longer celebration of anything but the remorseless instinct to examine language from the inside, with ruthless intellectual vigour. There is such gravity to Celan's celebration of language that it is always and everywhere an act of universal mourning for the great, the irreparable, loss.

Levi included Celan in his book *The Search for Roots*, published posthumously. That book also included *De Rerum Natu-*

ra by Lucretius. The nature of things is the title, and the poem seeks to discover and expound it. What is the nature of things, asks Lucretius in verse. What is the cause of thunder, asks Lear on the heath. He also asks a question even more germane to his situation: what is the cause in nature of these hard hearts? The answer he receives is provided by the plot, rather than any speech: the loyalty of Kent, the companionship of the Fool, and the love of the exiled Cordelia. The question is never healed by the answers, and by the end of the play Lear, Cordelia and the Fool are all dead. So what is the nature of things, then? Francis Bacon was discovering it when he acquired a dead hen, bought from a poor woman at the bottom of Highgate Hill, and stuffed it full of snow, to see if refrigeration would have the same effect as salt, and delay putrefaction. The snow badly chilled him, and he repaired to the Earl of Arundel's house at Highgate, where according to Aubrey he was put into a good bed with a pan, but it was a damp bed, unused for a year. Two or three days later he is said to have died of suffocation, which probably means he contracted pneumonia. The nature of things does not always invite inspection without penalty. Bacon had been interrogating nature for a long time; nature finally took her revenge.

But is there a fundamental difference between the use of language in scientific discourse and the use of language in fiction or poetry?

MODEL, FORM AND EXACTITUDE OF USAGE

DIFFERENT TYPES OF literary formality permit different types of pattern recognition. One of the satisfactions of satire, for example, is the discovery of a pattern where it had previously remained unobserved by us. Evelyn Waugh's *A Handful of Dust* finds a perfectly symmetric pattern of desire balanced by betrayal throughout the narrative and characterisation. Tony Last is comprehensively betrayed by his wife Brenda at the beginning of the novel; and comprehensively betrayed by the Dickens-obsessed Mr Todd at the end. Brenda betrays Tony and is betrayed in her turn by her young lover John Beevor, whose mother connives in the betrayal. She it is who arranges the flat in London where the adultery might take place; she it is who becomes the subcontractor for the obelisk set up in Tony's memory at the end of the book. Jock appears to be a true friend to Tony, but when it is supposed that Tony is finally dead, he it is who inherits Brenda. Brenda has loved one John (her adulterous lover) altogether too much. The other John (her young son) received far too little love from her, and dies. We can discern here a pattern recognition, a symmetric arrangement, as architectonic in its own way as the minuscule and majuscule worlds of Lilliput and Brobdingnag in *Gulliver's Travels*. There is a kind of 'truth' to these observations, or the novel would not engage us to the extent that it does. The verisimilitude is dependent on form; form in literature dictates usage. Usage can also decay into imprecision and convention when form has become the mere repetition of itself, to no purpose other than filling up the silence.

Swift we know was an avid reader of the *The Philosophical Transactions of the Royal Society*, and satirised the 'literalist imperative' in the Academy at Lagado in *Gulliver's Travels*. The notion that language could ever consist of a single unambiguous word with one unquestionable referent is mocked in the image of the Lagado academicians who carry a bag full of all the objects to which they might need to refer. Such unilateral referentiality, Swift was well aware, is a dream based on insufficient thought about what it is that language actually does, and language's inescapable implication in the fecund world of metaphor. The whole of *Gulliver's Travels* is on the stylistic level a mocking of the linguistic pretensions of the Royal Society, its wish to return to a golden age of plainness of usage and the banishment of ambiguity.

LET US TRY to clarify a field of force here. If there were an anode and a cathode to the circuitry of arguments about metaphor then at the near end we have the longed-for literalism and plainness of style of Thomas Sprat in his *History of the Royal Society*. Words should refer to one thing and one thing only. All ambiguity should be banished; it constitutes not enrichment but confusion. At the far end we have the notion, expressed by Owen Barfield among others, that language is inherently metaphorical and polysemous, and that 'the literal' is merely a late attempt at disambiguation. Now one argument regarding tropes is that all figurative language is a species of catachresis, and catachresis means misuse. Thus Johnson's Dictionary has this to say of metaphor: 'The application of a word to an use to which, in its original import, it cannot be put: as, he *bridles* his anger; he *deadens* the sound; the spring *awakes* the flowers.' And the entry on metaphorical tells us: 'Not literal; not according to the primitive meaning of the word.' So catachresis distorts the 'original import' and deviates from the 'primitive meaning'. And yet Johnson's own examples must surely alert us to the fact that, as Wittgenstein put it, the English language is a graveyard of dead metaphors. I may be a freelance writer. Well then, I am evidently related to those free lancers who were the mercenary soldiers of the Middle Ages. Perhaps I embrace the metaphor proudly and quote Voltaire to the effect that the pen is mightier than the sword. We should at least remember the Irish riposte: the pen is lighter than the spade. Or perhaps I feel I have just had a breakthrough. Good: the original usage here was the *Daily Express* in 1918 – the Allied troops had just broken through the German defences. Or maybe my new work is groundbreaking, as William James evidently thought when he used the word in its modern form for the first time in a letter of 1907. We are a long way from digging up a hole for the foundations, and even further from the original 'breaking the ground', which was the dragging of the anchor over the seabed.

No, there is no escape from metaphor, and therefore no escape from catachresis, even if we are required to disambiguate into the literal from time to time. The literal is itself a metaphor, meaning going by the letter. If we want primitive meaning, then the literal can only apply to texts; only that which spells itself out can be read literally, but riddling the literal meanings here, we shall find metaphors.

And the alternative? The alternative appears to be a world of interminable interconnection. It is what Coleridge thought was the realm of the imagination: he gave it the name 'esemplastic' a drawing together of all disparities into unity. This is the world where ambiguity is not a confusion but rather a proliferation of meaning. This is the world of the Doctrine of Signatures, where every object and being in the cosmos signifies itself through shape, scent, medical appliance. This is the world of Baudelaire's correspondences, a late return upon the Great Chain of Being. It is also the world of *Finnegans Wake*, where words refuse to remain in the compartments of their languages and climb out once more to intermarry with the words from all the other languages. It is most certainly the world of Shakespeare. 'That time of year thou may'st in me behold' he says. It would be a curiously cloth-eared reader who said, 'But you're an Elizabethan man, not a movement of the earth round the sun, or a calendar.'

So usage is dictated by form, not etymology. We can now return to our question: is there a fundamental difference between the use of language in science and that in fiction and poetry?

THE FINAL CHAPTER of *The Periodic Table* is the one devoted to the carbon atom. If we examine this chapter carefully we will see that some aspects of its language are taken from geology – the notion of deposits and strata – but a large part is surely taken from the notion of the migrating bird, one that has been ringed, so that we might track it. Levi actually writes at one point: 'We will let it fly three times around the world, until 1960.' Levi's dates, as he happily admits, are arbitrary. They are also meaningless. History does not exist in the atomic and sub-atomic world. There is an epistemological sleight-of-hand going on here, for the sake of the narrative, and it is hard to tell just how far Levi was aware of it, and precisely how much it troubled him. He certainly seems a little uneasy at one point, when he says: 'Is it right to speak of a "particular" atom of carbon? For the chemist there exist some doubts, because until 1970 he did not have the techniques permitting him to see, or in any event isolate, a single atom; no doubts exist for the narrator, who therefore sets out to narrate.' So here we appear to have come across a moment of clear separation between scientific usage, and the freer usage of the writer. But what can this actually mean?

Levi's is a great book, and this is no attempt to disparage it, but he himself would have been the first to acknowledge the need for precision in thought; the whole of *The Periodic Table* is a plea for precision in thought and expression. That, he implies, is the only possibility of redemption we have. Without it, you'll get fascism. So what does it mean then to set out to narrate in a world where narrative does not in fact obtain? It is a tenet of the world of quantum mechanics that we can only track atoms and particles within a specific field of observation. We cannot track them outside that field because in the atomic world there is no retention of identity, and therefore no history. There are only locations, quantities and states.

A practised astronomer could look at a picture of our moon and distinguish it from any one of the moons of Jupiter. Why? Because the celestial bodies retain identity; they are historical. Every collision up there that has been registered by a crater, every protruberance, tells one that here is this moon, not that one. This is not possible in the atomic realm. Whatever collisions take place, whatever distortions of the atomic structure there have been, once the atom regains its original identity, it is indistinguishable from any other atom of the same sort in the same state in the universe. And that is why it is only possible to speak of 'this atom' within a trackable field of observation, which is to say a specified apparatus. Outside that, one carbon atom is the same as any other. That is why Niels Bohr insisted that the apparatus must count as part of the phenomenon.

We can only speak of the atomic world as a world of statistics and probabilities. There is not, and cannot be, any dynamic or individual model on the grand scale; the science does not permit it. So, this life as re-constituted and narrated in *The Periodic Table*, as taken back into its origins way back then and its history more recently, is actually spurious. The 'life' of this atom is being told as though there were as much a retention of identity in the micro-world as there is in the macro one, but in fact there isn't. The terms of memory and history do not apply. We are applying the concept of 'story' to a dimension of material reality where stories don't obtain, because the discrete occurrences of matter in this realm, which we call particles or atoms, do not retain identity. They dissolve into statistical realities, not dynamic ones. The interesting question then is, do we do this simply because it is impossible for us not to? Because of the narrative requirements of the human imagination? Has our story-telling urge become, during the course of our evolution, effectively instinctual and unavoidable? Once again, Levi is evidently aware that the process of visualisation of the atomic world is essentially metaphoric: 'If to comprehend is the same as forming an image, we will never form an image of a happening whose scale is a millionth of a millimetre, whose rhythm is a millionth of a second, and whose protagonists are in their essence invisible. Every verbal description must be inadequate, and one will be as good as the next...' Coleridge wrote in a letter of 1800: 'A whole Essay might be written on the Danger of *thinking* without Images.' The problem is that a whole essay might be written on the danger of thinking with them, too.

LEVI MOST SIGNIFICANTLY ascribes agency to the carbon atom: '...it is the only atom that can bind itself in long stable chains without a great expense of energy...' This is a subject making choices: this is the classic impresario of a narrative. The figure of biography so overwhelms this reality, which in truth can only be scientifically spoken of in terms of statistics and probabilities, locations, velocities, quantities and states, that the disparate natures of the macro and the micro world become irremediably confused. It is of course this confusion, however deliberated or unconscious, which permits and enables the narrative. Another name for such confusion could be metaphor, or in this instance a whole congeries of metaphors. Metaphor is pattern recognition expressing itself in the fabric of language. The question, as ever, is do such visualizing and chronicling metaphors truly help us approach the reality of the sub-atomic world, or in effect do they simply remove us even further from it, while still permitting us the luxury of our narrative? Are we employing narrative at the expense of understanding scientific reality? In one sense, to be applying narratives like this to the atomic and sub-atomic realm is to misuse all formal proprieties which apply to the matter in hand, but we seem to find it unavoidable.

The metaphors applied to the atomic realm in most scientific writings will usually have a number of functions: they will permit visualization of that which is not in fact visualizable, and they will permit the recounting of a narrative in a realm, statistical and probabilistic, where narrative itself dissolves in numbers. They will invariably be uni-directional – out of sub-atomic realities and into the world of classical physics and Newtonian mechanics, into a reality that can be seen and followed. What the constant application of metaphor to atomic physics inform us most eloquently is this: we are creatures with a relentless compulsion towards narrative. We shape the data into images and tales. Even our accounts of science are fashioned by Coleridge's esemplastic power, the urge to fashion the disparate items into unities, to unite the realms. The disenchantments of modern science, the disintegration of our unities, the attempted literalisation of our myths and legends, all produce a return of the repressed, in the form of metaphor and narrative. We want it both ways. And insofar as we allow the 'play' between scientific and narrative language in *The Periodic Table* we get to have it both ways.

In the quantum world the wave is a visualization of the relationship between contingency and causality. The wave is a statistical envisioning of what must happen, given sufficient time and space, and in quantum mechanics, if it can happen, then it must. The quantum world, unlike the individual biography, never runs out of time. Now we can never say of this individual photon in the double-slit experiment: it will arrive here or there with the next emission. But give us enough photons, give us a sufficiency of data, and we will see the pattern of the wave, though it is a statistical wave, emerging. Bohr once called it a 'cloud of probability'. Contingency once-off might be called accident, since it is that which is neither necessary nor impossible. Physics insists that a contingency repeated often enough becomes a causality that can be expressed statistically, and in the form of the multiple 'journeys' made by photons such statistics express themselves in the form of a wave.

TO DESCRIBE THE behaviour of light as a wave is of course to transfer terms from one form of perception, one medium – water – to another, in this case light. A metaphor, as we have seen, represents a type of pattern recognition. We say the keels plough the waves because we have noticed the similarity between a plough's motion through the earth and a keel's through water. And here too we have noticed certain characteristics of the behaviour of waves through liquid: interference and diffraction, for instance. Observing similar processes in the superimposition taking place with light directed through two slits we recognise the pattern, we carry over the perception: we speak metaphorically of waves. Then the metaphor becomes a scientific observation. These days we are just as likely to speak of light waves or sound waves as marine waves. The metaphor has become fact. There is a curious footnote here in terms of waves and pattern recognition. The form 'wave' was only used for the first time in 1526 in Tyndale's translation of the Bible: 'For he that douteth is lyke the waues.' Prior to that the form was 'waw'. Now the interesting thing about 'waw' is that it is a palindrome. Although no wave is in fact entirely reversible, because of the law of entropy, the regularity of waves allows us to speak of their frequency and length, and this characteristic of symmetric patterning had in fact been captured by the original structure of the word. The store of language is a store of vast intelligence. We live amongst these metaphors, whether dead or alive.

Metaphor is in permanent dialectic with technology, and the extremities of perception which technology facilitates, which change from age to age. In the seventeenth century the development of the telescope and the microscope expanded the human imagination at both the macro and the micro level. The great vision of falling bodies which opens *Paradise Lost* would not have been possible without Galileo's development of the telescope. Milton himself pays tribute to Galileo in Book One. The science was soon incorporated into the narrative. No one would dispute this in terms of *Paradise Lost*. The curious thing is that, if we look closely, it is also true of *The Periodic Table*. No instinct, it seems, is stronger in us than the narrative one; that is why we resist death so fiercely. We want to carry on with the story.

X

THE VIRTUE OF PATRICIDE.

'In art one must kill the father.'

SO SAID PICASSO. The remark is frequently quoted, seldom analysed. The artist's father was José Ruiz, a painter and art teacher. It is said that on realising the prowess of his son, he handed him his brushes and palette when the boy was thirteen. Thus did mere talent bow to evident genius. No reason to kill him, though, surely?

Ben Nicholson had far more right. His own father, Sir William, a portraitist of considerable accomplishment, beguiled Ben's young fiancée away and married her. He would also ask of Ben whenever they met if the young man was still designing toilet seats – this being a reference to Ben's white reliefs containing sunken circles, now regarded as amongst the finest achievements of British abstract art. Ben could surely have been forgiven if he had sharpened one of his wooden brushes into a stiletto, and stabbed his progenitor through the heart, since this really did look like the primal father keeping the fecund womenfolk all for himself, thereby provoking his own fateful slaughter, the one Freud speculated about so freely in *Totem and Taboo*. But why the murderousness in Pablo's artistic heart? Is it not enough to transcend the lesser achievements of your forebear; do you really have to annihilate him too?

The word that now inevitably comes to mind is oedipal, but this is a recent addition to our lexicon, only recorded in English for the first time, according to the OED, in 1932. The nearest adjectives before that date would have been Oedipean or Oedipodean (always capitalised), both relating to the gift Oedipus displayed for solving riddles. And there was also oedipodic, a pedicurist's term for swollen ankles, which is relevant in its etymological way. But this father-killing business, and the universal psychic necessity it supposedly expresses, is undoubtedly Freud's contribution, when he finds a new way of reading Sophocles' play, not as one of the worst pieces of fateful bad luck ever recorded in fact or fiction, but instead as a universal allegory of hidden human desire, the secret murderous wish of every male child to kill the father so as to possess the mother entirely.

It is hard to imagine a Russian iconographer saying that in art one must kill the father. There the tradition, and its continuity, is of the essence. It is only when form is under dynamic interrogation, when art is turning itself inside out, when the new is in radical conflict with the old, that spiritual patricide appears to be in order. Modernism negotiates a crisis of form. The old realism had become, according to Brancusi, 'a confusion of familiarities', and the word familiarity is linked morphologically to the word family. So if you want to attack that effectively you will need to go for the head, which is to say the paterfamilias. So shall we modify Picasso's statement and say, in modern – and certainly modernist – art one must kill the father, because the father still commands that kingdom which represents our 'confusion of familiarities'? His is the old formality that must be broken up by those excluded from the Salon, the Young Turks of innovation and dissent stirring out there on the street.

Because Cronus had been told that he was bound to be supplanted by one of them, his sons were promptly swallowed by him at birth. Only the infant Zeus was replaced by a stone and escaped. In such circumstances patricide seems a reasonable option, as the only means of survival, in fact. The corrupt tycoon Robert Maxwell effectively engaged in different displays of torture for his sons, preferably in public, and it might have been interesting if one of them had in fact assassinated him to see how plausible his defence in court might have seemed. The revenge most of them took on this disreputable tyrant was to join him in the family business as soon as possible. Jeremy Bamber killed both his parents, together with the rest of his immediate family, but his sole purpose appears to have been the acquisition of a sizeable inheritance by pretending that his schizophrenic sister had been to blame; he killed her too, and left the shotgun in her hand. He is one of the few people sentenced to life imprisonment in Britain who will actually spend the rest of his life inside a prison.

BUT THE QUESTION of patricide is seldom so literal. We are normally looking at those figures who stand in a projected and secondary parental relationship: kings, priests, and ultimately, perhaps, God himself. Bolingbroke after all gets to be king by killing Richard, who was occupying the throne at the time. In the sacred wood at Nemi the resident priest had to be cut down by the new arrival, who then took over the priestly powers from his victim. This provided the title for T. S. Eliot's first book of essays, and also the gory details at the climax of Francis Ford Coppola's *Apocalypse Now*, which merges the details taken from J. G. Frazer with the plot of Conrad's *Heart of Darkness*. Here, though, Kurtz has not fallen through the interstices of brute imperialism; rather he represents a living protest against it. He has translated imperial slaughter and mendacity into a personal murderousness which at least has the virtue of being unillusioned about itself. Willard arrives to cut him down. He has been instructed by the military command to terminate

Kurtz 'with extreme prejudice'. Kurtz sees what is coming. He describes Willard as a messenger boy sent to collect an overdue grocer's bill. Thus does the inglorious future displace the inglorious past.

According to Freud's argument, God did not make us; we projected from the inner shadows of our psychic machinery a figure cognate with the authoritative figure of the father, but also related to all those other shapes of male power governing our lives. Presumably then, if we have been blessed with a loving father, loving teachers, loving probation officers and policemen, the figure of the deity might appear in our prayers as a vast source of charity. But if not, not. Studying scripture could surely take us either way. Yahweh, as Harold Bloom constantly points out, is an alarming God on more than one occasion. He tries to kill Moses in the Book of Exodus: *And it came to pass by the way in the inn, that the Lord met him, and sought to kill him.* The defence his wife Zipporah employs, wielding a sharpened flint, involves the blooding of both her son and her husband. Thus does she make of him, as she puts it, a 'bridegroom of blood'.

We are never told why this should have happened, but then the murderousness of Yahweh does not necessarily arrive bearing any explanations. After all, he decides to wipe out the whole of his new creation only six chapters into the narrative of its very first book, and all we are told there is that 'the wickedness of man was great on the earth', and he'd had enough. Angels might have been copulating with the daughters of the earth. Why the animals, reptiles and birds had to be annihilated too remains unexplained. They were presumably no better than they should be, but in their animalistic way, no worse either. This does look alarmingly like the principle of collective punishment.

William Empson's greatest accusation against Christianity was that it made a fetish of suffering in its ritual and iconography, and that a religion in which the anger of the father could only be appeased by the death of the son was a barbaric one.

Now the Trinitarian response to this would be (and has been) that the Son offers himself up for voluntary annihilation in order to counteract the catastrophic effect of the Fall, and the Father accepts this gracious offering; he does not want it, but he accepts it as the only truly redemptive solution to the dilemma Adam and Eve have brought about through their disobedience. The problem is that no modern account of the development of humanity can really posit a 'Fall'; it is incompatible with all that we have come to know about the development of our species. Even the choreographic skills of Busby Berkeley could hardly have coordinated this scattered species of ours into one coherent collective action which would so reject the will of the Creator. In other words, there was no Adam and Eve; and so our notion of a cosmic inheritance of guilt as a result of their primal sin is the ultimate filial projection.

So, for Empson, Christianity comes to represent a religion of the murderous father. It has been said that Judaism is the religion of the father; Christianity the religion of the son. This may be so, but the religion of the son is dictated by the created order of the father, nonetheless. One might recall that the last words of Jesus as a living man are a cry to his heavenly father, asking why he has abandoned his only son on the cross.

Empson returns to the theme obliquely in his thoughts on Eliot– 'My God, man, there's bears on it' – in *Using Biography*. This extraordinary essay argues that the figure of the hated Jew evident in the original version of *The Waste Land*, before its editing by Ezra Pound, was a displaced figure of Eliot's own father, who had recently died, and had made provision in his will that in the event of Eliot's own death, his English wife Vivienne should not inherit Eliot's portion of the estate, which would instead revert. Empson argues that the Unitarian figure of Eliot's father, denying the divinity of Jesus while being notably competent with money, has been conflated with a universal semitic persona: 'Now if you are hating a purse-proud business man who denies that Jesus is God, into what stereotype does he best fit? He is a Jew, of course…' On this reading, Eliot's subsequent espousal of Trinitarian orthodoxy was a posthumous killing of the Unitarian father from whom he had been alienated. The poet now becomes simultaneously the crucified son, and the primeval patricide.

IT IS OFTEN easier to make out curious symmetries and patterns in ancient myth than in our own psyches; that was one reason Freud made so much use of them. Berggasse 19 in Vienna was filled with artefacts and images from antiquity. Oedipus occupies a central figure among them. He has two equivalent significances for Freud: he is the solver of the riddle, the one who peers unhesitatingly into the darkness, and he is the slayer of the Old One. One simple enough reason why we might witness the slaying by the son of the Old One, the progenitor, is that he might have had it coming anyway, so best to keep the business in the family. Laius and Jocasta transfix the infant Oedipus's feet with a rod and send him out on to the mountain to be exposed, so that he will die. Now admittedly this is in response to a revelation from Apollo that if the boy grows up he'll kill his father, and ravish his mother, but even so: it can hardly be described as loving parental behaviour. The initial murderousness of his father towards him is equalled by his own towards the old fellow when they finally meet again: 'what goes around comes around'; that is the great mythic principle. The future never can be avoided. Perseus ultimately kills the father of Danae, his own grandfather, by throwing the discus. The prediction of the oracle has come true, however hard the old man tried to evade it by building towers.

We should remember the sequence of events regarding Oedipus: first he kills his father, then he answers the riddle. We could, if we so chose, view this as an early act of demythologization. First we debunk the myth of God, then our eyes are opened. Adam and Eve's eyes were opened to their own nakedness as soon as they ate from the tree of knowledge. Oedipus after all discovers the great secret hidden away inside our psyches: the incestuous and murderous desire that lurks in there, two and half millennia before Freud can catch a glimpse. Slaying the Old One, on this reading anyway, can yield certain epistemological benefits. Although we might remind ourselves that neither Adam and Eve nor Oedipus himself end up much happier as a result of their breaching of the paternal boundary.

How oedipal was the inventor of the Oedipus complex? Might he perhaps have fashioned this particular theory out of a complex darkness inside the labyrinth of his own psyche? We know that he was ashamed of his father, Jacob, because he had permitted gentiles to knock his fur cap off in an anti-semitic incident in Vienna. He was also adored by his mother, as was Picasso. Whether or not these biographical data are relevant, the fact is that Freud committed two of the greatest acts of oedipal violence, in cultural terms, of the twentieth century. First he assassinated William Shakespeare, then he went on to kill the Jew Moses, if in this latter case with the assistance of the anthropology of his day.

First he assassinated the great poet, to whose work he was devoted. He insisted that William Shakespeare of Stratford-on-Avon could not have written the works of William Shakespeare. They were written instead, he said, by Edward de Vere, the Seventeenth Earl of Oxford. This theory was propounded, not for the first time, by J. Thomas Looney in a book entitled *Shakespeare Identified*, which was published in 1920. Freud read it and was overwhelmed by its arguments. It solved a number of crucial problems for him. He had convinced himself that whoever authored *Hamlet* had lost his father before composition. This fitted de Vere, not Shakespeare. And at some point he appears to have also convinced himself that the man who wrote *King Lear* must have had three daughters; once again this fitted de Vere but not Shakespeare. There is remarkably little logic here. Why not argue that the fellow who wrote *Othello* must have been black with a white wife, or the one who penned *The Merchant of Venice* a Mediterranean Jew with a daughter who looked all set to marry out? And as for the home life of whoever wrote *A Midsummer Night's Dream,* even this expert navigator through the unconscious might have been baffled there, since the queen does not merely marry out; she miscegenates with a member of the animal kingdom, like Queen Pasiphae with the beautiful white bull. All this notwithstanding, Freud became a convinced anti-Stratfordian and could be remarkably acidic towards any who clung to the traditional position.

Harold Bloom speculates in *The Western Canon* that Freud first started thinking through the Oedipus conflict in relation to *Hamlet*. He had made it plain in *The Interpretation of Dreams* that he regarded *Hamlet* as a return to the theme of *Oedipus Rex,* after a further two and half millennia of repression. Hamlet cannot actually bed Gertrude, as Oedipus beds Jocasta, because the forces of cultural inhibition had become so much greater in the interim. Bloom reckons that Freud was intimidated by the genius of Shakespeare, which so frequently anticipates him in his perceptions, so he does to him exactly what Hamlet does to Polonius. The Old One gets slain.

THEN, IN THE 1930s, with European Jewry under lethal threat from Nazism, Freud publishes *Moses and Monotheism*, in which he argues that Moses, supposed author of the Pentateuch, the founding book of Judaism, was not in fact Jewish at all. He was an Egyptian, a follower of the monotheistic Akhnaten, or possibly even Akhnaten himself. All the narrative paraphernalia of the bulrushes, the reeds, the baby in a basket at the riverside, is a baffle for a child born in untoward circumstances, probably to an Egyptian princess. A similar argument had been made many times over the years, often by Jewish polemicists, about the genealogy at the start of the gospels of Matthew and Luke. They are so assertive about the royal identity of Jesus, going back all the way to David and beyond, because of the accusations of illegitimacy that dogged the man from Nazareth. Virgin birth, eh? No father in evidence, presumably.

Now these thoughts regarding Moses were not original to Freud; they were very much in the air at the time. Nevertheless, a number of significant figures pleaded with Freud not to publish, the most notable being Professor Abraham Yahuda, a Biblical expert. A man of Freud's status, attacking the founding author of the Judaic scripture, would surely play straight into the hands of the Nazis: this religion can be seen to be not merely repellent, but provably fraudulent. Freud would not hang fire. The book was published in 1939, just in time for the commencement of hostilities.

So, two old ones had been slain in two decades: Shakespeare is replaced by a dubious nobleman and courtier, and Moses, author of the founding texts of the embattled religion in which Freud had been raised, turns out not to be Jewish at all. The nearest he gets to being a true member of the chosen people is when Zipporah his wife circumcises their son and scatters the blood on Moses himself, addressing him for the first time as her bridegroom of blood. He is a surrogate; he even has a surrogate circumcision performed by his own spouse, not on him but on their child. Once again, as in the story of Jesus, the blood shed is all the son's. Father simply stands back and watches.

We might notice that on both occasions, Freud decides that what the text is overtly telling us about itself is not to be trusted. We must use our canniness as interpreters to get through to the real latent content; all the information is there, but it is not self-disclosing. In fact, it is self-disguising. This does of course mean that the interpreter now becomes an agent in the unfolding meaning of the text, however ancient and revered it might be. The text challenges our hermeneutic power to engage with it. It will only come alive if we give it some of our life, as an invitation into the philosophical dymanic of the present. Bob Dylan once summed up the situation with remarkable *brio:Oh God said to Abraham, 'Kill me a son'*

Abe says, 'Man, you must be puttin' me on'
God say, 'No.' Abe say, 'What?'
God say, 'You can do what you want Abe, but
The next time you see me comin' you better run'
Well Abe says, 'Where do you want this killin' done?'
God says, 'Out on Highway 61'

Now Bob Dylan's father was called Abraham, and his friends and loved ones knew him as Abe. Highway 61, where the scene of the promised sacrifice of Isaac by Abraham on Mount Moriah is here to be re-enacted, was the road that followed the Mississippi to New Orleans. But it was also just another road out of town. The young man then called Robert Zimmerman fled along that road as soon as he could, eventually landing in New York, where he almost immediately cut off his lineal patrimony by changing his name to Dylan – announcing in effect that he was now no man's son. Why not be your own father instead?

See how close Dylan brings the ancient story to him; that is the mark of genius. Midrash is a technique which makes scripture as personal as a diary entry. It demands that the ancient text answer the questions of the present, or what use is it anyway? One might as well have done and abandon it to the philologists, so it can be buried along with them in a library. Midrash renders any text, however ancient, immediate by translating it into the desires and disasters of the present. A man called Abe from Duluth, Minnesota, had a son named Robert, not Isaac. And God instructed him in the song to take this boy down to Highway 61 so he might be executed, as a way of demonstrating God's authority. A bizarre story, for sure, but perhaps no odder, all the same, than the one in which Yahweh orders the ancient Abraham to take his own beloved boy to Mount Moriah and there offer him as a burnt offering, a holocaust. Neither boy died in the event. Isaac was replaced by a ram, and Robert Zimmerman found a substitute in Bob Dylan, who wrote the original's work for him under another name, just as Freud came to believe the

Earl of Oxford had done for William Shakespeare of Stratford-on-Avon.

The problem midrash always raises is this: does not the midrashist in effect engage in his own poiesis? Is he not doing to the original material what the poet and novelist might do? Freud was only too aware of the accusation here, and also the implied danger. He told Arnold Zweig that he had initially planned to call the book that became *Moses and Monotheism, The Man Moses: A Historical Novel*. But then Freud believed he had discovered many of his greatest 'scientific insights' in literature, in the work of Sophocles and Shakespeare – or rather Edward de Vere. He did not look upon the literary as a second-class form of discovery. Thomas Mann, one of Freud's greatest readers, would write *The Tablets of the Law* a few years later. In this re-telling, Moses has a Hebrew father, but an Egyptian mother, so according to the law of matrilineal descent, he is not a Jew either, though at the time of Moses it was the patrilineal line that dictated Jewish identity. This tale is Thomas Mann's midrash on the story of Moses, as *Fear and Trembling* is Kierkegaard's on the story of Abraham and Isaac.

SO WE RETURN to where we started: the confrontation of the modern with the tradition that preceded it. Let us kill the artistic father and be free. The Dadaists called for the museums to be burnt to the ground; Duchamp painted a moustache on the *Mona Lisa*. Henri Gaudier-Brzeska declared that classical sculpture was all wrong. It misunderstood what sculpture was for, pretending that one medium was really another in disguise. Brancusi took Rodin's *The Kiss* and re-made it several times in that modernist form which reverts to the earliest art rather than any later realist tradition. The confusion of familiarities is instantly abolished and instead we are given significant form. They are figurative fathers who are here being killed. But we can find an oedipal situation with an actual biological genealogy if we go back one hundred years, and visit Prague.

Franz Kafka effectively invented his own Oedipal father figure in his *Letter to my Father*, using a great deal of immediately available biographical data to do so. Hermann Kafka was hardly the ideal reader of demanding modernist literature. He does not appear to have been much of a reader of anything, including Hebrew scripture, and his mighty efforts to make a living and maintain it did not leave much leisure for any vivid interest in the arts. But for Kafka he nevertheless becomes the invisible barrier to everything preventing his fulfilment – physically, morally, sexually, and intellectually. He does not read the son's work, despite an invitation to do so. The actual father, with all his strengths and inadequacies, metamorphoses into an invisible sky god guaranteeing failure and frustration. He would appear to need killing if there is to be any serious progress made. The only problem is that Franz, physically fragile and tubercular, is evidently not the man to perform such an execution. In his fiction, the father always tends to win. Gregor the giant cockroach starves to death, while beautiful music plays in the next room. Georg in *The Judgement* throws himself into the river after his father has sentenced him to death by drowning.

Picasso probably picked up from his father the basic rules of realist verisimilitude, which in its own defence claims to copy nature. Then, once he had proven his mastery here, in his own words he learned to make his art 'against nature'. His response to the natural was from this point on no longer mimesis but inventive combat. His zestful imagination offered alternatives to the shapes available in the street or the field, not to mention the bedroom and the *corrida*. Why make do with the repetitions of mimesis when primary creation is an alternative possibility? Why simply follow in your father's footsteps? You might end up spending your life painting pigeons, as José Ruiz had done. Oddly enough, Picasso did go on to paint the most famous pigeon of twentieth-century art, but he called it a dove, and stuck an olive branch in its beak.

Picasso took the brushes his father had handed over and with them re-painted the world of western art. Why imitate nature when you can create afresh? There is at least one sense in which Oedipus owed it all to his father, the Old One whom he will slay: he might be able to answer the Sphinx's riddle because for a while in infancy he did not in fact walk on four legs, but three. He noticed such things because he had been rendered unnatural, against nature, by his father, who had had both his feet riveted together with a rod, thereby giving him his illustrious name. His Highway 61 was the route from Thebes to Corinth. It was only on his journey home again, his treacherous return into the past, that the catastrophes started rolling. First he kills his father, then he solves the Sphinx's riddle, and by the time he arrives back at Thebes, a womb is awaiting his triumphal re-entry, since it is the same one from which he originally emerged.

But Picasso does not burn down the museums, though he might occasionally deface a masterpiece or two in his exuberance; the masterpiece is always there still when he's finished. He does not kill the real fathers; instead he wrestles them, the way Jacob wrestled the mysterious angel some believe to have been Yahweh himself. He takes on Rembrandt, Velasquez, Ingres, Goya. He becomes them on paper and canvas, the way Bob Dylan in Greenwich Village became Woody Guthrie, having now claimed a new patronymic from a drunken Welsh bard. The real father here can never be killed, since his work is too strong for that. One can only be agonistic, furiously agonistic perhaps, but not patricidal.

TO SOME EXTENT, we are all still in the sacred wood at Nemi. The difficulty is establishing whether we should be engaged in killing the Old One, or in protecting his memory. Are we saying, he who made me I shall now unmake, for only then can I be truly free? Or are we saying, you who claim in the form of so many institutions this plenipotentiary power are lying through your teeth? In which case, all that needs killing in this dark wood is the shadow of an illusion, the great shambling beast of our projections. But should we decide to post ourselves as cultural guards instead, then we say, in effect, that the Old One is not the fount of all deception and disgrace, but rather the mighty shape, however incoherent, of what went before us in our great evolutionary and historic journeyings. Perhaps we are condemned, all of us, to an endless dialectic between the two positions. Lord Reith, after years of running the BBC, was asked what system of government he had come to think best. He replied, without hesitation: 'Dictatorship, tempered by periodic assassination.'

XI

CONSTELLATIONS.

IN THE MOUTH of a cave stands one of those men whom we call prehistoric. He lives, that is, before history begins recounting its narrative to itself through written records. His bones might speak to us, should we ever find them, but nothing else will, except for the marks he has made on stone and bone. Should some unforeseen miracle of science and technology bring our caveman back to life one day, cloned into movement and utterance, we might even hear the noises that once emerged from his larynx, but we wouldn't understand them. He stares out now at the night sky, where he sees a shape, a form that comes into being if you join up the miscellaneous lights out there with your own eyes. And he remembers. He saw such a shape in that same corner of the sky the last time it was as cold as this, the last time it grew dark before he could find his prey, the last time leaves fell so wetly on his face. So it's a shape that returns then; one of nature's recurrent themes; a leitmotif. Not only in the sky but in his mind, where the shape is now fast transmuting to a horse. The scattered lights from millions of years before are forming, with the help of his neural synapses, a constellation.

This is a speculative moment, though a highly possible one. This might be the furthest we can go back in time through the development of our species to find the rudiments of representation. What is being represented, mentally, mnemonically, is one of the extremities of perception, not simply because our prehistoric man is here seeing the furthermost objects in his universe, signals sent from the far edges of our reality, both in space and time; nor because this represents an outer boundary where we might find the origins of the patterned world we once created and still create daily, where we endlessly orienteer ourselves in regard to the ceaseless flow of stimuli and perception that surrounds and engulfs us. This is also an extremity in another sense, because if this is one of the places where representation begins, then it is also where mere sensation and instinct are transcended; where we begin to construct inside ourselves those constellations of perception we call thought. This is where organized perception begins. Organized perception is dependent on memory. If a retainable perception is to separate itself from the sentient flux, it must form a memorable shape; it must recur, if only in consciousness. In this one manoeuvre we have seen our early ancestor give birth to organized perception, pattern-recognition and organisable memory. And in the process what he has just created is the first constellation. This might be the moment when both art and science are born.

What does it mean to constellate? We fill the heavens with ploughs, goddesses and horses, and we know that the shapes are both there and not there at the same time. We join up the dots in our minds; we relate stars which are otherwise unrelated except by the weakest of the four forces controlling our cosmos: gravity. In populating the skies with creatures both real and mythic, and then, after the Neolithic revolution, with agricultural implements that can't be too much use for ploughing through all that inter-stellar dust, we are engaging in what we will ultimately call science and what we will one day call art, since this is what they both ultimately do: constellate data into meaningful shapes and recurrent patterns, so that they may be considered, reflected on, and measured. Both science and art shape the world into patterns of representation, and feed off one another endlessly in the process.

CONSTELLATION AND REPRESENTATION.

AT THE HEART of our word constellation is *stella*, the Latin for star; con-stellating is bringing stars together into patterns. We constantly constellate ourselves inside the cosmos; we situate ourselves here where we seem to have found ourselves living for a time. We orienteer ourselves in regard to stars, planets, and whatever other type of constellations we discover and construct.

The constellation in its widest sense was one of the guiding concepts, the cynosure effectively, of the thought of Walter Benjamin. He believed that our earliest star-patternings were related to our extraordinary facility for mimicry. We mimic what we find on earth, the origin of both the dance and the Palaeolithic cave painting; and we also mimic what we find in the heavens. We turn the lights we see at night into creatures and implements. We populate the skies with creatures from the menagerie of our imagination. We map ourselves inside the universe through those constellations which, in Wordsworth's phrase in 'Tintern Abbey' we 'half-perceive and half-create'. Astrology begins with a mimesis. Benjamin came to believe that the ultimate store of non-sensuous similarity, the greatest mnemonic cave of mimetic devices, is language.

The nature of any representation changes as the constellation in which it is situated alters. So the constellation itself changes with every shift in intellectual life, though sometimes imperceptibly to those actually living through the transformation. Let us take a vivid example.

THE YEAR IS 1584. Let us place a dinosaur tooth in Prague, in the *wunderkammer* of Emperor Rudolf II of Bavaria. This wonder room or cabinet of curiosities is growing larger by the day. So here we have an unimaginably large tooth from an unknown creature of preternatural size. How to situate it in this particular European constellation? According to the Emperor's lights, it might well be a freakish expression of nature, something created by the left hand of God. Let's say this one had been worn as a fetish by a shaman encountered in Siberia; Rudolf has agents bringing him outlandish wonders from all over the earth. Perhaps he even asks the opinion of John Dee, newly arrived from England this very year.

Dee examines it closely but he can assign it to no actual creature he knows, and so speculates that it might well be the incisor of a dragon, or even part of the dentition of a mutant elephant, perhaps one encountered on the moon by an astral traveller. There are points of comparison here. The wunderkammer already contained the remnants of a dragon, and a bone (six-foot long) from a narwhal. No point having a cabinet of curiosities unless you have curiosities to put inside it. Back home in England one of the sources of local discontent around his home in Mortlake is that Dee, who is reputed to have developed special techniques for locating treasure, might provoke the wrath of the dragons traditionally thought to protect the trove. Part of his laboratory will be despoiled before his return.

But there is no constellation in which our tyrannosaurus tooth can be meaningfully situated. That intellectual constellation is yet to be constructed.

Now we travel forward by three centuries. The same object is placed inside a different constellation. In the first place we now have the word dinosaur, only coined in 1841 by Richard Owen, the first Director of the Natural History Museum, and coined by him originally in Latin – *dinosaurus*, meaning terrible lizard. The constellation has now changed so much that the object to be contemplated is effectively a different object. In the wake of Lyell, we have a conception of the world as a place of enormous antiquity, one in which whole species have become extinct. Both Leopold II and Dee would probably have assumed that any part of a creature obtained today probably belonged to a creature still living today, however obscure its habitat might be, like the dragon or the unicorn. But now we have another new coinage which indicates a change in our constellations: *fossil*. It once meant anything dug up; its modern meaning arrives in 1665, when it comes to signify the remains, often extremely ancient, of an animal or plant. The nineteenth century has been piecing together these vast creatures that last walked the earth sixty-five million years ago, before one of the great extinctions consigned them to evolution's cellar.

The constellation in which an object appears changes the nature of that object; it becomes differently faceted, under changing lights and a changing optic, like a Cubist painting. Let us reverse the process. Go back to Emperor Rudolf's court with a film and some projection equipment. Show them Stanley Kubrick's *Dr Strangelove*. Screen it on the wall of the emperor's darkened wunderkammer. Say they are all about to witness a wonder, a phantasmagoria as elaborate as any ever assigned to that travelling magus Faustus. But what would they make of those B52s flying through the clouds with hydrogen bombs in their metal intestines? They would surely have to seem to these people of the pre-aeronautic era like vast and malign birds, armoured pterodactyls with lethal eggs inside their bellies. These creatures would be as real to Rudolf and Dee, precisely as real, as those dragons who were said to live deep inside caves, protecting buried treasure from rapacious men. And this is despite the fact that Leonardo has already sat in his garden watching sycamore leaves spinning to the earth, and dreamed of helicopters.

We have been thinking primarily about how new concepts alter the constellation, or shift the paradigm by challenging its capacity to absorb new data. But sometimes the alteration can come about by registering something old, rather than adding something conceptually new. So Aby Warburg came to understand that the primeval forcefulness encoded in the symbolism of western art, which in one formulation he called the afterlife of the antique, was never soluble in contemporary rationality. Such primal power can never be dissolved in the pellucid solution of reason. It must be negotiated, constantly. It persists and can express its longevity, not merely in the symbolism of astrological devices, but more lethally in certain types of modern state. Nazi Germany would soon be proving his point. The preternatural powers embodied in the emblematic constituents of the constellations must never be underestimated.

THE CONSTELLATION AND THE ESSAY.

WALTER BENJAMIN PRIZED contemplation over taxonomy. What he called the mystical gaze permitted subject and object to become one; then unanticipated correspondences began to occur. Benjamin was fascinated by the ecstatic trance which in antiquity connected us to the powers of the cosmos, but which has been marginalised by modernity into mere aberrant behaviour, addiction or derangement. The Great War returned to this ancient trancelike communion, and mechanized its unforeseen potencies into continent-wide slaughter.

Benjamin was one of the greatest essay writers of the twentieth century, and there is a relationship between his concept of the constellation and his genius for the essay. One of the central concepts in Benjamin's unfinished *Arcades Project* is the figure of the collector. In this conception the collector seizes objects from out of their utile continuum, and places them solely in relation to one another and the collector's gaze; in other words, the objects are placed in a constellation, a constellation now dedicated to the dynamic interaction of their own significance. The constellations we inhabit, whether in the wunderkammer of the collector, or on the pages of the essay, represent the latest configuration of our reality.

Benjamin was constantly aware of the effect of technology on our constellations. For example, I might note that in the transition from the word *besetzung* in Freud's original German to the word *cathexis* in the final English version, a huge change has taken place. James Strachey wished to make the common terms throughout the English Collected Works sound as impressive as possible, so Latin and Greek were employed: *ego, superego, id, cathexis*. But the original *besetzung,* with its sense of filling up a space, also carried some implications over from thermodynamics – the image of energy, in the form of steam for example, filling up whatever space it finds available. This was a meaning entirely lost in *cathexis*, since the Greeks had no science of thermodynamics. Benjamin noted how in the arcades an artificially vaulted heaven contained its own artificial stars. As soon as street lighting began to be commonly used outside, the arcades started to fade. They were no longer so eerily present, glowing away to themselves in the evening.

The Arcades Project is in effect a vast series of interconnected essays. Each inhabits a slightly different constellation. Vladimir Nabokov, in criticising Thomas Mann's *Doctor Faustus*, referred to that novel's 'super-essayism'. It is true that there are whole sections of this book which can be separated off so they stand alone: disquisitions on medieval music, for example, or polyphony, and this for Nabokov constituted a drift away from the true purpose of the novel, which should never deviate so discursively from its narrative commitments. But why not? *Moby-Dick* can be accused of exactly the same freedom in following certain themes in self-contained sections, or essays. In his novel *The Man Without Qualities*, Robert Musil has his alter ego, Ulrich, proclaim the superiority of the essay to other forms of writing or perception. In Chapter 62, Ulrich announces that his stance towards reality is essayistic, a form of thinking he connects up with 'hypothetical living'. Ulrich seems here to be aligning himself with that anti-systematic bias we find in both Kierkegaard and Nietzsche: you can construct holistic philosophic systems, but no one can authentically live inside them, not even their creators. We are all condemned to live essayistically, however axiomatic our credal subscriptions.

An essay reveals its constellations in its structure; it also admits their provisionality. In any case, the constellations are never in precisely the same place the next time we look at them. What goes around comes around, but never in precisely the same way.

THE FRAGMENT AND THE ESSAY.

WE HAVE CHANGED our mind about the fragment. Once it was thought to be part of a whole which, for one unfortunate reason or another, never managed to complete itself, or completed itself, and then was broken apart by time, military vastation or the perils of transit. Now we believe that the fragment often takes fragmentary form because that was the only meaningful form available to it, particularly in modernity. Coleridge's 'Kubla Kahn' is not the tragically interrupted long poem the poet pretended it was, perhaps even to himself; it is the poem it is, having found exactly the form it needed to express its vatic rhapsodic ecstasies – which could not have continued long in any direction. Eliot's *Sweeney Agonistes* is a more complex case, perhaps. Here Eliot was experimenting with a new dramatic form, one which fed upon the demotic rhythms and conventions of street talk in the jazz age. He could find no way to continue with this, and after the ascesis represented by the writing of *The Hollow Men* and *Ash-Wednesday*, he abandons this whole mode, and opts instead for the full dress theatre of *Murder in the Cathedral* and the plays that follow. *The Waste Land* is a poem of fragmentary voices, overheard in the fast-moving streets of the city; *Four Quartets* is a discursus in a philosopher's study; no cockney voices break in, no snatches of song from the music hall. The urgency has gone, along with the demotic edginess of the language. *Sweeney Agonistes* is jagged, urgent and sinister. The plays that follow are, in comparison, completed, rounded out; they fulfil the expectations of a well-established dramaturgy. They have abandoned the fragment, and lost an enormous amount of linguistic energy in the process. *The Waste Land* inhabits the same mental world as *Les Demoiselles d'Avignon*; *Four Quartets* and *Murder in the Cathedral* inhabit an earlier one, where the writerly conventions were not being put so severely under interrogation. Between October 1926 and January 1927 the only two fragments of *Sweeney Agonistes* that were ever to appear were printed in *The Criterion*. It is intriguing that at this point Eliot thought this was some kind of beginning, not the end it in fact turned out to be; but then perhaps Coleridge spent years planning to complete 'Kubla Khan'. There was one other possibility: the sequence called *Coriolan*, but only two sections of this were ever written, then Eliot abandoned it, to join *Sweeney Agonistes* in the section of his *Collected Poems* called 'Unifinished Works'.

One of the greatest tributes to the fragment ever written is Walter Benjamin's *Arcades Project*, not merely because it remained uncompleted at the time of his death; one might easily argue that such a work was uncompletable in any case. The quotations that make up the bulk of this mighty book are torn from their contexts, the way objects assembled in the collector's gaze have been torn from their miscellaneous locations, so as to form their own constellation, and find their genuine significance in relation to one another. Benjamin seems constantly astounded by their vividness. It was one of Adorno's complaints against Benjamin that he tended to present his material in an unmediated manner. It had not, that is to say, been translated through the terms of the necessary discourse. Such a facility for unmediated and vivid apprehension might also be called 'essayistic'; it does not necessarily philosophize itself, and tends not to systematize itself at all.

The age of modernity is the age of perceptual fragmentation. We have speeded up the world to the point where there is no time to connect up all the fragments of information hurtling towards us. It was for this reason that Benjamin started to use two different concepts to register the impressions of experience in the modern age. *Erlebnis* was the lived experience, no sooner encountered than largely dispensed with; *Erfahrung* was that deeper level of experience that could not be disposed of so easily; it had perceptual longevity. These two categories bear some relationship to contingency and causality. And they are evidently also related to Baudelaire's insistence, in 'The Painter of Modern Life', that modern art needed to be made up of two hemispheres, the one relating to artistic tradition and classical beauty, and the other to the speedy disposability of the present. The whole of his poem 'The Swan' is an exploration of this theme, examining how Paris demolishes and rebuilds itself. A city can be rebuilt faster than the human heart, he says. The demolished forms survive as allegory. Benjamin, Baudelaire's greatest student, believed allegory was the continuance of certain meanings and forms beyond the death of the original form. As he put it in a letter to Horkheimer: 'Allegory is in the world of ideas what ruins are in the world of things.' Classical antiquity had lived on into the Christian Renaissance in the form of allegory; a resurrection of the old forms in a new context. And the old Paris of ruinous tenements and tiny streets lived on, after Haussmann's urban redevelopment and the building of the boulevards, in the allegorical forms of Baudelaire's poems.

We tend to see representational fragmentation as the falling apart of an existing order. This is most famously expressed by Donne:

> *'T'is all in pieces, all coherence gone...*

The visual equivalent of this are those broken implements lying on the ground in Dürer's engraving *Melencolia*. For Donne the agent of demolition here was the new philosophy, which would soon enough express its own coherence. This is also the feeling of *The Dunciad*, where fragmentation rules the ruinous psyches of the metropolis:

Round him much Embryo, much Abortion lay,
Much future Ode, and abdicated Play…

That which is designed, teleologically, to be whole, is in fact in pieces, either through violence or interruption. That is one sense of fragmentation, but there is another one, more in tune with the modern temperament . Here we discover anew the components, and structure, of our perceptions. Picasso's great Cubist portrait of the art dealer Ambroise Vollard is not the trace of an existing image being broken up; it is the articulation of a new way of seeing, which constructs the image on the canvas in a parallel manoeuvre to the way the mind constructs the image from the data supplied by the eyes. There is no abdication here, and no abortion either. Here the fragmentation of the surface represents a breakthrough, not a breakdown. It might remind us that when the man of the Upper Palaeolithic stared up at the sky and saw the constellations, then went down into the deep darkness of the cave and painted horses and aurochs on the wall, both constellations only existed at all because they had been configured inside his head.

THE ESSAY AS A FORM OF MODERN PERCEPTION.

WHAT WE ARE edging towards – essayistically, it goes without saying – is the notion that the essay might be the most authentic form for registering and recording the fabric of our experience in modernity. The characteristics that make it so can be listed: provisionality, improvisation, speed, and an acknowledgment, even in the form of the essay itself, of fragmentariness not as an absence in a desiderated whole, but as an inherent aspect of the nature of modern life itself. Montaigne's invention of the essay is an announcement of modernity; it arrives at pretty much the same moment. Shakespeare read Montaigne in Florio's transla-tion, and Hamlet becomes his own essayist, though we usually refer to his excursions in the genre as soliloquies. Heisenberg's Uncertainty Principle acknowledged that our precise knowledge of the position of a particle is in inverse proportion to the precision of our knowledge of its velocity, and vice versa, not because our present apparatus is inadequate, but because that *either/or* is inherent in the nature of the phenomenon being observed. And we might find a parallel in the omnipresence of the fragment in the findings and makings of modernity. So much is represented as fragmented, not because something completed has been broken up, or an achievable whole not completed, but because this mosaic of discrete pieces actually constitutes the perceptual world of modernity. The camera was designed to capture this kaleidoscopic panorama visually; the essay attempts to capture it linguistically and philosophically. The essay is the formal expression of a world of fragments. Fragments can be connected, of course. They do not have to take the form of fossils, being re-assembled into a form they initially exhibited; they can be chips of stone in a mosaic, each effectively complete in itself. Or they can take the form of the facets which, once assembled, compose the figure of Ambroise Vollard in his portrait by Picasso.

XII

THERIANTHROPES AND VENTS.

PREFACE.

TWENTY THOUSAND YEARS ago someone painted images on a cave wall. This display of mimetic ability seemed breathtaking for its formal audacity to spectators in the twentieth century. The ability to capture with such vivid economy of means the presence of certain animals, like the auroch and the bison, struck modern artists as uncanny. Picasso on re-emerging from one such cave remarked, 'We have invented nothing.' Like the ouroboros swallowing its own tail, it seemed that art had taken 20,000 years finally to arrive at where it started: a formal simplicity and audacity without the distraction of unnecessary surface detail.

It is not merely mimesis that we are witnessing on these cave walls, but also mimicry. What appear to be human figures are entirely human only from the waist down. Above that they are dressed in animal disguises, including antlered headgear. The resemblance here to shamanic costume has led some to suppose that the Magdalenian artists must have been shamans, and that when they went down into the terrible and dangerous darkness of the caves, they were also entering a trance. The trance might help explain the astonishing vividness of the represented images. The cave's darkness was then the outer manifestation of that inner occlusion permitting the hallucinatory realities of a shamanic transport. The parietal walls are the walls of a cave; they are also, as a matter of nomenclature, the walls of a skull.

So in some of the earliest representations of ourselves that exist, we have presented ourselves as therianthropes — part human, part animal. We are engaging in that mimetic activity we have subsequently named art, and we are also engaging, as therianthropes, in the impersonation of other creatures or beings. This we can call mimicry, but it is also the activity at the root of ventriloquism, a sacred activity in our earlier history, and since ventriloquism is ultimately the craft of displaced voicings, we have also entered the realm of allegory, which displaces identity, genus and species, giving one type of being the voicing of another, or even personifying an abstract entity. It is possible that the creatures portrayed in the caves were *ex voto* offerings to a nature god or goddess which needed to be appeased for the hunt's takings. This we don't know, and perhaps never shall; nor do we know if the painters were in fact shamans. What we do know is that our preternatural gift for mimicry, imitation and disguise lies at the root of much of our artistic tradition.

It is our gift for mimicry which makes learning possible. One of our curious vulnerabilities as a species is the extraordinary amount of time the human child requires for its nurture. Our weakness here is also our strength, since it is during this time that what biologists sometimes call the exogenetic or exosomatic inheritance is acquired. In other words, we learn whatever is on offer at the time in the form of culture. Our remarkable aptitude for this process of learning, often cognate with mimicry, is now being explained by some neuroscientists (if tentatively) as a result of the configurations of mirror neurons in our heads.

These represent a neurophysiological explanation of our ability to anticipate, respond and copy; to shadowbox in a lightshow of neurons and synapses whoever or whatever our interlocutor might be. And then we remember. Without memory there is no learning. Mnemosyne (memory) was the mother of all the muses, including Clio, the muse of history. A great deal of our history takes the form of rear-view mirror imitation, sometimes disastrously.

MIMESIS AND MIMICRY

THE FIRST THINGS we 'read' had never been written, Walter Benjamin pointed out, since they were venatic and stellar. We read the vestiges of the hunt, prints, spores, feathers and fur, because otherwise we could not have survived. And we read the constellations, in order to situate ourselves on land, in the ocean, and inside the seasons. Otherwise we would have had to stay wherever we were. In reading the constellations we were also inventing them; they had no existence before we gleaned those particular patterns in the night sky. The stars did not group themselves together to look like ploughs or winged horses. We imposed the patterns on the heavens; the heavens did not volunteer them. The constellations can be seen to represent our first version of allegorical thinking. One species of thing becomes another by metaphoric transfer and, once entangled in our manifold facility for generating meanings and interpretations, it then starts to become semiologically fecund. Our meanings proliferate to such a degree that they sometimes seem to outrun their creators. Thus can the fetishized products of our own makings become reifications, thing-like immutabilities that appear to have created us.

Other animals hunt by instinct , even when they do so in groups, like wolves or hyenas, or dolphins or sharks, but we employ projective mimesis. We mimic the future actions and reactions of the creature. We don't merely pursue our prey: we construct the landscape through which such pursuits will take place. For example, that form of hunt known as the *battue*, where we dig the hole, spread the net, then drive the animal towards it. Here, we are not merely following the venatic traces: we have to think ourselves into the mind of the animal beforehand. We are mapping out the route the venatic traces will take. We are not operating purely instinctively, like a lion on a scent; we engage instead in conscious mimicry. And the consciousness here, to use Gerald Edelman's distinction, is not primary but of a higher order, connecting up the past, present and future, employing symbolism in language, and perceiving self as integrated into community. Our success in this regard comes from an ability to mimic the other creatures, so as to hunt, or employ, or escape them, and then memorise the contents of the mimicry as part of a symbolic system. It is essentially the same activity as the employment of black propaganda in time of war. We have to think like our opponents, in order to ensure their defeat. Our endless fascination with secret agents and particularly double-agents could be an extension in time of the mode of the therianthrope on the walls of the Palaeolithic caves. We need to point both ways, like a herm stone on a boundary line. We are, as Claudius says in *Hamlet*, to double-business bound.

We ventriloquize other humans, other creatures, and sometimes gods too. Here we make a decision, depending on credal subscription, or the absence thereof. To put the matter crudely: was Moses ventriloquized by God, or was he ventriloquizing Him? Did the Almighty direct the hand that chipped out the stones up there on the mountain that gave us the Decalogue, or did a leader of men go up a mountain and decide that on his return he would sort out a number of troublesome problems, having claimed for himself a much higher authority with which to do so? It is possible that the answer here is not straightforwardly either one or the other. We are presented with the same problem when the Sybil provides messages from Apollo. Who is ventriloquizing whom? In the Judaeo-Christian tradition, when someone is addressed directly by God they tend to be alone at the time. No photography permitted. At Cumae or Delphi, there was an audience. But the messages delivered also tended to be ambiguous to a remarkable degree. Gods spoke in riddles; the ingenuity of the human mind was required to fathom them. If God decides to riddle, then man has no choice but to play the hermeneut.

ALLEGORY

IT IS THE mechanical quality of allegory that Coleridge objected to, particularly in *The Statesman's Manual*. Unlike the symbol, the allegorical emblem does not have an organic unity connecting it inevitably with its point of origin and its meaning. This makes it disjunct; the esemplastic seamlessness of the imagination is interrupted, breached. It was precisely this breaching which Walter Benjamin most valued in allegory, since such breaching, the overt mechanical quality of the allegorical image's construction, permits the crucial perception that sign is always separate to some degree from origin and meaning, that they are not organically unified except by sleight-of-hand, and that there is therefore a rupture between representation and truth. Truth is only constructed through representation. Only by acknowledging this can we understand the functioning of representation, and stop representation itself from occluding the sources of light, as it does in Plato's parable of the cave, the shadows on its wall, and the monochrome puppets which thus become gods in men's minds. The representation is constructing 'truth', even as the representation itself is being constructed.

Baudelaire was the last great allegorist, as far as Benjamin was concerned, and the allegorical image was so potent in the verse of this poet precisely because it mirrored the fate of the commodity in capitalism: wrenched from its origins, or from any context which would traditionally bestow holistic or ritualistic meaning upon it. The albatross is clumsy on the ship's deck, and reflects the fate of the poet in modern times; the swan with its clipped wings, escaped from the circus, clatters through the streets of Paris at dawn, and makes the poet think of Andromache, the wife of Hector, ripped from her noble context in Troy, and now employed as a Greek conqueror's sex slave. She is a commodity, of the antique and pre-industrial variety. All becomes allegory for me, Baudelaire wrote, and he never disguised the process of manufacture of the images. They were wrenched from their original contexts and translated to Paris, the way commodities from all over the world were transported to the World Fairs being held at the time in the same capital city. Allegory presents us with the perception of two radically different planes of meaning now conjoined. A figure from *The Iliad* is embodied in a dirty swan in nineteenth-century Paris; a seabird is mocked by sailors on deck who have captured it, and so the albatross becomes a figure of the poet in the modern age, ungainly since denied his true element, the heavens. It is precisely the disjunctiveness of image and identity that gives the allegory strength, not the apparently uncontrived naturalness of the symbol. An allegorical emblem is a symbol that advertises its own factitious manufacture, and to that extent makes itself symbolically problematic. It is in Coleridge's sense mechanical, but not thereby rendered weaker, but actually more potent. In an age of the mechanical mass production of commodities, why should poetry hark back to an earlier age in the technologies of making? That could after all seem nostalgic. Mayakovsky had hoped for a poetry to be read on the factory floor at lunch time, or to workers in city squares. For a few years after 1917 this actually happened. Factory workers anticipated Mayakovsky's visits with the same avidity that Greeks did the rhapsodes who recite what we now call Homer. He made no bones about the fact that his images were manufactured. They had that in common with tractors, though he reckoned the latter could at times be more useful. When he put a bullet through his heart in 1930, he was saying that the signifier had now been separated permanently from the signified; that the agreement which makes an allegory – particularly a revolutionary one – possible, had snapped. The hoped-for constellation had fallen apart. This moment was to be memorialized allegorically by George Orwell in *Animal Farm* as the moment that the pigs, standing in for Stalin's *nomenklatura*, start to use language for control rather than elucidation. Constellations, we recall, are more like allegory than any straightforward mimesis. Like Tinkerbell, they are only there if you believe they are. Mikhail Bulgakov wrote a different allegory about the same events: it was called *The Master and Margarita*, and in it Woland beguiles and bewitches the imaginations of Soviet citizens in the 1930s. Only the devil himself, it seems, can convince these programmed citizens that a man called Jesus actually existed. In the novel he is called Yeshua, and he confronts Pontius Pilate, truth speaking to power, as the Master confronts the might of the Soviet state, even though he does it from the inside of a psychiatric hospital.

ON THE TITLE page of Bunyan's *Pilgrim's Progress* there is an epigraph from Hosea: 'I have made similitudes.' This is of course from Hosea via the English language, and before that via Latin and Greek. The Greek form for parable was rendered into Latin as *similitudo*, and this was then turned into the English *similitude*. Bible translators from Wycliffe to Tyndale used similitude to mean parable. So Jesus spoke in similitudes, as had the prophets before him. And this dark speech, as it is sometimes called, was deliberately riddling. It often baffled its listeners but always caught their attention. One of its functions then would appear to have been defamiliarization. We think harder when faced with the unfamiliar. Narrative estrangement is always a beckoning to the far country of the unknown. The parables are at their most riddling in Mark, the earliest synoptic gospel; they tend to become smoothed out and comfortingly glossed in the later texts. They explain themselves as staging-posts towards the *eschaton*.

One of the meanings given for similitude in the OED is allegory. So we can say that Jesus was either constructing allegories or repeating and adapting already available versions. St Augustine is unapologetic in his reading of these parables as allegories. In the Good Samaritan pericope he tells us that the traveller was coming down from Jerusalem to Jericho. This then is the fall of man. The inn is the church; the innkeeper St Paul; the Good Samaritan Jesus; and the two coins (pennies in the English version) are the sacraments. The last detail made this exegesis particularly welcome to the Reformers, who had reduced the sacraments from seven to two, thereby restoring the faith to something more like its vibrant state in primitive Christianity.

A parable can be viewed as an allegory miniaturised, just as an allegory can be viewed as a manifold of metaphors extended into narrative.

ALLEGORY IS A hinge that lets us swing from one plane of meaning to another. This, as the image suggests, goes both ways. We can convert the unknown into the known, allegorise it into the recognisable landscape of our own mythology, or we can discover meanings in the text to which our intellectual world made us previously blind. The technique of reading the Old Testament typologically permitted Christians to see in the Hebrew Scripture a series of promises of the coming of Christ. This was an allegorical reading Talmudists found perverse. Blake read Milton as an allegory, though one the original author himself had not intended – or not consciously, anyway. (Can you intend something unconsciously? Is that not a little like intending something unintentionally? Freud reckoned you could, as we shall see in the next paragraph.) Now Blake spoke disparagingly of allegory, always contrasting it with vision, which seems closer to our symbolism. And yet he constantly engages in what we might normally call allegorical readings. For him Satan in *Paradise Lost* is the hero of energy, thrusting against the frigid and delimiting power of reason. Blake read the Bible as if it were allegory too; or in his own terminology, a visionary text to be understood as such by any visionary reader who has not succumbed to the Spectre. Once again we have energy versus reason; fulfilment versus law; the centrifugal force of imagination ever pressing outwards, while the centripetal force of ratiocination and law-making repression attempts to draw a circle round it and shrink or delimit its power. Life forces versus death forces.

Freud read both *Oedipus Rex* and *Hamlet* as allegories of a universal conflict between infantile desire and familial and social inhibition. This is an allegory in which the unconscious is dictating the text in such a manner that it gets certain crucial meanings past the censor, raising a number of important questions regarding what we mean by writing, and how conscious that process is. Here we appear to be faced with an intentionality which is unintentional as far as the conscious ego is concerned. Wallace Stevens often said that in poetry the imagination needs to outrun the intelligence, if only just. Imagination here might be Blake's energy; it is the force that outwits the superego. The writing of the allegory, it would appear, is being prompted by the unconscious, and permitted by ego and superego, neither of which would permit the same subject matter to be treated overtly or 'realistically'. Freud's unconscious is evidently choosy about genres. And here we touch upon that transition in Freud's thought from *unbewusst*, the adjective signifying the state of being unconscious, to *das Unbewusste*, the noun signifying the unconscious. When Elizabeth Barrett writes to Robert Browning, early in their relationship, that he has '…a habit of very subtle association; so subtle you are probably unconscious of it…' she is not saying that some agency called the unconscious is swallowing his awareness, unbeknownst to him. She is saying that he has a habit of mind and work, of making multitudinous connections, of which he himself is not necessarily overtly conscious while he actually writes.

Freud allegorises the functions of the psyche. Whether in his economic, his topographical or his structural model, he presents different agencies as commanding different planes of activity. The ego, in its prouder days the captain of the soul, now tries to hold sway as best it can amidst a sea of troubles. This is the area where the unconscious must come to consciousness if it is to be known and analysed at all. Meanwhile the superego keeps delivering the riot act, laying down the law. The id acknowledges neither time nor constraint, but only desire, however perverse such desire might be deemed to be by the powers focused in the superego. The forces of repression cast out of the arena of the ego those dark urgings of the id which the superego cannot tolerate if it is to stay in business, the civilizational business, and these are then cast into the unconscious, there to foment until some of them launch commando raids into conscious life in the form of the return of the repressed.

We should be clear about something here, significant in terms of writing. The unconscious in Freud is a cryptographer. Sophocles imagines he is writing plaintext, as cryptanalists call it, but actually, according to Freud, he is encoding cyphertext. This way the unconscious can express its Oedipal desires without alerting the police agency of the superego. The superego is evidently kept in the dark about the real content, the incestuous and murderous allegory, as is the conscious ego. It is as though William Cecil and Francis Walsingham have hunted through the suspect epistles in the offices of state, but spotted nothing; a new Jesuit codemaster fresh from Rheims has managed to outwit the pair of them. Until, that is, Freud comes along and, with his psychoanalytic insights, discovers the secret of the age-old cypher. Oedipus has enacted a universal wish by killing the father and sleeping with the mother. This desire has been hidden away in the unconscious for all this time, and only now, two and a half millennia after the writing of the play, has cyphertext finally yielded up its meaning into plaintext. The allegory has been detected; the secret message of encoded illegal desire has been revealed at last. The criminal can be exposed to daylight, finally, and it is every single one of us, blinking with incredulity at the obscene circus being performed each night on our own psychic premises. There is a problem here, as Wittgenstein noted: how precisely can the unconscious manage to function as an autonomous agency? Who is actually speaking when it speaks?

Not only does Freud start to read certain great works of art as allegories, he creates his own allegory, in the form of the dream dance of the human psyche, which vanishes at dawn, like Hamlet's father, or a vampire making for his pinewood coffin. Prosopopeia or personification is one of the indispensable devices of allegory, which produces narratives out of metaphoric displacements and the concretisation of abstractions, drives, urges. If mythic identity intensifies and condenses as metaphor, the drama of allegorical action enacts a sequence of metonymic displacements. Just as in a medieval allegory the knight rides away to confront personified evil, in the form of a bad king who imprisons and hides in his castle a personification of good in the form of the alienated princess, so Freud gives us these personifications of the conflicting regions of the psyche: id, ego, superego. They are engaged in a civil war without any foreseeable ending in the kingdom of the psyche. They must cohabit, but they do so with a bad grace which in the case of the neurotic ends in illness; in the case of the psychotic it ends in murder and madness. That is the message the alienist from Vienna delivered.

VENTRILOQUISM

ETYMOLOGICALLY, THE WORD comes from the Latin *ventriloquus*, from *venter* (belly) and *loqui*, speak. Speaking from the belly, or in the belly. This is really a matter of technique, for that theatrical business sometimes known as voice-throwing. For our purposes, the term is wider, and it means something remarkably similar to either allegory or parable, since it means speaking otherwise. Expressing another identity than the one assigned to you by what has been called interpellation, which is to say, finding yourself in the interstices of the great web of a linguistic community. You are given your name, and are named by it, before you can utter the word. Speaking otherwise is a kind of escape from this, but then the therianthropic figure on the cave wall had perhaps already found a way of being not entirely entrapped in the condition of singular humanity. Another way of making the self other is to have a piece of wood talk to you, often infused with what seems to be something like demonic intelligence.

So in the wider sense being used here, ventriloquism is a term for one identity speaking through any other. At the very end of this tradition, no more than its vestigial trace, the vent sits with the figure on his knee. The vent gives his voice to the piece of wood, and the piece of wood then appears to take on an identity of its own. This process was known to Marx as commodity fetishism: the created object appears to be autonomous, independent of its own creator. It had a concomitant as far as Marx was concerned: reification. Here the actual relations between people appeared ossified as thing-like and immutable. History presented itself in the guise of nature, which is one of the ways in which myth often hides its human origin. The more real the puppet becomes, the more shadowy the ventriloquist must appear. The legendary British vent Arthur Worseley never spoke at all. His figure did all the talking for him, and at one point confided to the audience: 'All vents go nuts in the end, you know. He thinks I'm real. Don't you, my son?' Here the unreal, the ventriloquized, is the only figure potent enough to diagnose the full extent of its own unreality.

When Moses chisels the laws on stone, or when (according to tradition) he writes the Pentateuch, he is taking dictation. It is not his voice we are listening to, but the Almighty's, whose intonations he does his best to capture in lapidary style. He is being ventriloquized, however willingly. He is God's secretary and amanuensis, like one of Milton's daughters, copying the words of the greater figure uttering them. I am that I am, he repeats.

We might note here the passage from *daimon* to demon in our culture; it is a passage from the preternatural as opportunity to expand perception, if hazardously, indeed sometimes lethally, to the preternatural as degradation and possession in an entirely negative sense. The Sybil was possessed and provided answers sought by pilgrims for their questions; the demonically possessed can provide answers only to trained inquisitors, and that frequently under torture. Here we might note some curious parallels. The exorcist's task is to get to the true voicing, and get it to admit (despite itself) to being a demon, not merely the paltry human frame it has inhabited. This is the task of the inquisitor. Your behaviour, which has come to our attention, leads us to believe that you are not letting on as to what it is that is actually going on inside you, particularly on the midnight of the sabbath. And this process has its secular equivalent in the forensic process of prosecution in a court of law. The aim is to stop the villain ventriloquizing innocence; to entrap the authentic voice of guilt into confessing itself. Torture has frequently been used to facilitate this process too, and in many parts of the world it still is. The words of Elizabethan indictment can be heard to resonate: the imposture by which one pretends to be other; the cozenage by which many are convinced; the daubing of the exterior with a plausible but duplicitous appearance, so that the true interior remains undetected. A whited sepulchre, in short. All this could be brought into the light of day whenever 'the conscience was scraped'.

THE MIRROR NEURONS, if we accept the latest interpretation of their agency, seem to present us with an opportunity to escape our psyches, or at least to permit a multiple occupancy of them. Thus do we engage in mimicry, mimesis and ventriloquism. Thus do we, chameleon-like, take on the colour of our surroundings, if only for the sake of survival. And realising that one being can stand in for another, as the (perhaps) shamanic figure on the caves of the Upper Palaeolithic has become an antlered beast, we also register the world of representation. If this can be that, then the world of representation called art has now been inaugurated, as has the world of symbolic logic. If I can be a reindeer or a snake in a shamanistic dance, then the rudiments of allegory are being articulated. One species can ventriloquize another. This can not only be that, but be it so convincingly, that torture might be called upon to separate the two once more into discrete identities. If they have been fused for long enough, such separation may no longer be possible. In the British film *Dead of Night*, the ventriloquist played by Michael Redgrave has so merged his own psychic energies with those of his puppet that at the end they fuse irrevocably into an irreparable psychic unity, as the identity of Norman Bates fuses into the maternal super-ego at the end of *Psycho*.

We are fascinated by spies, as our books and our films testify. The agent and in particular the double-agent engage our minds so much because of the way in which mimicry and ventrilo-quism here cease to be a matter of mere material agency, and ap-pear to become instead a matter of spiritual reality. Which side is the double-agent really on? The answer is frequently: both. It all depends on the state of play, the flow of money, the pres-ent location and lover, the latest interlocutor. The two identities are permanently ghost-dancing one with another. And as Yeats put it, 'How can we tell the dancer from the dance?' Mr Verloc in Conrad's *The Secret Agent*, the first full-blooded version of this genre, is effectively a different human being, depending on which room he happens to be sitting in at any particular time.

One conclusion we might draw from all this is that the hu-man psyche appears to find it difficult to be inhabited with any tranquillity by a single stable identity or agency; perhaps the pay-off for the extraordinary evolutionary success of our mi-metic facility, or the obverse of those advantageous mirror neu-rons and the mimicry they give rise to, is a chronic dissatis-faction with any unitary and tranquil occupancy of the psychic domicile. Freud fragments our psychological identity into ego, superego and id, and shows how these forces ventriloquize one another, often with catastrophic effects. Most of Freud's discrete agencies within the psyche are mimics, ventriloquists, and frequently double-agents. The arena in which they act out their conflicts and desires, often when the lights have gone down and the subject stares only into his own dark auditorium, presents us with a theatricality of possession and exorcism. One only has to think of Lady Macbeth sleepwalking. Now her guilt can finally utter itself, once the control of the conscious ego has finally been suspended. Out on the heath in *King Lear*, with all social laws suspended, Mad Tom becomes a legion of demonic spirits bespeaking themselves without let or hindrance .

EGO (CHARACTER'S CITADEL)
AND ITS ESCAPE ROUTES.

HAMLET, IMMEDIATELY AFTER his meeting with the Ghost, splits himself in two; he ventriloquizes himself into his own antic disposition. Thus does he acknowledge that – with the new and terrible knowledge he has just acquired – he cannot inhabit only the one psyche any more; certainly not the one expected of him. There is not enough space in there to accommodate the disparate voicings now making themselves heard. So like an amoeba he splits into two. He now becomes his own Fool, a character not provided for in the *Dramatis Personae*. There are buffoons here, such as Polonius and Osric, but no Fool like the one in *Lear*, who is 'all-licensed' to ridicule the status quo. It is immediately after the ghostly meeting too that he writes in the play for the first time: 'My tables. Meet it is I set it down.' And yet what he sets down is utterly trite. He reminds himself that one may smile and smile and be a villain. And a moment later his revelation appears equally banal when in answer to Horatio's urgent inquiries as to what it was the Ghost imparted, he replies that there's ne'er a villain living in all Denmark but he's an arrant knave. Horatio, sensible as always, replies: 'There needs no ghost, my lord, come from the grave to tell us this.' Horatio, unrelenting rationalist that he is, is missing the burden of the play's turning-point here. Language is now fracturing. All common usage is under suspicion. Hamlet has begun his impersonations. He even learns how to impersonate himself, and only gives this up entirely in the soliloquies.

Some happenings exceed the terms of representation. The Weird Sisters in *Macbeth* perform a deed without a name; their preternatural palavers lie beyond the community of language. The Ghost says he could a tale unfold 'whose lightest word would harrow up thy soul'. He doesn't though, and at the end Hamlet himself indicates that his story has never been told either: 'O, I could tell you...' but this fell sergeant Death has already finished his paperwork, and it's time to be off. Since the entry of the Ghost into his psyche, there is in fact no conventional language in which Hamlet can speak meaningfully to others, so he speaks mostly to himself instead. The soliloquies here are unprecedented in world literature, and they are the effect of the Prince's ricochet from the possibilities of any social intercourse which might permit the utterance of such truths as he has been witnessing. From now on he mocks all social pieties: Polonius's elder statesman routine, Ophelia's love-and-marriage prospects, even Laertes' rhetorical effusion of grief at his sister's graveside. The Prince is having none of it. Instead he deepens the grand vault of consciousness inside himself, and this he vocalises authentically, mostly to himself, alone on stage. Beyond that he treats the world to his antic disposition. In other words, since what he finds in the world is grotesque, he provides it with a grinning gargoyle face to suit its wretched purposes.

It is the word 'antic' that should alert us. It derives from that *antike* which became antique in one lineage, while becoming antic in the other. Grotesque behaviour, of the sort Hamlet engages in when he puts his antic disposition on, was a form of the grotesque, derived from the word grotto, and the recent discoveries of the lurid sculptures inside and outside them in some late Roman sites. It was appropriate to the *bizarreries* which Hamlet starts to contrive for those all around him. The whole theatre of the Danish court is nothing but a show anyway, so why not add one's own garish spectacle?

Hamlet here does something remarkably similar to Yeats, in his creation of the self and the anti-self, though without Yeats' evident relish for the procedure. And we might remind ourselves about a few things that were going on at the beginning of the twentieth century, in the world of art and literature. This was the first period of reception of Freud's work. T. S. Eliot annnounced that the function of art was not the celebration of personality, but the necessity of escape from it. Ezra Pound discovered his true energies when he wrote *Homage to Sextus Propertius*, in which he ventriloquizes the ancient poet, lending him a modern voice in which he might reincarnate himself. Eliot too in *The Waste Land* falls back on an ancient voice: that of Tiresias, who is brought to contemporary London so that he might 'view' in his blindness what in modernity he has already viewed in antiquity. James Joyce discovers that if he is to write great rather than merely brilliant literature, he needs to escape the consciousness of his alter ego, Stephen Dedalus. By creating Bloom and then H. C. Earwicker, he flees the confines of his own defining ego and his own experience. Who, after all, would want voluntarily to remain inside them, if an escape route were available? Eliot's accounts of the experience of the conscious ego in his early poems is usually a description of unrelieved mental agony.

What Freud's work had shown was that the greatest energies of the human psyche lay outside the realm of the conscious ego, and tend to be distorted and repressed by the alliance between ego and superego, when they are exerting the full powers of their *entente cordiale*. If we could get into the unconscious realms and explore them, said the Surrealists, then we might be on to something. Freud could never bring himself to approve of the Surrealists; they seemed altogether too cheerful at the prospect of entering the unconscious, like cavers with spotlights and cameras. André Breton managed a meeting, but found it very disappointing. Freud himself often seems appalled at what

he had been discovering, and certainly was in no mood to celebrate. When he encountered Salvador Dali he felt he had at last
come face to face with bona fide Iberian lunacy. But they could
agree on this one thing, Freud and the Surrealists, perhaps the
only point of agreement between them: the ego likes to pretend
to itself that it represents the main site of psychic activity, the
ground zero of psychic energy, but it is wrong. If you want to
discover the real cauldron of energy, you are going to have to
devise a means of getting beyond the conscious, rational, controlling personality, either as analyst or as artist. You are going
to have to leave the city square and the library, and head for
Nighttown. Which is precisely what Joyce has his characters do
in *Ulysses*.

Blake was here a curious precursor. Reason is constantly
portrayed in his writing as the circumference placed around
energy, its perimeter fence. It is the ligature of character and
personality which church and state connive to impose upon the
eternal delight which energy represents, when it is allowed to
function untrammelled. Blake reads the Bible, Shakespeare and
Milton allegorically, but then he reads the streets of London allegorically too. He can do this because he has a universal vision
in which energy and the forces of law, repression and retribution
are endlessly fighting it out between them.

There might be a possible confusion of usage we need to
address. Allegory is here being used as a means of reading otherwise, speaking otherwise, leading to the possibility of living
otherwise, while always accepting that no representation ever
grows seamlessly and organically from the flashpoint of its own
signification. For Blake it was a negative word; he shared that
sense of it with his contemporary Coleridge. Both think of it as
something mechanical, cerebral, over-intellectualised, not natural enough. Blake is explicit: 'Allegories are things that Relate
to Moral Virtues. Moral Virtues do not Exist; they are Allegories and dissimulations.' Allegory for Blake represents literary

or spiritual inauthenticity: 'The Last Judgement is not Fable or Allegory, but Vision…'

Blake understood with remarkable proleptic powers how the division of the psyche leads to mental entrapments, and the squandering of the greatest psychic energies. What he called the Spectre is the fate of a rationalistic selfhood which comes to feed only upon itself. This form of reason is not reasonable; it exerts a more and more terrifying power until it consumes itself. Chesterton used to say that the phrase 'He has lost his reason' is an unfortunate one, since the case is often the contrary: the person concerned has lost everything else, human contact, warmth, affection, but reason now whirrs away like a mighty machine obeying its own rules. This vision of untrammelled reason seems to be remarkably like Blake's. This is the reason with which we calculate the profit that might be made from global warming; the new possibilities being opened up for mineral mining and oil-drilling in the Arctic. This is the reason that celebrates every expanding line of zeroes, without noticing the vacancy at the heart of each one.

HEADING FOR THE PRESENT.

ALTHOUGH OUR OWN skin is a matter of sufficient pride and provocation to have a whole set of industries devoted to its vivid display and renovation, we spent much time in prehistory and history wearing the skins of other creatures. This is not merely the practical matter of letting what's left of the bear keep us warm in winter, since we've already killed him anyway. Nor is it merely the fashion display of the mink coat or the foxfur stole. We have climbed into the skin of animals so as to assume their power, in rituals that locate us inside a sacred space of uncanny interaction. The shaman in a snake headdress summons the necessary rain. This is visual ventriloquism. As for the verbal sort, well that has been used not merely to tempt birds into our nets, but also to summon the gods into our minds and scriptures. We have ventriloquized the god's voice, since he has always needed us, if only as an instrument through which to speak. On the one side, we impersonate the animal powers, thus taking on their uncanny instincts. On the other, we articulate the voice of the god, speaking through the Sybil or the priest. Either way, we exit the confinements of the single human psyche. We might manage to be, blessedly or otherwise, out of our minds for the duration. Through mimicry we hope to achieve transcendence.

The discontents of which Freud spoke as the concomitant of civilization constitute confinement within the parameters of the ego. Denied the free expression of instincts, we endure repression in order to construct bridges, churches and aeroplanes. A brief respite from such singular imprisonment is ecstatic trance, the visions achieved when consciousness escapes confinement. At the top of the brain stem we have some ancient configurations that go back a long way in biological history. Is it possible that we still have the ghost of primeval memories, memories of what it once meant to have a consciousness that was unconstrained by repression, individual or social? When we ventriloquise either the animal or the god might we be craving a union with nature that was once ours? Now instead we have separated ourselves from nature, in order to achieve mastery over it. We have conquered the forces in our world, at the price of our own alienation, and that alienation is a form of solitary confinement in the psyche. We want out, and one way out is the egoless transport of ecstasy, whether its form is animal or divine.

All we tend to see are the vestiges of these traditions. The ventriloquist with the figure on his knee is one. It is too seldom pointed out how the vent's dummy is always brighter than the vent himself: his function is to outwit the human. Such ventriloquism is blatant; less so is the actor becoming through voice, gesture and body someone else even as we watch. We notice how the actor playing Hamlet becomes an actor self-consciously playing the self he is simultaneously putting into question and suspension. We have a tendency to find Hamlet at the heart of our modern theatrical tradition, but perhaps that place should be shared with Bottom in *A Midsummer Night's Dream*. After all, he becomes a therianthrope through enchantment, and in consequence dreams a dream so transcendent that there are no words to express it. His name is a pun, for the word 'profound' comes from *pro* and *fundum*, and the *fundum* is the bottom. He dreams a dream that has no bottom; he makes a note to himself that someone needs to put it into poetry, this depth beyond depths.

The therianthrope is an expression of doubleness in our nature, and of the animal rooting of our intelligence. Picasso recreated the minotaur for our times. He becomes a creature baffled by his own passion, imprisoned by his circumstances. In engraving after engraving, the artist pursued this child of unholy lust, this monster who had come from the miscegenation of two species. He believed this was the condition of man. And then there is Marsyas, the satyr, a therianthropic fusing of man and goat, who starts to play the flute as beautifully as Apollo can play the harp. The animal is competing with the god, and so the god contrives a terrible punishment: he is to be skinned alive, reminding him what finally tends to happen to animals, however elevated their spirits might become. The god is giving him a 'dressing down' – the first meaning of which was a butcher's initial hacking into the carcass.

It is the minotaur's fate to become the trophy of Theseus, as Marsyas becomes the trophy of Apollo. They both ultimately fail in taking on the attributes of another species, whether human or divine. They are doomed therianthropes; stuck in the middle between competing powers. We are entitled to regard the ventriloquist's dummy as an externalisation of our own gift for mimicry. Here mimesis triumphs, and we can note that in the mimesis of art, we turn into play those attributes which were originally the condition of survival. Though Plato tends to regard mimesis as a reflection and an unnecessary one, a deviation from the pursuit of the truth, Aristotle regards it more as a form of work, a productive endeavour constitutive of human identity, formative endeavour more than empty echo.

In allegory the therianthrope owns up to his assumption of a double nature. The man in the headdress on the Palaeolithic cave wall steps down for a moment and shows us how the headdress was made; from the remains of which animal. What Coleridge meant by the mechanical quality of allegory is the fact that it owns up to its own manufacture. It admits that the headdress only works when there is a man inside it, conducting the ritual. In the artistic tradition, allegory is said for all serious purposes to have pretty much disappeared in the late Romantic period. Visually it has its epitaph in Delacroix's *Liberty Leading the People* of 1830, though it continues obliviously in the academic paintings of the salon, and has a curious twilight life later on in the symbolists. And yet we can argue that it doesn't disappear so much as find itself internalized, or even introjected. *Dr Jekyll and Mr Hyde* is an allegorical re-mapping of the interior of the psyche, as is *The Picture of Dorian Gray*. So too is Freud's new mental topography. This psychomachia is battled out by agencies as potent as self and soul had ever been, centuries before: ego, superego, id. Now mimesis has been taken over by the manoeuvres of identification, representing various forms of psychic cannibalism. And the figure on the vent's knee would have to be discussed in terms of projection. Though once again the dialectical complexities of the situation require some talk of the death drive, *destrudo* or *mortido,* which Freud tried to negotiate in *Beyond the Pleasure Principle*, his post-war meditation on the significance of human destructiveness on an apocalyptic scale. Destrudo and Mortido would be good, if Latinate, names for the ventriloquist's figure, which more often functions as a psychic assassin than a moral prop.

And as for the role of Satan in our allegorical scheme, he has been swallowed whole only to be vomited back up again, out of the depths of the psychological interior; Hyde is a Satan who had been lurking all the while within the good doctor Jekyll's psychic shadow. The right chemical mixture springs him from his narcolepsy. He jumps right back out of the ventriloquist's belly finally, not merely as a voice, but a body too, like the creature appearing from the chest of John Hurt in *Alien*.

THE INTERNALIZATION OF allegory could be presaged by an exploration of 'the double' in semi-allegorical form. Certain figures are presented to us as twins of some sort, and we find ourselves asking if they are really psychic rather than physical or sexual twins, psychological alterities departmentalised diegetically into separate bodies. Geraldine and Christabel in Coleridge's poem share the same bed. Geraldine, it transpires, is therianthropic, being at least partially serpentine. She has that much in common then with Lamia in Keats's eponymous poem. The latter is not so much therianthropic as one species masquerading as another, or vividly transmuting into it, as happens so often in Ovid. Her identification by Apollonius ends the masquerade, unweaves the rainbow, leaving reason triumphant and everyone except the philosopher utterly miserable. Lizzie and Laura in Christina Rossetti's 'Goblin Market' share the same bed, and come out of the same womb, and seem more like one psyche divided between addiction and sobriety than two sisters divided merely by a moral *habitus*.

When allegory returns, blinking into the light of day, in the twentieth century, it does so in a newly problematized form. Kafka writes an allegory minus any guaranteed referents. The mode of his writing seems clearly allegorical, but the key has been misplaced somewhere in the fragmented interstices of modernity; which is another way of saying that there is no key. And the same is true visually of Picasso's *Guernica*. If we ask of it specific allegorical questions, what does the bull represent, what does the bulb represent, we soon find ourselves cut loose from any anchorage in codified and guaranteed meaning. This makes the work more not less effective. We can no longer allegorise as we once did. The urge continues, but the epistemological underpinning was demolished sometime between 1848 and 1918. The allegory now is a text searching for a philosophy to explicate it; a riddle that introduces us to riddling, but can indicate no way of concluding the activity, or exiting the labyrinth of clues.

The worst possible approach to allegory would be to imagine that we construct a uni-planar narrative and then add different layers of meaning to it; the spiritual; the moral; the eschatological, etc. That is not the way allegory works. Allegory is an embodiment of a multi-layered, polysemous world, which exhibits different levels or aspects of being in the multiple possibilities of its text. It is an expression of the Doctrine of Signatures, and that Doctrine's sister, the Great Chain of Being. Both of these modes of seeing find manifolds of meaning in every inch and every moment of the universe. Such a world of multiple significance finds alien what modern linguists call 'lexical priming', where one word is privileged with a single meaning, which then excludes others. In the allegorical world, words have different meanings, which need not be mutually exclusive; they can instead be complementary, even if on the surface they appear to be contradictory. This was part of William Empson's argument regarding ambiguity in *Seven Types of Ambiguity*. Modern physics had discovered a fundamental ambiguity at the heart of nature in the form of wave/particle duality. Literary texts could embody equally potent ambiguities, so the act of reading a play like *Measure for Measure* ceased to be a question of either/or, and became instead one of both/and. The mind of Angelo, wearing the regalia of power and religion as a mask for lust, confronts the piety of Isabella, provocatively taunting the ethos of puritan denial with her advertised virginity. They can be seen as two hemispheres forming one world. They belong together; they need one another. Neither can exist for long without the other.

When Haeckel formulated the notion that individual lives recapitulate the life of the species, that the ontogenetic recapitulates the phylogenetic, he was recovering the older dialectic of the microcosm and the macrocosm, two different planes of meaning which echo and reflect one another. Freud employed this notion to the end of his life, though it is a way of thinking abandoned by modern biology. But then Freud's whole world view was based on polysemous utterance, and polysemous psychic tracings. His reading of *Oedipus*, after all, is that in restricting ourselves to the single manifest meaning for so long, we had been missing the allegory of infantile desire and social repression which is the hidden, reverse meaning to the obverse and evident one; and where exactly can the lexical priming be said to operate here? Lexical priming would be the work of the censor, or that of Bishop Sprat wishing to expunge all figurative language from the lexicon. Obverse and reverse are not separate and sequential alternatives; they are two sides of the same sheet of paper. They arrive simultaneously.

But in a manoeuvre which would surely have brought the Irish Bishop up short, modern physics moved out of the uni-planar world of meaning he adumbrated, when it discovered complementarity, or wave/particle duality. Sprat had thought that all meaning could be singular and uni-planar, if only it could rid itself of decorative distractions, in the form of 'the poetic'; that lexical priming could be the order of the day for all rigorous scientific thought, that figurative language, with its additional and supererogatory layers of meaning, could be definitively excised. But the realisation that light could be seen in one mode of observation and measurement as particle, and in another as wave, meant that the very facts of nature must be perceived as inherently polysemous. In which case, the allegorical world might contain a greater truth than positivism could ever have imagined.

When Baudelaire formulates his notion of correspondences, and employs the synaesthetic results of these transcendent colloquies between categories in his verse, he is rediscovering in modernity the multiplicities afforded by the allegorical vision. And if nature is multiple, then what of human nature? Is our notion of the singular self inhabiting the unitary psyche not as positivistic in its way as the notion that all energy can be transmitted either as particle or as wave, but never as both simultaneously? Why should the process of selving always issue in a singular identity? Why cannot the process issue in selves, rather than a self? When the Portuguese poet Fernando Pessoa finally 'selved', four primary poetic identities came out. There were to be many others.

We can all end up with selves, of course, but we tend to treat the matter as one of psychopathology. The word schizophrenia signifies a splitting of the psychic energy and identity into multiples and manifolds. We have to study hard to achieve and maintain a singular psychic identity. Much of that lengthy period of exosomatic inculturation during our childhood is devoted to using all our notable gifts for mimesis and mimicry in order to become one single personality. We copy ourselves into being, both linguistically and culturally. We have to study hard to become the human singularity. But we are constantly assailed by the temptations of unconfined variety. The loss of that singular identity can be categorised medically, schizophrenia being one such designation. But it can also be celebrated, as it is in various forms of religious devotion and ecstasy; in our many mutating versions of the shamanic trance; in various forms of glossolalia; or simply in our notion of reformation. He is a reformed character, we say, meaning that the psychic shape and formation that went before have now been re-mapped, and the revised psychic profile should be applauded. Basic training in the armed forces re-shapes someone's instincts, drives and responses, so as to re-configure the individual into an efficient agent of self-defence and aggression. At a push, it can all be done in six weeks. Sixteen years of pre-formation can be radically revised by six weeks of reformation. We are made of mutable stuff, and we remember that when the Sybil used to throw out leaves on which were written the message from Apollo, in answer to the pilgrim's various questions, the letters on each individual leaf had to be assembled into the right words in the right order. Some even blew away in the wind. The messages that come to us from the mightiest powers need not be unambiguous. They can be construed as multiples of possibility.

WHEN THE VENTRILOQUIST ventriloquizes he does not simply effect a reflection of himself; instead he engages in a dialectical relationship with his own protean identity, and his own language use. The voice of the figure is always distinct from that of the vent. But more intriguingly, the identity of the figure becomes radically disjunct from that of its apparent initiator. Apollo loses control of the words being assembled in his name by the wooden Sybil on his knee. The model for dialogue between vent and figure is not that between master and disciple so much as the separate voices in Marvell's dialogue poems, where the progress of the argument increases the gulf between two identities defining themselves in counterposition, one to another. The different voicings may have had their origin in one being – the body and the soul being one of its variants – but they become aspectival, contrary, at times multiple in their possibilities, like allegories, which might be similitudes, but can never be simply translated into equations.

Certain figures haunt the modern imagination. *Dr Jekyll and Mr Hyde*, obviously. Yet despite the chemical inducement, Hyde is there as a fully-formed alternative to Jekyll; he simply needs to be released from his socially inhibited host. This psychic alterity is also a register of psychic multiplicity. Here civilisation rids itself of its discontents by abolishing the constraints that make it possible in the first place. *The Picture of Dorian Gray* is another example; the charmer whose dark identity can be assigned to a painting and a locked room. The room containing the painting is parallel to Bluebeard's special chamber, where he hides the past, the true past, the murderous past, the past that – if revealed – can only mean the death of the present. The earliest self-portraits we own up to are still to be seen on the cave walls of the Upper Palaeolithic, and there we appear to have at least two identities. We are therianthropes, pointing in two directions at once, towards two different species. So it seems that we saw ourselves from the beginning allegorically and as multiple identities, and continued to shape our therianthropic possibilities as minotaurs or centaurs, sphinxes or lycanthropes. After his early phase, all of Picasso's most compelling self-portraits are minotaurs. His iconography indicates that he felt his power and his torment could not be entirely contained in that single word 'human'. But then the word is surely therianthropic anyway. What Darwin explained was that the animal from which we grew is still here: every time we smile we are being therianthropic. The expression, according to him, is a vestige of a baring of the teeth in aggressive warning to show that the flesh of an opponent will soon be bitten and torn.

Empson, in his famous discovery of the extent of ambiguity in poetry and drama, was discovering that there is in effect no ultimate hierarchy of meaning, no lexical priming; all meanings are primary. It is a question not of which is generated first, but only of which is accessed first; to which we assign priority to at any particular moment. Light arrives as a particle, but leaves as a wave. Lexical priming is a self-imposed limitation, even if it might well appear in the guise of a necessary prioritisation, or disambiguation. Nature itself, modern physics informs us, has ambiguity built into its inner structure; it is neither univocal, nor disambiguated, but polysemous, polyvalent, multi-planar.

YEATS CONTINUED MARVELL'S tradition of dialogue poems, and formulated his notion of antinomies, and also of self and anti-self. This is another way of saying that identity itself consists of process rather than the achievement and expression of a fixed quantity. Our psychic energy is delivered by an alternating current; this is dialectics brought alive, as we see whenever we watch a skilful ventriloquist animate his figure, or when we see Shakespeare make a contrived psyche appear unquestionably real by uttering its authentic soliloquy. And Robert Browning's realisation as a poet that identity is to be discovered and explored in alterity had preceded Yeats's by decades. Why adopt a persona? Why become someone else? Because the motivation and therefore characterization of that created other might be more coherent than attempting to characterize ourselves from within; we constitute an incoherent region at the best of times, even though we insist we are situated in the centre of the combat zone known as human identity.

Niels Bohr often repeated this discovery: that the opposite of a fact is a falsehood, but the opposite of one profound truth may very well be another profound truth. Light is both particle and wave. Freud became intrigued by the way certain words embody their opposites: cleave is one example. We cleave something in two, and yet when a man marries a woman he should, according to the Bible, leave mother and father and cleave unto her. It is as though one meaning gains its intensity from the echo contained in its opposite. We see light only in contrast to darkness, after all. Two words Freud did not examine, but might well have done, were *anathema* and its doublet: *anathemata*. These curious words going back to the Greek idea of setting something apart, making something sacred, then take on the notion of an object or person set apart in a different way, something accursed. The ambiguity seems to reach its plenitude in Tucker's *Light of Nature*: 'Saint Paul wished to become anathema himself, so he could thereby save his brethren.' This is a theme explored with characteristically vivid brilliance by Borges in his story 'Three Versions of Judas'. There Nils Runeberg comes to understand that the key to salvation was not Jesus so much as Judas; that the great traitor had taken on the ultimate burden of darkness in which humanity was mired; and that it was he who was therefore the true salvific agent. Milton, we might remind ourselves, ventriloquized Satan into life in *Paradise Lost*, but he failed to do the same with God, who remained a lifeless and sententious abstraction, despite being allowed to laugh three times. Milton found what Yeats would have called his anti-self in the demonic figure, not in the divine one. Prosopopeia is choosy regarding its incarnations.

THE VENT'S FIGURE is frequently, if not exactly demonic, then certainly *daimonic*. The *daimon* in Greek thought was a divine spirit, whose collaboration means success, and whose antagonism means inevitable failure. Heraclitus internalized this force by announcing that an individual's character is what is meant by his *daimon*. Destiny is character; fate is inscribed throughout your own psyche, but it may not necessarily be under the conscious ego's constant control. All successful ventriloquists operate figures who are contrarian, who oppose the will and the interpretations of the vent. They put the old man right, with something approaching gleeful malice. And yet what is most curious about the ventriloquist's figure is that it is not a mere amplification or spilling over of the unitary identity of the ventriloquist. It always sets itself up psychically in opposition to the source of its own original voicing. It takes delight in goading that spirit. It takes the animating force, and grins as it turns the anima into animus. It is in Yeats's sense an anti-self. There is a parallel here: the voicing of the parodist, turning the original words into a mockery of themselves, even a potent self-criticism. Charles Dodgson, the stuttering mathematics don of Christchurch College, Oxford, behaves like the most fluent literary ventriloquist, who constructs for himself a figure, and he gives this figure the name Lewis Carroll.

The inhibitions and repressions of the vent are now metamorphosed into the fluently acid repartee of the dummy. The figure comes to life and creates an allegorical circus of Victorian society, a surrealist inferno of absurdities. It is, we might remark, a skittish inferno since, as in a Tex Avery cartoon, no one ever dies, however dire the circumstances that crush them. The Queen might continually call for a subject's head to be removed, but all the heads nonetheless remain in place, and that fact registers a distance between being monarch in Queen Elizabeth's time and being the same in Victorian England. (We might also note that Dodgson, though a permanent deacon of the Anglican Church, did not actually believe in hell. He wisely kept quiet about it.) Carroll is now endowed with a daimonic, if not exactly demonic, force never recorded in regard to any of Dodgson's own activities in or out of college. He also becomes one of the most lethal parodists who has ever lived, taking Wordsworth's verses on the leech gatherer from 'Resolution and Independence' and subverting them with the sort of forensic exactitude, of both tone and phrasing, which the figure all too often directs back at the ventriloquist who is his progenitor and present employer. Here is Wordsworth. The old man on the moor has been asked by the poet how someone as old and frail as he makes a living in such difficult circumstances. This is his reply:

> *He told that, to these waters he had come*
> *To gather leeches, being old and poor;*
> *Employment hazardous and wearisome!*
> *And he had many hardships to endure:*
> *From pond to pond he roamed, from moor to moor;*
> *Housing, with God's good help, by choice or chance;*
> *And in this way he gained an honest maintenance.*

And here now is the Knight in *Through the Looking Glass*:

> *He said "I hunt for haddocks' eyes*
> *   Among the heather bright,*
> *And work them into waistcoat-buttons*
> *   In the silent night.*
> *And these I do not sell for gold*
> *   Or coin of silvery shine,*
> *But for a copper halfpenny,*
> *   And that will purchase nine."*

The text has been turned over, turned inside out, and finds new possibilities for itself. In fact it has been obliged to testify against itself; to become its own anti-self; to switch from defendant to plaintiff. A parody is a sort of allegory, translating the text through ironic manoeuvres into a series of reversals. This procedure is not necessarily hostile, and can indeed be loving. The sacred parodies of Robert Southwell, John Donne and George Herbert borrow the motifs of profane love, in order to celebrate divine communion. This is not far from that multi-planar move from literal narrative to anagogical implication in medieval allegory. In each case we move from one region of meaning to another, while retaining the same personnel and *mise-en-scène*. The figure and the ventriloquist always share the same space and the same language, but one is anode to the other's cathode .

What metaphor tells us linguistically, in its unavoidable prevalence, both before Bishop Sprat's anathemas and after them, is that we cannot rest content trapped inside a single psychic identity, or any uni-planar level of meaning. We seek to find the porosity of borders. Our language insists that it believes in Baudelaire's correspondences, even when our science flatly denies them. But where metaphor provides us with similitude, however elastic, allegory also provides contradiction and contrariety. Allegory is constantly bearing out Bohr's observation that the opposite of one great truth may often be its apparent contradiction. When Lear and the Fool exchange their banter in the storm, their dialogue may seem at any instant an instantiation of duality, but it will ultimately turn into a tragic complementarity. Shakespeare's glossolalia finds a unity by hearing all the dissonant voices in the snake pit, not suppressing them.

Is contradiction reversal? And might reversal be a modality for the revelation of truth? The reversal of circumstances in tragedy is what brings out the truth, where the status quo ante had concealed it. In Aristotle's terms the natural development, the unimpeded growth of character, would be called entelechy; but what halts that process, diverts it, overturns it, brings about another outcome altogether, is peripeteia. Lear's life has to be turned inside out, so he leaves the palace and finds himself instead in a hovel on a heath, and then the revelations begin. He finally starts to see through to the truth of things, a truth that was denied him while cosseted by privilege. His palatial protection was a form of asymmetry; a prophylactic against a balanced view. Only by being cast down himself, becoming outcast, can he see the other side of things, the other hemisphere, which kept the privileged sphere in which he lived parenthesized in power and prestige. By turning this whole world through 180 degrees, we now see the underside of life, its symmetric underpinning:

> *Poor naked wretches, wheresoe'er you are,*
> *That bide the pelting of this pitiless storm,*
> *How shall your houseless heads and unfed sides,*
> *Your loop'd and window'd raggedness, defend you*
> *From seasons such as these? O, I have ta'en*
> *Too little care of this! Take physic, pomp;*
> *Expose thyself to feel what wretches feel,*
> *That thou mayst shake the superflux to them,*
> *And show the heavens more just.*

Contra–dictare: to say against; to utter something which, if accepted, negates the statement that precedes it. The Fool endlessly contradicts Lear, but by the end Lear has absorbed those contradictions into his own psyche. Either/or has become both/and. The reversal of the specific situation of the King has established the truth of the whole situation in his kingdom seen globally. The reversal establishes a truth, though it can be a terrible one. The reversal of Gregor Samsa's situation, from human back to animal, and vermin at that, reveals a terrible truth about the dynamics of human family life, and its necessary economy. Good parodies always supply an element lacking in the original.

Tragedy seems to insist that a situation can be inhabited, but it can never be entirely understood as a structure – moral, psychological, political, economic – until it is reversed. And here there is a startling precedent in ancient myth: the story already mentioned of Marsyas and Apollo. Marsyas finds the flute discarded by the goddess Athena because blowing on it distorts her face and makes her nymphs laugh. She throws it away; the satyr Marsyas picks it up. He then becomes so proficient that he challenges Apollo, the god of music, to a contest. It looks as though he might win, until Apollo pulls a celestial fast one: he reverses his lyre and plays it exquisitely the other way around, commanding Marsyas to do the same with his flute, but this is impossible. The muses deem Apollo the winner, and the punishment is now the god's to choose. He chooses the most terrible one of all: Marsyas must be flayed alive, inch by inch. So it seems that Marsyas can reverse (briefly) the ordering command of music, but he can never reverse the scheme of cosmic mastery. It is this lethal symmetry that flays Marsyas, the mathematic symmetry of power. When Apollo turns the lyre back to front and still plays it, this demonstrates that his power extends all the way from heaven to hell. This is a power that can be turned inside out and still obtain. In demonstration of the fact, Marsyas shall be turned inside out; he must be flayed alive.

Whenever the ventriloquist's figure outsmarts the man on whose knee he is sitting, Marsyas is playing his flute once more, and self concedes power momentarily to anti-self. The civil war between our differing psychic identities resumes, to the sound of laughter in the auditorium. Each of us ultimately constitutes an auditorium of our own, as the act of solitary reading proves.

MODE MINUS CODE.

LET'S SAY THE allegorical impulse continues into modernity, but the idea of a master code against which the allegorical personages and emblems can be correlated has withered almost to vanishing-point. Ontology has become problematical. We are no longer sure there can be any master code for us to check our world of emblems against. So we retain the great quest, together with some mighty questers; we have a dangerous, even desolate, journey for the questers to make. We have enormous hazards and dangers thrown in the way. And we have the obligation, as Bob Dylan once put it, to keep on keeping on like a bird that flew. But the grail itself remains utterly elusive, not merely its whereabouts, or the means for acquiring it, but its very meaning and identity. What would a modern grail be should we ever recover it? Would we find the chalice, having forgotten the ceremony which first bestowed meaning upon it? Does this set of specific confusions, the questing deprived of any ultimate code, in fact conjure up one of the forms of our modern literature?

The allegory abandons external topography and heads inwards to the psyche. Alice heads down below, just as Dante Alighieri did in the *Inferno*, but we have seen that the Reverend Dodgson did not actually believe in hell, so what we encounter is a place of infernal confusion, without eternal punishment or any truly potent devils. In *The Hunting of the Snark* the quest is undertaken with all the ceremony of one of the polar missions of Dodgson's day, but what is the quest? To encounter the Snark. And what is a Snark? Well this one was a Boojum. And that's it.

In *Childe Roland* Browning provides us with all the allegorical paraphernalia. A knight, a horse, a wasteland to be crossed, seeming dangers all around, unreliable informants, but what is the goal that is finally to be achieved here? Only the ceaseless journeying over hostile terrain remains to be celebrated. As Thom Gunn once put it, one is always nearer by not keeping still.

In Kafka the law grinds inexorably on, but to no purpose any of the participants can ever perceive. Some are accused, some are arraigned, some alienated, some dispossessed. The law is too distant now for comprehension; it appears infinitely remote in both time and place. Like a midrash which has lost the scriptural text from which it sprouted, or a remnant of rhyming slang which has forgotten the keyword with which it originally chimed, the texts become vestiges, hieroglyphic traces, the sites of ceaseless speculation. Sometimes, they turn into interpretation machines for generating dread; the dread that can fill a reader before a text he cannot decode.

And there is the strategy of James Joyce in *Ulysses*: the use of fictive parallels. This is not allegory, but it has a certain allegorical resonance. We end up, as Borges put it, reading Homer through Joyce. It would appear that even Joyce came to read Homer through Joyce, since we now know that he added 30% of the Homeric allusions and references during the proof stage of the book. The writing of *Ulysses* had turned into a form of auto-suggestion for the mythic patternings that represent the text's ultimate cartography. Thus did the waters of the Aegean finally reach the Liffey.

AN ALLEGORICAL FUTURE?

WALTER BENJAMIN POSSESSED a picture by Paul Klee. It portrayed an angel with his wings outspread, and a look of horror, or at least dark astonishment, in his eyes. The title of this watercolour was *Angelus Novus*. So who or what was this new angel? Whatever the artist had intended the image to be, Benjamin lived with it long enough for it to yield intimate meanings to him. *Angelus Novus* distilled its own allegoric revelations, and Benjamin always claimed that the only potent antidote to melancholy was allegory. For him the angel became the angel of history. He was staring at the accruing mountain of wreckage and detritus that history was heaping before him. He would have turned away but a mighty wind from paradise had caught in his wings and was propelling him backwards into the future. This wind, Benjamin informs us, is what we call progress.

In reading his account of this image, we start to see why Benjamin found allegory so potent. In such an allegorical reading, we bring as much to the interpretation of the significant manifold before us as we take away. We are negotiating a constellation, certainly, but we are also reading the void between the stars. Like that distant man in the cave mouth, inventing art and science in the same instant by perceiving the first recurring cluster of stars, we situate ourselves at the first moment in history, as well as the last. And allegories are never univocal.

XIII

WILLIAM BLAKE.

LUX, LUMEN AND THE LIGHTS OF SCIENCE.

WILLIAM BLAKE DIED in 1827, exactly one hundred years after Newton. In that final year he described the atom as 'A Thing that does not Exist'. Plenty of people, including a lot of scientists, would have agreed with him, though it would take more than another decade before the word 'scientist' would actually become usable, patented by William Whewell, who also gave us anode and cathode. As late as 1900 Ernst Mach still thought of atoms as a convenient fiction without any physical basis in nature.

But with Blake the matter is truly complex; it is not merely a question of establishing whether or not atoms exist. Blake railed against what he thought of as materialist science, or mechanical materialism. He loathed Francis Bacon, whose mode of analytic scientific enquiry renders him an intellectual anti-Christ as far as the poet is concerned. His feelings regarding Newton seem considerably more complex. Newton is finally redeemed in Blake's various mythic schemata, and Blake's portrait of him with a pair of compasses has a magnificence of its own, even if the vision of the author of *Principia Mathematica* might be altogether too circumscribed, premised on the measurements of reason, not the delights of energy, and his crouching body represents a closure, not an opening. Blake has a horror of that intellectual model of the world he believes connects Newton with the ancient atomists: the notion that the cosmos is merely a vast arena in which lifeless atoms bounce around and collide, one with another. The outcome of such a 'nature' would appear to be fortuitous; any forms we have finally achieved can only be construed as accidental. Not teleology, but random formation. So how could one ever get from such a theatre of the statistically arbitrary and lifeless to our existing, intelligent, creative and creating forms? How evolve from that haphazard abecedary to this dynamic shaping spirit? The same question greatly troubled Blake's contemporary Coleridge. That Newton might conceive of the vastness of space as God's sensorium did not help either of them, nor could they have known anything of his hermetic obsessions, or his relentless apocalyptic calculations.

One wonders what Blake might have made of the quantum states, whose meaning was formulated precisely one hundred years after his death, at the Solvay Conference in 1927. These states now present themselves to us as the fundamental forms of nature. We know, as earlier atomists could not, that the atom has a structure, despite the etymology of the word, which indicates indivisibility. We also know that the wave patterns which particles display have certain definite forms; that would surely have pleased Blake, had he ever been cajoled in any way by materialist science. Classical physics posited a world of infinite attenuation, without gaps; and certainly without quantum leaps. Between the absolutes of space and time, all forms could be infinitesimally eroded and accrued; so there were no ultimate edges to states, but rather a statistic winnowing as one state attenuates into another. But nature, the quantum revolution taught us, is formally shaped in its very texture. Its warp and woof is fashioned from essential forms; these we call quantum states. Matter is either thus or thus. It cannot be endlessly attenuated; cannot be negotiated in some infinitely graded scale of material attrition. We have a ground state, and an excited state above it. Between the two forms is nothing, or something even less specific than that. As Wallace Stevens said of his Snowman, he sees the nothing that is not there, and the nothing that is.

IN THE PERFECT city of Golgonooza, as constructed by Los and Enitharmon, Blake tells us there is both Art and Science. And in *Jerusalem* he tells us: 'The Primeval State of Man, was Wisdom, Art, and Science.' So it is not science per se that is the enemy, it would seem, and yet Blake is explicit: 'Art is the Tree of Life. Science is the Tree of Death.' What could have happened in the hundred years since Milton's writing that has made of science such an irrevocable enemy? It was no enemy for Milton, after all, who gleefully incorporated as much of the Galilean discoveries as he could into the opening of *Paradise Lost*; who goes to visit Galileo while under house-arrest in Tuscany, and writes about that visit with a certain pride in *Areopagitica*. Here we have an exemplary case of art learning all that it can from science, grabbing the scientific swag, and turning it to booty in the verse. One might almost hear Blake's ghost calling out to ask, and when does science ever learn from art, then? There is an answer there too. When Galileo looked through his newly-fashioned telescope in 1610, and saw the dark patches on the moon, he realised they must be protruberances; lunar mountains. He knew this because he had studied the techniques of chiaroscuro in the country that was then at the technical forefront of explorations regarding the representation of the effects of light and shade in two-dimensional images. He knew the spotty patches were the effect of an occluded light source. Thomas Hariot in England had seen exactly the same spotty patches the year before through his own telescope, but lacking Galileo's knowledge of chiaruscuro, he had been unable to make the same sense of them.

If science did not seem to conflict with the most mythic sto-ry ever told for Blake's greatest avatar Milton, it would appear to have threatened his own imagination with nothing short of death. Science was for him a radical diminution of vision, with-out which there could be no true perception at all. In its merely single vision, its one-dimensional analysis, measurement and comparison, it occludes the twofold, threefold and fourfold vision which together constitute Blake's mental world. It rep-resented a cancellation of the essential intellectual force in its visionary multiplicity. In the intellectual Armageddon where Blake spent most of his life, as a faithful if frequently battered woodkern, trying to escape the massacre, science was the lethal devourer that wished to consume the prolific as a dragon might eat a princess.

A few contextual moments might be of assistance here. Blake was working for Joseph Johnson at St Paul's Churchyard at the same time that Joseph Priestley was being published by him. They might easily have met. Johnson was a sociable fellow, of-ten inviting people to join him at his table. Priestley as a dis-senting minister was involved in the same world of the conven-ticles that Blake seems to have frequented, at least for a while. Priestley was also fiercely pro-revolutionary, and his house and laboratory were duly burnt to the ground in Birmingham by a King and Country mob, as they celebrated their traditional ver-ities and virtues. But apart from a reference to Dr Priestley in 'Auguries of Innocence', and the famously disparaging remarks about gas and gasbags in 'An Island in the Moon', Blake ap-pears to have nothing further to say about his contemporary. And Priestley has nothing whatsoever to say about Blake. It has been speculated that Blake's Urizen could have gained his name from Priestley's habit in heated discussion of demanding 'Your reason? Your reason?' in which case we would be able to say with even more confidence that the one was not much enam-oured of the other. From all that we do know of the pair of them, Blake and Priestley might have been expressly designed so as to miss the point of one another entirely. But it is at least a curiosity worthy of remark that Priestley was discovering his laws of contraries in relation to electrical charge at the same moment that Blake was discovering his laws of progress through contrariety in relation to spiritual development. One expresses itself as the second inverse square law, and the other as *The Marriage of Heaven and Hell.* Contrariety, in and of itself, does not represent cancellation; it is a generator of energy. Contraries, as Blake tells us, are not negations.

PRIESTLEY BELONGS TO that Unitarian moment when all of creation appears to be subject to minute scientific scrutiny; when every inch of the Lord's creation can be expected to yield up detailed information about the divine intention. Otherwise, observable nature would have to be seen to contradict the findings of true theology, and how could that ever be? That would make of the Almighty an incoherent Creator. So Priestley speculates in *Disquisitions Relating to Matter and Spirit*, published by Blake's sometime employer Joseph Johnson in 1777, that the soul could well be made of atoms of an exquisite fineness. It must obviously be made of atoms of some sort though, or the framework of scientific enquiry in which Priestley is situating his theology would entirely collapse. Man would be in danger of becoming soulless; a survival machine, however effective, with no prospect of redemption. And just to remind ourselves how strong some of these cross-currents at the time could be, Joseph Priestley, the man who isolated oxygen on these islands, and dialogued so impressively with Lavoisier, also believed that Jesus Christ would return within twenty years, to inaugurate the millennium. Jesus didn't return, and Lavoisier in Paris was decapitated by Madame Guillotine during the Terror. So, no more well-informed remarks from that particular head. Millenarians are always navigating towards disappointment.

The matter is perhaps best summed up in Blake's question at the start of *Europe* in 1794, the year of Lavoisier's death: 'Then tell me, what is the material world, and is it dead?' Dead material: how could true life ever come out of that? This was also the burden of Coleridge's question, when he writes in *Joan of Arc*: 'It has been asserted that Sir Isaac Newton's philosophy leads in its consequences to Atheism: perhaps not without reason. For if matter, by any powers or properties *given* to it, can produce the order of the visible world and even generate thought; why may it not have possessed such properties by inherent *right*? and where is the necessity of a God?' How can thought come out of lifeless matter, unless it is inspirited by the divine breath, that *pneuma* or *ruah* which the Book of Genesis tells us hovered over the waters? Nature can never provide Form; that must come from the divine spirit. It was this that led Blake to say of Wordsworth, whose greatness he acknowledged, that his devotedness to the material details of Nature made him in effect an atheist. And in a Notebook entry in the 1790s Coleridge speaks of Newton as a 'material theist'. The emphasis would seem clear, in Coleridge as in Blake: there is a gap which philosophy, including natural philosophy, cannot bridge, between those inert material atoms, cold and lifeless as they are said to be, and the life of the spirit. One of Blake's most crucial words for the spirit's vital animation, along with imagination, is vision, and vision is an ambiguous word. Like the Proverbs of Hell in *The Marriage of Heaven and Hell*, it points both ways. Its obverse and reverse meanings could be seen as contradictory and dualistic; or they could be seen as complementary. Does the vision pour into us, or is it always in the process of pouring out?

PRIOR TO NEWTON, there had been two competing views of how we see: we can refer to them as the *lux* and *lumen* optics. Lux and lumen are now terms used to define degrees of luminosity. But in that older tradition, which was long-lived, lux was thought to be the light that shines from us and delineates the objects out there to be perceived. This then was an optic of the inner light, and therefore also of the inner fire, one that was ignited by spirit, and is therefore the first cause of inspiration. Newton in his *Optics* firmly established that it is the lumen, and not the lux tradition, which appears to be verified by modern science. It is the light that comes from outside which we register with our ocular equipment. The light starts from elsewhere, then, not inside us. We are its recipients, not its generators. Otherwise, as Newton asks, how would we be able to see the image fading on the inside of the lid when we close our eyes?

Now what shines and what doesn't shine is very important to Blake. Where, he constantly asks, do you think this shining ultimately comes from, the light that provides the source of vision, that permits the delineation of its forms? Do you really believe it can arise out of those dead particles of matter, what Newton had called corpuscles? He asks his question most pressingly in these polemic verses:

> *Mock on Mock on Voltaire Rousseau*
> *Mock on Mock on 'tis all in vain —*
> *You throw the sand against the wind*
> *And the wind throws it back again.*
>
> *And every sand becomes a Gem*
> *Reflected in the beams divine*
> *Blown back they blind the mocking Eye*
> *But still in Israel's paths they shine.*
>
> *The Atoms of Democritus*
> *And Newton's Particles of light*
> *Are sands upon the Red sea shore*
> *Where Israel's tents do shine so bright.*

THE OPPOSITION HERE is a vivid one: between particles of light, those cold or dead bits of stuff that appalled both Coleridge and Blake, and that both resisted as the posited rudimentary elements of this universe of ours, and the luminous gleam, the visionary brilliance that Blake sees perennially all around him. The grains of sand here become gems, and they do so because they are 'reflected in the beams divine'. In other words, Blake would appear to be recovering the lux tradition from its Newtonian depredations, simply by insisting that the light that shines from within actually comes initially and eternally from God – who for Blake is always within, since, for Blake, God existed inside each one of us; project him into some realm above and beyond and he becomes Old Nobodaddy, Milton's unloveable heavenly Father; the fictive Boss of a cosmic deistic machine. So Blake translates his antinomian inheritance, the abrogation of the Law so often preached in the conventicles he and his father seem to have once moved amongst, into an alternative science. Not one of passive reception, then; not one of Lockean perceptive blankness awaiting the world's stimuli to inscribe its material signature, but one of active visionary discovery and creation. God said *Fiat lux* not *Fiat lumen* and Blake is still seeing light generated before his eyes. In its ultimate form it is uncreated light, since he tells us elsewhere that what is merely created also dies. Priestley speculates whether the light that radiates from Jesus during the Transfiguration might be uncreated light, but for him this triggers another problem in its turn. How exactly would mortal vision manage to perceive uncreated light? Blake would have had no problem here: the true artist transcended mortal vision, to see instead the forms of the imagination. In twofold, threefold or – on blessed days – fourfold vision.

Blake translates this divine vision into his verses and his paintings. The science of Golgonooza is in effect an antinomian science. It had abrogated the law of passivity of the human receptor, and replaced it with the lux tradition of a radiant and radiating body, emitting energy, often in the form of light. We see it in Blake's image of Albion and Christ. This hermetic tradition can be observed in any number of places: when the woman touches the hem of the garment of Jesus in the gospel account, she is healed, but he feels the power simultaneously going out of him. At this moment, Jesus is a form of divine radiation. In Rembrandt we frequently see the sacred figure emitting light. And when Einstein was monitored with electrodes attached to his head, he had been asked to think about relativity. The observers were expecting, presumably, a particular emission of energy through wave-form cerebretonics, and so had set up the equipment precisely to monitor such a radiant emission from the physicist's brain. The aureole around a saint's head is the commonest form of this tradition, along with any form of laying on of hands. The notion of a radiant and healing energy continues its eccentric course when the youthful Samuel Johnson is taken from Lichfield to London in order to be touched by Queen Anne. Scrofula, or the King's Evil, could be dispelled by contact with the anointed monarch. It didn't work, sadly. The Great Cham remained scrofulous to the day he died.

When the Berlin Wall fell, accompanied by the collapse of the Soviet Union, Francis Fukuyama announced the end of history. He has since acknowledged that he was perhaps underestimating Clio's longevity, but the notion of an apocalyptic time, an era of such radical change that everything is utterly transmuted by it, was there for Blake too. The French Revolution was seen as the end of the old history, the third and final age had now begun, and this was to be the age of the spirit. At last. The antinomian tradition here traces its genealogy back to Joachim of Fiore, as well as Swedenborg and Boehme. The first age of Moses was over; the second age of Christ had recently ended; the third age, the spiritual age, the endtime of the Holy Ghost, had now begun. Law had had its day; it was now no more than a dead husk of death-delivering prohibition. Love could at last replace it. If the prolific was now at last coming into its own, then the devourer might no longer consume the children of the light.

That was the essence of all inherited antinomian beliefs for Blake. Time might at last have been re-united with eternity, after their long and acrimonious separation. Part of that belief is his hatred of what he calls 'Creeping Jesus', a phrase he marvellously invented; this false Messiah is addicted, he reckoned, to 'Yea and Nay'. Now we are told in the New Testament: 'Let your yes be yes and your no be no. All else comes from the Evil

One.' But Blake insists that his Jesus, not the Jesus of history, that chronicle of the man named Yeshua from Nazareth, but rather the translucent redeemer of apocalyptic times, includes both yes and no, not as separated realms of existence, but as the obverse and reverse of the coin of genuine existence; not dualism then, but complementarity. Here obverse and reverse are no longer 'opposites', but different aspects of the same indivisible reality; contraries not negations. This aspectual inclusiveness characterises the redemptive thought of the Everlasting Gospel, which states explicitly that with the death of Christ and the harrowing of hell, the reign of sin is now ended for ever. It is no longer Antigone who dies in this new drama; but Creon. And good riddance too.

BLAKE HAS AT least one thing in common with modern physics: for both the word energy is a sacred term. Energy, *energeia* in its Greek form, meaning work, including all the infinite possibilities of doing and making, is the source of many of the radical discoveries of modern physics, as well as many of its continuing mysteries. (Its first use to signify mechanical or electrical energy is in fact recorded during Blake's lifetime, in 1807, and obviously relates directly to the kind of work Priestley had been doing. The previous definition of energy, that of Johnson's great Dictionary of 1755, was: 'Power not exerted in action.' In the terminology of physics today, this would mean that energy was potential, not kinetic.) And Blake is of course explicit: 'Energy is Eternal Delight.' Energy is for Blake the centrifugal force ceaselessly pressing outwards, to escape constraint, limit and inhibition. It is the prolific, radiating out of itself its own ceaseless exuberant creation. Reason operates as a centripetal force, a force of limit and circumscription, and although this is not simply an opposition of positive and negative, the reasoning force when deprived of its dialectic with energy becomes for Blake the Spectre, the dead and malign reason that hangs like a mephitic vapour over the Land of Ulro. A line of circumscription can still be a celebration of form, a liminal frontier between the prolific and the devourer, as Blake's own fluent line so often is in his visual work, but it can also be the container of mere measurement, the geometric vector that circumnavigates a vacancy, indeed the outer filament of a gas-bag. Your reason, sir, your reason.

Blake's Newton as he portrays him is luminous, but he is entirely intent on measurement, and his vision has been constricted to a downward gaze. Like Nebuchadnezzar he is being pulled down by the gravitational pull of dead materiality, where Blake's more glorious figures always move upwards and outwards. They are presented to us as the source of their own energy – God is only ever alive through his vital being inside the living creatures of imagination – and it is the light of themselves that illuminates their vivid landscapes. Their bodies are luminous with their spirits; indistinguishable from them. They radiate energy continuously. Their flesh is the irradiated form of their souls.

Blake presses himself here to an extremity, which threatens him with incoherence. He insists that nature has nothing to do with his art; that his images all come from Imagination, not from any exterior act of copying; that the visionary daughters have nothing to do with the daughters of memory. And here we have no alternative but to stop taking the terms of his vision on trust for a moment, for here we encounter a problem, which links up fatally with the dilemma of the utter negation of materialist science in his thought. How could we recognise Blake's figures, his trees, his streams, if his art has no commerce whatsoever, as he insists, with nature? How could we recognise his drawing of Catherine putting on her stockings? He would reply that those who can paint with true vision, not the single variety which constitutes Newton's sleep, create forms which can be recognised immediately by those who can *see* with true vision. He might also argue, in semi-Platonic manner, that the spiritual form is what is embodied, though in degraded incarnations, in the natural body. Nature is itself neither more nor less than a copy of those purer forms. He has another ace up his sleeve too, when he writes to Flaxman on 21st September 1800: 'In my Brain are studies & Chambers filled with books & pictures of old, which I wrote & painted in ages of Eternity before my mortal life…I look back into the regions of Reminiscence & behold our ancient days before this Earth appear'd in its vegetated mortality to my mortal vegetated Eyes.' Memory does play its part, then, but in the form of extra-mundane reminiscence. If the visionary forms were first perceived in a prenatal existence, then they obviously have no business being checked for accuracy by post-natal measurers.

But let us momentarily risk empiricism and single vision so as to choose a specific instance and test the matter. This test, we had best admit immediately, would have struck Blake himself as utterly repellent.

THE SPECIFIC IMAGE for examination is 'The Ghost of a Flea'. The creation of this image has been documented for us. Varley, an early spiritualist, recounts how Blake perceived the flea's ghost in the room. His visitor requested him to limn it, so the artist called for his materials and began to draw. Soon before us appears a remarkable image. This is evidently what Blake, with extraordinary vividness, saw appearing before him. No one else could see anything at all. But a number of people, including Kenneth Clark, have pointed out, with patient shrewdness, that we can in fact provide an iconography of this image. It did not come solely out of the Imagination, but out of Blake's hoard of remembered forms, many of which had been provided by others during the course of his life. There would appear to be a reference to nature, after all. An image from Robert Hooke's *Micrographia* had become rooted so firmly in Blake's mind that he no longer realises it is even there to be called upon. And another image, a somewhat coarse reproduction of one of the howling devils from the Sistine Chapel ceiling, also seems to have found a roosting place in Blake's inner menagerie of images, his iconographic mental catacomb. His visual imagination has so entirely internalised these items that they can now reappear at will, and Blake's noted 'eidetic imagery' appears adept at externalising previously internalised material, whether iconographic, Biblical or literary. Blake's imagination has previously stored all it will need from nature, it seems, so he no longer needs to make any direct observations of it, though he must have at least registered some natural forms as he made his way about the world, or he would have continually collided with them. The image of the flea (or its ghost) had arrived through a microscope, through Hooke's eye, not Blake's. Hard to think of Blake spending much time staring through a microscope. He would probably have agreed with Pope:

> *Why has not man a microscopic eye?*
> *For this plain reason: Man is not a fly.*

In the extremity of his protest against that materialist science he sees as void of life, multiple vision or interest, Blake is pushed to a position of vigorous polemic opposition. Like Swedenborg, he insists he can journey in the realm of the spirit and find all the forms he needs there. And with that word 'forms' we do seem finally to have summoned what Yeats called Plato's ghost. In speaking of Plato, in a letter to Butts of 6th July 1803, Blake is prompted to one of his rare uses of the word allegory which is not entirely abusive. He says of Plato's notion of poetry that it is not unlike his own: 'Allegory address'd to the Intellectual powers, while it is altogether hidden from the Corporeal Understanding.' However, Blake soon exhibits his usual genius for ambivalence, in his comments on Berkeley: 'Plato did not bring Life & Immortality to Light. Jesus only did this.' And even more firmly: 'What Jesus came to Remove was the Heathen or Platonic Philosophy, which blinds the Eye of Imagination, The Real Man.'

BUT WHATEVER CAVEATS he might have expressed in other respects, Blake seems never to have baulked at Plato's ideal version of form. He tells us in *Milton*:

> *The Oak is cut down by the Ax, the Lamb falls by the*
>   *Knife,*
> *But their Forms Eternal Exist Forever.'*

Once again he seems to be in agreement with modern physics here, though he undoubtedly arrived at the agreement by a notably circuitous route. The forms of matter might be smashed to bits in particle annihilation, modern physics tells us, but the amount of matter and energy must remain constant. And the quantum states are always there, glowing away even in our ultimate entropic sump. Blake believed the forms outlived their temporary hosts; and so did Niels Bohr. The *nihil* at the heart of the word annihilation is deceptive; it is not a rendering to nothingness we are observing, but a species of metamorphosis. 'Every force evolves a form.' Thus Mother Ann Lee, the founder of the Shakers. Blake would have agreed with his contemporary as, in a radically different register, would Darwin years later. Form was never inexact for Blake; only inadequate and inexact representation could make it so. No *sfumato* for this artist. The form was the precise expression of the force.

IT IS A world of passive perception that is Blake's sworn enemy. Dead matter measured and circumscribed by a reason which has detached itself from the perpetual delight which is energy, which has submitted to the life-hating commandments of Old Nobodaddy, which has etherialised itself into the grey abomination of the Spectre, and which now wanders in perpetual lament through the drear ruins of the Land of Ulro. Nature which is not animated by the visionary fire is for Blake a form of death; this he comes to call simply Nature, in an intellectual manoeuvre which we have to admit can be ultimately confusing. This quirk of Blake's separates altogether too absolutely the exterior from the interior, the daughters of memory from the daughters of inspiration. And it is this region of lifeless form that he adumbrates when he declares that Art is the Tree of Life and Science the Tree of Death. He is not prepared to be a mere receptor of stimuli and data, as the lumen tradition seems to suggest that the perceiving subject is. Instead he says that the light does indeed shine within us all. God did, after all, say, *Fiat lux*; not *Fiat lumen*. He was uttering the light that, according to Blake, was nothing less than the ceaseless radiation of his own visionary identity, though to those enlightened by this last age of the spirit, he will appear in human form. Logos is inseparable from lux. And that's why Israel's tents do shine so bright. The particles of luminosity enlighten the visionary. Their blowback in a world of dull materialism blinds the mockers who imagine they are in fact the true seers. Instead they are fact-men; the intellectual functionaries of Caesar, the clerks notating the stately actions of the Beast.

Niels Bohr used to start his lectures by saying that every sentence was to be taken, not as a statement, but as a question. Just as Blake's visionary forms in his etchings and paintings tend to open out, and rise up, so one of Blake's most characteristic linguistic forms is the question, which is a trope of syntactic opening, not closure. How often we find Blake asking, rather than answering: 'And did those feet in ancient time…?'; 'What immortal hand or eye could frame thy fearful symmetry…?'; 'Little Lamb, who made thee…?'

The light couldn't just be particles, Blake insisted. And it turns out that he was right. Just over ten years after Blake wrote *The Marriage of Heaven and Hell*, Thomas Young conducted his famous experiment at the Royal Institution, which established that light propagates itself as a wave, creating patterns of diffraction and interference. His demonstration elicited a certain amount of derision at the time, particularly from an anonymous review by Brougham in the *Edinburgh Review*, because if true it would have appeared to disparage the findings and conclusions of the mighty Newton, and his corpuscular theory of light. God, according to the Bible, had said, *Fiat lux*; let there be light. But if Alexander Pope is to be believed, then he subsequently changed his mind, or at least modified it. In 1727, the year of Newton's death, Pope wrote:

Nature and Nature's laws lay hid in Night;
God said, Let Newton Be! and all was light.

It would appear that Newton, born on Christmas Day in 1642 without an earthly father, since he was a posthumous child, represented some kind of intellectual redeemer, a veritable messiah in the world of natural philosophy. Blake of course was having none of this. And the masters of memorials in Westminster Abbey seemed a little dubious too: Pope's couplet was never incorporated into their memorial stones.

IT TOOK EINSTEIN'S paper on the photo-electric effect in 1905, followed by twenty years of laborious intellectual toil, before it could finally be established that light was both wave and particle; that it wasn't made simply of particles, but nor could it be described entirely as a wave. Waves are after all forms of perception; and all forms in nature are perceived through pattern recognition. Their shapes continue even after all the individual particles temporarily constituting them have departed. The matter may be created, and is therefore, according to Blake, perishable, but the form can be seen to be eternal.

Only through contraries comes true progression, Blake told us. And Bohr said something complementary. The opposite of a small truth, he said, is merely its contradiction; but the opposite of a great truth might well be another great truth. Contrariety is not negation. Light is both wave and particle, even though those two modes of transmission had previously appeared to be inherently contradictory. Blake said in *Milton*: '…there is a place where Contraries are equally true.' We need to be careful too whenever we use the word 'opposition'. It is a tricky word, and its modern usage, as Empson reminds us in *Seven Types of Ambiguity*, is a relatively recent coinage. In its origin it was straightforward and exact enough: one planet on the far side of the sun is in opposition to ourselves at an angle of 180 degrees. But how loose the term can sometimes now appear. In any book of antonyms, black will be given as the opposite of white. But the absence of all light is hardly the opposite of the combination of all colours in white light. The opposite of white light could more aptly be considered to be coloured light, which can be refracted, while remaining itself, while white light can only be refracted by rainbowing into separate colours, and therefore vanishes as white light at the precise moment of its own refraction. And the opposite of any colour should be another colour, not the entire absence of colour. Whatever might be the opposite of a man, it is surely not a woman. Macbeth understands this all too clearly when he says, 'I dare do all that may become a man. Who dares do more is none.' And Lady Macbeth is not the opposite of Macbeth, but his lethal complement in dark ambition. Blake would presumably have added that the opposition between an angel and a devil would disappear should they ever embrace; they represent hemispheres of a single mental world. The energy would begin to flow between the bright spiritual anode and the dark spiritual cathode, should they ever reach out and join hands. The antinomian circuit of energy would then complete itself.

C. S. Lewis says in *The Great Divorce* that he does not understand what Blake means by the 'marriage of heaven and hell', and he suspects that Blake didn't either. I think Blake did, actually. In 1790 we know Blake acquired Charles Wesley's *Hymns for the Nation, in 1782*. His dated autograph appears in the copy he acquired. So he would be contemplating the contents of this book around the same time that he starts work on *The Marriage of Heaven and Hell*. Wesley thinks the American rebels are a bad lot, and he is in no doubt whose side the Almighty is on in this particular battle. America is Sodom, and the Congress is described as 'like Lucifer in its rage for power and its blind fury of insurrection'. Blake, we might recall, reckoned it was the King of England who had sent over to America his 'punishing Demons'. And so once again, we can hear Blake thinking, not for the first time, we populate Hell with our enemies, just as Dante had done in the *Inferno*. And each pantheon of villains in the form of hell needs another hemisphere to sustain it, in the form of virtuous heroes aligned in heaven. It all depends on which side Albion is on in this conflict; which is to say, it all depends on who and what you reckon Albion is. Wesley's Albion was certainly not Blake's. But what would happen if one hemisphere stopped seeing the other as a Manichean negation of itself, and embraced it instead? We know that if you bring matter into the presence of anti-matter the energy generated is so huge that, could such generation continue to be sustained, we would have enough light and heat to overturn the Second Law of Thermodynamics. Entropy would give way to a visionary universe. Energy would indeed be eternal delight. The prolific and the devourer would be happily married in perpetuity.

THE TRUE SPIRIT of Blake's opposition to dead forms, and intellectual passivity, his contrariness whenever confronted with what he believed to be the forms of the Spectre, might be captured most compellingly in David Jones's beautiful poem, 'The Tutelar of the Place', where the Ram is the figure of geometric lifelessness, calculation and oppression; the global obliteration of all locality and differentiation. This is Blake's Beast updated, wielding state power only to achieve the greatest possible uniformity. Set over against it, in an iconographic opposition Blake would have understood only too well, is the Lamb, and the womb that brings forth that Lamb:

> In the December of our culture ward somewhere the
>   secret seed,
> under the mountain, under and between, between the
>   grids of
> the Ram's survey when he squares the world-circle...

When the technicians manipulate the dead limbs of our culture as though it yet had life, have mercy on us. Open unto us, let us enter a second time within your stola-folds in those days – ventricle and refuge both, *hendref* for world winter, asylum from world-storm. Womb of the Lamb the spoiler of the Ram.

LIBRARY, UNIVERSITY OF CHESTER

ACKNOWLEDGMENTS

I would like to thank the following for their help:

Denis Boyles, Ann Denham, David Elliott, Andrew Hedgecock, Steve Lloyd, Michael Moorcock, Jenny Newman, Emma Rees, Anthony Rudolf, Bernard Sharratt, Chris Simon, Chris Steare, Chris Walsh.

All errors are mine.

Note: The essay on Blake was originally delivered as the lecture 'William Blake: Lux, Lumen, and the Lights of Science' to the William Blake Society at St James Piccadilly on 9th December, 2013.

ABOUT THE AUTHOR

Alan Wall was born in Bradford, lives in North Wales, and studied English at Oxford. He has published six novels and three collections of poetry. His work has been translated into ten languages. *Jacob*, a book written in verse and prose, was shortlisted for the Hawthornden Prize. He was Royal Literary Fund Fellow in Writing at Warwick University and Liverpool John Moores and is currently Professor of Writing and Literature at the University of Chester.

Printed in Great Britain
by Amazon.co.uk, Ltd.,
Marston Gate.